Harmattan, A Wind of Change

Carolyn Johnston is the daughter of Tim and Berrice Johnston and she spent much of her childhood in Northern Nigeria. She is an integral part of the story and has edited her parents' letters with skill and sensitivity. The collection is much more than a fond duty to parents – it is both a love story and a significant contribution to the documentation on the end of empire.

Harmattan, A Wind of Change

Life and Letters from Northern Nigeria at the End of Empire

Edited by

Carolyn Johnston

The Radcliffe Press
LONDON • NEW YORK

Published in 2010 by I.B.Tauris & Co. Ltd
6 Salem Road, London W2 4BU
175 Fifth Avenue, New York NY 10010
www.ibtauris.com

Distributed in the United States and Canada Exclusively by Palgrave Macmillan,
175 Fifth Avenue, New York NY 10010

ISBN 978 1 84885 143 6

A full CIP record for this book is available from the British Library
A full CIP record for this book is available from the Library of Congress
Library of Congress catalog card: available

Typeset in Caslon by Dexter Haven Associates Ltd, London
Printed and bound in India by Thomson Press India Ltd

CONTENTS

For Andrew and Tim and Ellie and Olivia

LIST OF ILLUSTRATIONS

INTRODUCTION

In the early years of the twentieth century West Africa was known as 'the white man's grave' because each year one in five Europeans either died or had to be invalided home. People living and working in the remote areas could be a hundred miles away from the nearest doctor and when sickness struck the only way of contacting him was to send a runner with a message. The doctor then had to make his way – on horseback, bicycle or on foot – along narrow bush paths, and in the rainy season there would be rivers to negotiate as well, so by the time he arrived the patient had often given up all hope and died. Apart from the health considerations and primitive communications, many Europeans lived in one-man stations with no immediate help and few comforts other than basic camping equipment, and it could be a very lonely life. So why would anyone want to go and work there? For Tim Johnston it was a case of wanting to do something constructive and worthwhile on the one hand, and following the family tradition on the other, for his father James and two of his uncles had served in the Indian Civil Service.

Tim, the youngest of five children, was born in Belfast in 1913 when the family were on leave. He was christened Hugh Anthony Stephen and how he got his nickname is an amusing family tale. During the voyage home from India his sister Alma, aged three, befriended the ship's cat which was called Tim. Back home in Belfast she missed her little companion and when she asked if she could have her own Tim, they put her new baby brother in her lap and told her: 'Here you are, here's Tim'. The name stuck.

Tim spent the first five years of his life in the Punjab and was then sent to boarding school in England. When they were growing up the five children rarely saw their parents and spent school holidays with various aunts and uncles. Luckily for them, Tim and

1

Alma usually stayed with their mother's cousin Iva Sturton whose husband John was the vicar of Market Lavington in Wiltshire. They lived in the large Vicarage which, in Tim's words, was: 'a terrific house to play Murders in, because it has two staircases, and a passage upstairs which makes a complete circuit'. The Sturtons had no children of their own and Iva loved having them to stay. She was a very special person and they were devoted to her.

At a very young age Tim set his heart on working in Africa. After gaining his degree at Brasenose College he stayed on at Oxford to do the Colonial Administrative Service course and having completed it in the summer of 1936 he set sail for Nigeria.

His first tour was in Sokoto, in the north-western corner of Northern Nigeria where the landscape is savannah and where daytime temperatures in the hot season soar to 45°C and do not come down below blood-temperature until late at night. His second tour, by contrast, was in Oturkpo near the Benue River, a land of thick forests and high humidity.

Soon after war broke out in 1939, Tim secured his release from the CAS and returned to England. He joined the RAFVR and was trained to become a fighter pilot. In 1941 he met and fell in love with Berrice Lincoln and they were married the following year after he had served in Malta where he was awarded a DFC.

Berrice's background was very different from Tim's. Whereas he came from a professional, highly educated and privileged family, she had had to leave school when she was only thirteen years old because her father had abandoned the family and her mother was unable to pay the school fees. Berrice never saw her father again, which must have been traumatic for her as they had been very close. On her fourteenth birthday she started work in a dress shop and a few years later she joined the ATS.

Throughout the war, and after it, Tim and Berrice wrote hundreds of letters to each other, which are the basis of this book. In 1991 Berrice told me:

> I'm in the process of re-reading the letters that Dad and I wrote to each other – incredible how so many survived our frequent postings in the war and the vagaries of the mail. Some day you will probably read the letters and you will understand that I was the most fortunate woman in the world to have loved, and been loved

by, Dad. And you will see how, at my request, he helped so patiently to fill in the gaps in my education.

After the war Tim returned with her to Nigeria and they were sent to Nassarawa, a one-man station. Subsequently they were in Makurdi, Kafanchan, Birnin Kebbi and Sokoto where Tim became Resident. In the mid-1950s Tim was posted to Kano, first as Senior District Officer and then as Resident. It was there, in 1956, that they received the Queen and the Duke of Edinburgh on the last day of their Royal Tour of Nigeria. The following year Tim became Permanent Secretary to the Premier of Northern Nigeria, Alhaji Sir Ahmadu Bello, and Head of the Northern Civil Service. Two years later he was made Deputy Governor of Northern Nigeria and when the Governor went on leave he was the Officer Administering Government.

Nigeria gained its independence in October 1960 and Tim retired from the service at the beginning of 1961. He then took charge of the Overseas Service Resettlement Bureau in London, which helped officers returning from the Colonies to find further employment. He also found time to write two serious books, *The Fulani Empire of Sokoto* and *A Selection of Hausa Stories*, as well as *Zomo, the Rabbit*, a book of Nigerian stories for children, published under the name Hugh Sturton. He was working on another book about the explorer Denham when he died. *Denham in Bornu* was later completed by David Muffett.

Had Tim not died so prematurely – two days after his fifty-fourth birthday – he would undoubtedly have written a memoir. In fact, he set out his idea for a book in a letter written in 1960:

> What I have in mind is an impressionist picture of this country built up with many diverse and apparently unconnected blobs of paint which I hope, when viewed from a distance, will build up into a coherent whole. My blobs will consist of episodes, sketches, stories, anecdotes, ... historical incidents ... [although] I think too much history would pall ... My idea is to have as much diversity as possible ... For title (and sub-title) I thought of: HARMATTAN – *A Wind off the Desert*.

I hope that this book, with all those ingredients, will give the reader a really good impression of an era that is not only long gone, but almost forgotten. It is derived from Tim's papers, his early letters to his aunt, Berrice's diaries of her first tour in Nigeria, and the letters they wrote to each other over a period of nearly twenty years, whenever they were apart. The reader will get an impression of what the officers did and the kinds of problems they were faced with; what it was like for the wives and how they coped in the primitive conditions; and what happened to the children who often had to be left behind in England. Some of their comments may seem, by today's standards, offensive or racist but I have deliberately not edited them out because my parents were products of their period and that is how it was then.

Eventually I intend to offer Tim and Berrice's letters and diaries to the Colonial Records Archive at Rhodes House Library, along with the copies of Tim's official papers returned to me by the late David Muffett.

I have been incredibly fortunate throughout this project in the support I have received from friends old and new. Firstly, I am grateful to the late Richard Barlow-Poole who recognised the potential of the letters and encouraged me to try and get them published. Secondly, I want to thank all those of Tim and Berrice's friends who took the trouble to contact me and tell me their memories, some of which are included in the Envoi. In particular I am indebted to John Bolton-Maggs and the late David Muffett and Nigel Cooke who helped me to understand what was going on in the background. Thirdly, I would like to thank my old friend Colin Bodrell who spent some long hours with me delving into the National Archives. Next, my heartfelt gratitude goes to John Smith who read each chapter as I completed it and put me right when I got things wrong, and who gave me encouragement and the confidence to keep going. And finally, my thanks go to Anthony Kirk-Greene who also encouraged me greatly and helped me with the technical aspects of editing a book.

– 1 –

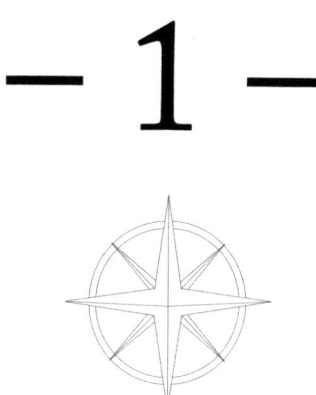

The Land and the People

Northern Nigeria forms part of the savannah that stretches right across Africa from the horn to the bulge. It is sandwiched between the Sahara in the north and the rain-forests in the south and within this belt it occupies the sector which lies between Lake Chad to the east and the Middle Niger to the west. It is a land of rolling plains that stretch away in every direction to apparently limitless horizons. Its towns and villages nestle in the valleys where water is plentiful and the soil fertile. Round them cultivation has cleared away the bush and left the land open but studded with fine trees like an English park. The intervening heights, by contrast, are still well clothed in bush which sometimes rolls away as far as the eye can reach. This pattern of the tamed and the untamed tends to repeat itself again and again. Only occasionally does a black granite inselberg or a range of red laterite hills, a shallow river with wide sandy banks, or a considerable town of flat-roofed houses, encircled perhaps by a great mud wall, now crumbling into ruin, appear to give variety to the scene.

The picture is saved from monotony by the extraordinary changes which the seasons bring about. In March, when there has already been a drought for five or six months, the hot weather arrives. The sun then shines fiercely out of the brassy sky and dust-devils stalk across the parched landscape. But by July the rains will have transformed the scene: there will now be a soft wind coming from the south-west and the country will be looking as green as Ireland. Four months later, however, by November, another transformation will have taken place. The Harmattan will then be blowing out of the north-east, bringing crisp days and chilly nights, and the landscape will have resumed the tawny colouring which is the real livery of Africa.

The people are a mixture of the ancient indigenous tribes and immigrants who crossed the Sahara Desert by one of the well-established caravan routes. When Islam swept North Africa in the seventh century, the Berbers, a liberty-loving people who did not want to submit to Arab domination, headed south and slowly infiltrated Northern Nigeria. Legend indicates that the union between the Berbers and the indigenous peoples was a peaceful one and led to inter-marriage. This seems inherently probable because the Berbers, arriving a caravan at a time, would not have been numerous enough to attempt a conquest or to impose themselves as an alien aristocracy. Of necessity, therefore, they would have had to settle down among the local tribes to earn their livings.

The first product of the union was probably the Hausa language in its embryonic form. This derived its form and structure from Hamitic, or Berber, as well as from Sudanic sources, and later borrowed some of its vocabulary from classical Arabic. The second product of the union, which in point of time probably emerged at the same time that the language was evolving, were the Hausa city-states. The original seven, which are known as the *Hausa Bakwai*, were Daura, Kano, Rano, Katsina, Zazzau, Gobir and Garun Gabas, sometimes given as Biram. And the third product was the civilisation which blossomed in these city states. Some of the crafts, such as smelting iron and sinking wells, certainly flourished there before but there can be little doubt that the Berber immigrants, who had been exposed to Mediterranean culture, introduced new arts and raised the general standard of skill and sophistication.

Once the Hausa language had emerged and the Hausa way of life had been evolved, they became powerful influences in the central Sudan and soon began to make their magnetism felt. Before long other neighbouring states, to a greater or lesser degree, were drawn into the Hausa orbit. In distinction to the original seven, these satellites came to be known as the *Banza Bakwai* or Upstart Seven.

From the eleventh century Islam filtered in and there was a steady process of conversion among the Hausa dynasties. Islam is not only a religion but a whole way of life, and in Hausaland it had a profound influence on the lives and thoughts of the people. It tolerated slavery and slave-raiding, it is true, but then so did Christianity until a very late stage in its evolution. As against this, Islam was an important factor, perhaps the most important one of all, in the advancement of learning and the general spread of civilisation.

In the centuries that preceded the coming of the Europeans, the Hausa States came under the sway of three empires, Bornu, Songhai and the Fulani Empire of Sokoto. Considering that the Hausas are a virile and hardy people, it is surprising to find that they were almost always under the domination of some other power. In all their history they themselves only threw up one man, Muhammadu Kanta of Kebbi, who had imperial ambitions. He created an empire in the sixteenth century but it disintegrated within a few years of his death. The main reason for this historical paradox probably lay in the fact that the six leading Hausa States were roughly equal in strength. The result was that they were constantly fighting one another but none of them ever became powerful enough to dominate and absorb the others. Another reason is probably to be found in the nature of the Hausas themselves who are an easy-going people who do not take themselves too seriously. They can fight if they have to (as they showed in both World Wars) but in normal times they are more interested in trade and talk than in war.

By the middle of the eighteenth century Bornu had reasserted its suzerainty over Hausaland but, apart from collecting tribute, it exerted little real authority. The result was that the states continued to bicker and fight among themselves.

The civilisation of Hausaland may still have been as advanced as any in black Africa but it was showing clear signs of decadence. Politically the Hausa States had been unable either to maintain their independence individually or combine together to gain greater strength. Militarily, except for Gobir, which had now emerged as the most aggressive and powerful of them all, they were ineffective. In religion the peasants were still largely pagan, in outlook if not in observance, while the upper classes were lax and insincere. Learning, which of course was closely bound up with religion, was making no headway and even trade was greatly hampered by the constant wars.

There now appeared upon the scene one of the most remarkable men whom Africa has ever produced. His name was Usuman dan Fodiyo but he is usually known to history as Shehu, the Hausa corruption of Sheikh. He was a Fulani whose family had originally come from Futa Toro, near the Atlantic, and had been settled in Gobir for at least three hundred years.

The Fulani, as a people, present one of the great enigmas of Africa. Physically they run remarkably true to type and the typical Fulani has good clear-cut features, a reddish brown skin, and a slight but very tough and wiry frame. These physical characteristics, combined with their undoubted talents, have given rise to all sorts of romantic theories about their origins. The most widely accepted theory is that they came originally from the Middle East or North Africa and gradually worked their way round the bulge of the continent to the region of Senegambia. There they are believed to have sojourned for some time before drifting eastwards down the great corridor of the Sudan.

Shehu came of a long line of scholars. He showed exceptional promise as a boy and as a young man he soon made a name for himself as a Muslim divine and preacher. He was austere in outlook and his uncompromising puritanism at length brought him into conflict with the Hausa Chief of Gobir and his worldly court. This conflict came to a head in the year 1804 when Shehu, like the Prophet Muhammed, took refuge in flight from the persecution which threatened him. The war which followed is known as the *jihad* because for Shehu it was waged for religious and not secular aims. Nevertheless it had sweeping political and social consequences.

When the Fulani emerged from this struggle as the victors they took over the whole apparatus of power, not only in the capitals of the States, but in almost every town and village as well. Although they had imposed themselves on the Hausas as a ruling aristocracy, they were still only a minority and in the end the weight of numbers told against them. By the close of the nineteenth century most of the settled Fulani were speaking Hausa as their mother tongue, and in their manners and customs, though not in

8

their looks, had become almost indistinguishable from the Hausas themselves.[1]

This was the land where Tim would spend most of his working life.

* * * * *

Sokoto 1936–37

There were about thirty cadets going out together for the first time, each with a mountain of luggage; half of them had been at Oxford together for a year, so knew each other pretty well. Tim met his great friend Peter Scott on the platform; just before the train left Mrs Scott handed over an enormous bunch of keys and, turning to Tim, said 'I suppose you've got just as many'. Tim smiled in a sickly sort of way because it suddenly dawned on him that he had left his behind.

They sailed from Liverpool in the RMS Apapa, of the Elder Dempster Lines. It took five days to reach Madeira, from where Tim posted the first of many letters to Aunt Iva.

My dear Aunt,

We approach Madeira and the first post so I thought you might like a line to let you know how I am. Well, so far it is as good as can be – eating like a horse and sleeping like a log. We are the despair of our unfortunate Steward because we never spend less than three-quarters of an hour over a sit-down meal and for dinner it mounts to one and a quarter hours!

She is a nice little boat and gets along quite well. Yesterday we did 361 miles, the exact figure I prophesied but as the tickets in the sweep are sold by auction and it went up to over £2, I couldn't do anything about it. The man who bought it – a fat and pursy businessman – won £12.10s.

Thank you very much for bringing my suit to the station. I am sorry I sent you away so brusquely but I am sure you understood. Apart from the suit I haven't been too clever because

9

I seem to have left a shirt in the Hotel and I also forgot all the keys of my kit. What do you know of that!

They went ashore and later bathed off the ship in incredibly clear water. It took another day to reach the Canary Islands, after which it began to get hot and at Bathurst it was steaming. Some people came aboard from the shore and the first thing any of them said was 'Poor old Gerald's dead'. They felt sorry for poor old Gerald, but otherwise rather exhilarated, because it showed it was 'the real McCoy'.

It was cooler when they got to sea again, pursued out of the harbour by a lot of sharks, but the best of the voyage was over; Freetown was as hot as Bathurst and they were never really cool again. Drinking iced lager and trying to win the sweep on the day's run was about as much as they could do; a few hardy souls still danced on deck after dinner to 'These foolish things', but not Tim. At Takoradi there was a little bay, with a raft and diving boards, where they bathed; it reminded him of a line from a hymn – 'Where Afric's sunny fountains run down its golden sands' – but it was the first and last golden sand he would see in Africa.

Two days later they left the ship at Lagos, the capital of Nigeria. Tim had heard that it was usually the worst day of a tour, because of problems getting through Customs, and that many a man had resigned forthwith and gone sadly home. Without his keys he had an especially tough time. In the evening the new boys were bidden to Government House to meet the Governor and Lady Bourdillon; they were charming and welcomed them with champagne. Tim was told that he was going to Sokoto, and everyone said 'My God, poor devil', but he was delighted; the real McCoy again. At midnight they said good-bye to the 'poor devils who had to stay behind on the civilised coast' and got into the sleepers of the night mail which was to take them up country.

It took two nights and one day to get to Zaria, where they arrived in the early morning. On the platform he heard someone enquiring for him and saw a tall, thin type, rather eccentrically dressed, and wearing a monocle; he could hardly believe it, he was Hollywood's idea of an Englishman in the tropics all over. Gordon

Wilson took him in tow and put him up for the weekend until he could get a train to Gusau.

At Zaria Tim got an idea of what a good station was like. The bungalows were widely spaced, each standing in its own compound; the roads were well looked after and planted with trees; the grass was kept down by gangs working with

1. Tim during his first tour in Sokoto

matchtes; there was a Club with tennis courts, and a golf and racecourse.

Houses were of two sorts: permanent ones built of stone and roofed with galvanised iron covered with thatch, and temporary ones built of mud and roofed with thatch. He stayed in a temporary one and found it rather fun. It had no such things as doors or windows, just openings which might have a mat or a Tuareg blanket hung across them; the floors were beaten clay strewn with more mats. Insect life seemed pretty vigorous: flies by day and mosquitoes by night, and dozens of hornets busy building their nests up in the bamboo joists. He asked what the subdued murmur from the roof was and Wilson, who was a most kind host, told him white ants; they always eat the middle out of everything so you never see them except when one is too voracious, bites his way into the open and falls down to the ground.

The most important part of the weekend's work was securing some staff. There were a lot of applicants for the honour, but, after long examination of references and on advice, he finally chose a cook called Maiholi at two pounds a month and a steward-boy called Sule at thirty-shillings.

On the Monday, shepherded by Maiholi, Tim took the train to Gusau, the rail head. It was still 150 miles to Sokoto and the post lorries, Albions, took all day to do the journey. However, they were lucky and found a Bedford going through the same day. The country was dusty and hot, at times monotonous, at times rather forbidding, but it was Africa and it made Tim frightfully excited. Just as it was getting dark they found a big Packard waiting for them, and it whisked them the rest of the way to Sokoto.

Once he had settled in, Tim wrote again:

At last a tardy line to tell you how I am. Here I sit in my mud-house, with a kitten on my knee and bat whistling up and down in front of me. The house is a big one and the ground plan is something like this:

On the side of the lounge is my dressing room, with my bathroom behind it. On the other side there is a room devoted to my unwanted boxes and to nesting house-martins. I am at present seated at the table shown in the very middle of the house and the bat is doing his endeavour along the veranda in front of

BACK

STORE		BATHROOM
BOX-ROOM	LOUNGE (table)	DRESSING ROOM
	VERANDA	BED
	FRONT TERRACE	
WALL		

me. I hear him doing flat turns over my bed at night. The central lounge is where I spend all my time except when sleeping, dressing or bathing. It is a high room with three (sort of) Moorish arches supporting the mud ceiling; the floor is of tile and no match for the 'gará' (white ants) the emphasis I find should be on the last syllable. It is tastefully furnished with my pictures, a deck chair, a collapsible chair, a divan made out of a crate, some cushions and a blanket, a sideboard made out of a packing case covered with a green-check tablecloth (upon this are my cutlery set and 2 candlesticks, giving it the appearance of an altar), a small drinks table (price 1/6d) and two open cupboards (price 2/-each). I forgot to mention the mats decorating the floor (4d each).

I have a staff of four: 'Sule' my steward is a distinguished looking creature with good features and a short goatee – a local fashion but worn square not pointed – and a commendably quiet efficiency. In a way he is a swart Jeeves. My cook is called Maiholi: he is a fatherly old man and has chits dating right back to the early days of Northern Nigeria – 1903 and 1904! The small boy is called Audu Bernin-Kebbi: he is not a shining intelligence but amusing. Finally there is my water and garden boy of whom I know little, beyond that his name is 'Gado', which means 'bed'. Odd.

On arrival I was given one day to find my legs and then I started work in the Provincial Office. Today I took over the

13

Local Treasury and am now responsible for about £6000–£7000. In the last fortnight I have been discovering what a file is and have now also taken over all Mining correspondence. I was amazed to find so much gold-mining going on in the Province. It is nearly all alluvial and small but still applications for Leases come in constantly. By the end of the month I shall have taken over the whole office. The Resident, whose office it is, is socially very nice but officially something of a holy terror.

Within a month Tim had been moved to another house which he described in his next letter.

I am now installed in a bungalow near the office. It is quite a different type altogether from the 'Provincial Palace': concrete floor, doors and windows and a corrugated iron roof, mercifully concealed under native thatch. The plan is this: with A forming the drawing-room, B the dining room, C the bed-room and D the bathroom. E is the veranda of which C and D are really a part. I have only been in four days so will hazard no opinion yet. It is however furnished which for me is a great advantage. As soon as I can get some carpets and curtains it will begin to look quite handsome. There is also a punkah over the dining-room table

2. Maiholi with Dela (left) and junior wife and children

14

which is quite a luxury; they seem to be used much less here than in India (as far as I remember) in spite of the greater heat. I haven't seen or heard of any bedroom punkahs.

First let me tell you of the locusts and then of the white ants. A swarm of locusts passed over just after I last wrote and, after circling round for some time, came to rest. In the 'Provincial Palace' – my last house – I was just on the edge of the swarm but even so the sky was quite darkened by them. I noticed some large tree-bats, almost as large as crows, flying among them; they had evidently been dislodged from their trees and carried along in the tide, which they were quite unable to stem. My small boys, Audu and 'Bed', enjoyed themselves hugely, dashing in among them barefoot and raising great clouds with their cries and contortions. I expected the greenery to disappear before my eyes but strangely enough when the swarm moved on it seemed to have left no indication that it had ever passed, except a few strays. I had always understood that locusts cleaned up a countryside while you were ringing up the fire-brigade.

My experience with the white ants was a little more intimate. When young, the brutes have large wings and they behave in the rather foolish fashion of moths if there is a light about. The first night a reasonable number emerged from one of the many holes in my walls and started their maddening circumnavigation of the lamp. We had a reply for them however. About eight frogs were mobilised and grouped round the lamp at the points and intermediate points of the Compass and each time a white ant stalled and fell to earth, a long tongue flicked out and all was over. In quarter of an hour there was nothing to be seen but eight enigmatic frogs. A few days later however, instead of 50 we had 5000. The frogs were mobilised but couldn't cope with the situation at all and so the only thing to be done was to take the lamp outside and put burning straw over the myriad that at once collected round it. Rather jungle law, I fear, but the gará deserves and gets little sympathy.

I don't think I told you, last time, about the sultan, Sultan Hassan. He is the most charming old man you could wish to meet anywhere – very jolly but dignified withal and a man of considerable piety, as befits the 'Commander of the Faithful'. I met him on the occasion of the opening of a new Dispensary in Sokoto and hope I shall have a chance of renewing my acquaintance with him.

On Monday we went to the local school sports. They have just got a beautiful new running track, probably better than that of any English Public School, and the boys seem to be very keen on it. This is rather a 'good thing' because the chief trouble with the local seems to be that he isn't really keen on anything; very charming and very dignified of course, but not keen. In a way, of course, it seems a pity to disturb such dignified and natural slumber but the answer I think is that for good or evil they have entered the 'Great World' and it is better that they should run their own country rather than have others doing it for them. Education is rather booming locally and a girls' school is going to be built in Sokoto, starting almost at once.

In his next letter Tim described, among other things, the Chief Commissioner's visit to Sokoto.

The Chief Commissioner[2] arrived and conferred the C.B.E. on the Emir of Gwandu and a Certificate of Honour on my Chief Clerk. I must say he is a most unimpressive little man for a Lieut. Governor; no presence and no conversation. On the night of his arrival all the Administrative people were bidden to the Residency to dinner to meet the old boy and later the old boy himself invited the whole station (in relays) to drinks or dinner in the house I had so laboriously prepared for him. At dinner on the first night, after the port had gone round, the Resident rose to his feet and said 'Your Honour – I give you the King'. I threw my head well back and set down my glass quite empty; what I hope no-one realised or noticed was that it was quite empty when I took it up! The dinner being an unofficial one, I had anticipated no toast and had therefore passed the port on without taking any. What is more, the glass I so feverishly seized, putting my hand right round it to hide the nakedness of the land, was not even the port but the liqueur glass. However, I don't think anyone noticed except the hostess and she wouldn't mind.

Next day we played tennis with His Honour and I regret to say that I struck him with a ball at very short range across the net. But it wasn't a hard shot luckily and next set I played with the great man and we won 6–1 so I think I was forgiven. Both he and his Private Secretary felt the heat very much up here; the N.N. HQ at Kaduna is apparently cool in comparison.

You will observe from the line above that I am falling into the local habit of abbreviating. It is something of a vice, I must admit, but useful if you have someone who talks the same language. For instance instead of saying: 'on arrival I was met on the Elder Dempster boat 'Apapa' by the Private Secretary of the Governor and taken to Government House' you would say 'on arrival by E.D. I was met by HE's P-S and taken to G-H'. The office jargon too is hardly English sometimes. One communication we received read: 'Undernoted please find the above'. That's all – except for a heading and a thing they are pleased to call a 'sub-joined schedule', to which the single mystic sentence in the body of the letter referred.

Like India, Nigeria is rapidly sinking beneath mountains of correspondence, all growing rapidly. By the same mail and from the same source we received (1) a letter drawing our attention to this remarkable fact and soliciting suggestions for overcoming it and (2) another letter calling for yet another monthly return to the Secretariat, thereby adding yet another little mountain to an already extensive range. There are altogether three Secretariats in the country and yet a great deal of the work they should do has in fact to be done in the Provincial and Divisional Offices. In the case of cadets fresh from home, it doesn't much matter because it is a very good training, but it is criminal (in most people's opinions) the way DOs are tied to their offices instead of being left free to look after their native staffs. The manner of governing is all right: it is just the technique that is at fault and here too I think there will be a progressive improvement. The service can be divided into three 'age-grades', as the anthropologists call it: first the immediately post-war group who were deprived by the war of their three or four years at the University and in many cases of their last years at their Public Schools as well; the second group belonging to the middle twenties who enjoyed their University careers but rather drifted out for want of something better to do; and the third group (to which I suppose I belong and should therefore perhaps not discuss), which seems to regard the job more professionally. The people in groups 1 and 2 are very nice but I don't think the country will be as well governed as it might be until the people who started coming out say eight years ago get to the top of the tree.

You will be glad to hear that I am as fit as a fiddle. It is a perfectly dry heat now and although it goes up to over 100°F in the shade every day, it is not in the least oppressive. The nights are delightfully cool and I sleep out with a blanket on. It is most impressive waking up in the early morning when it is still dark and hearing 'Allah, ila-Allahu...' from the town about 2 or 3 miles away.

Meanwhile, back in England, Edward VIII had abdicated and Tim wanted to know what the opinion was there.

Well, what does everyone think of our King, as was? The wires have been humming out here with a vengeance as the result of his doings. I heard his speech last night on the wireless and thought he did it very well under the circumstances but all the same I think everyone is terribly disappointed in him. I for one never thought for a moment that he would abdicate, I must say; it seemed to me that he was just bluffing and that when Baldwin called it, he would climb down and be a good boy again. One can only hope Albert will be like his father and increase in stature as he grows older. It is an ill wind that blows no good and at least the crisis spared us the Governor's visit. What is more I heard there is a public holiday tomorrow.

The month of Ramadan is just drawing to a close. Luckily for those observing the fast the weather is quite cool but when it comes in April or May, which (their months being lunar) it sometimes does, the strain must be considerable. They are not even allowed to swallow their saliva according to the strictest orthodoxy, but, being fairly lax locally and therefore doubtless dead in sin according to the ideas of puritans like Ibn Saud, I have no doubt they do when no-one is looking. There is a pathetic story told about the Muslim sailors on a polar expedition; as soon as they got into the region of the midnight sun they were unable to eat or drink anything at all because it happened to be Ramadan and so persistent were they in their abstinence that the Captain had to put down his helm and come dashing south to save their lives!

Tomorrow there will be enormous excitement trying to spot the new moon. If it isn't visible from Sokoto messengers are sent

out to the villages where some of the villagers are said to be able
to see it in water even if it is invisible to the naked eye in the sky
and if *they* fail despairing telegrams are sent to see if it has been
seen anywhere else in Nigeria. The day after the end of the Fast
is a great Feast Day. There are Public Prayers, which by courtesy
Europeans and even European women are allowed to attend,
and after that the usual festivities, chaps galloping about and a
good deal of singing and dancing and horse-play. It should be
rather amusing.

The men here (or all that can afford it) wear long flowing
robes of white cotton and turbans of either white, dark blue or
occasionally red and white or yellow. Only the very up-stage wear
shoes but all manage to look very dignified. The little beards they
grow on their chins, like goatees only not pointed, become them
very well. The women wear dark blue almost always – just a length
of cloth swathed round them – but they let themselves go with
their headwear which is often very flamboyant. The small children
are most attractive: the boys run about without anything on but
the girls, except when very small, are dressed to the nines. There
was a very amusing incident at the school sports. The girls' school
arrived to watch and were taken in crocodile to their seats. Just
as they were passing in front of the Europeans all a little girl's
clothes, except her multi-coloured and enormous head-wear, fell
off but she carried it off with perfect composure and just pulled
them up again as if it was the most natural thing in the world.
As indeed it was.

In his next letter Tim was able to describe the festivities.

I will tell you first about the local festival marking the end of the
fast of Ramadan. It happened just before Christmas and the
Europeans were by courtesy allowed to attend. It was a most
impressive spectacle, beginning with Public Prayers on a hill-side.
These were attended by thousands of people, all dressed fit to
kill, with their donkeys, horses, camels or whatever else had
brought them. The 'hoi poloi' assembled first and then came the
procession of notables, their turbans getting bigger and bigger as
they became more and more notable. When the Waziri (Vizier)
arrived, with what might have been a vulture's nest perched on
his head, we knew that we were getting warm. Next came the
'Commander of the Faithful' in a white turban (all the others
wore shiny dark blue ones) with the lower part of his face veiled.

The whole procession was mounted and the Commander of the Faithful had three remounts behind him to assert his position. Behind these came the personal bodyguard, part modern, part ancient. The modern section was made up of Native Administration Mounted Police in olive green uniforms and carrying lances; behind them rode more NA Police dressed up like the Middle Ages. They wore enormous helmets, about 4 ft high and chain mail. Some of the chain mail is genuine stuff from the Crusades and until 40 years ago they still fought in it. The helmets are less historical, being made from kerosene tins.

After prayers the Sultan asked some of us, of which I was lucky enough to be one, to his Palace. There we climbed into his very high gateway – it easily dominates the low-lying town – and watched the antics of the loyal populace below. The most delightful thing about it was the absolute spontaneity that you saw everywhere. Men galloped up, with their long robes flying out behind, shook their fists up at us in salute and then galloped off again. There were a lot of drums and wind instruments in the crowd but no co-operation: the owners simply banged or blew them unmercifully, incessantly and with enormous enthusiasm.

We also visited the tomb of Usuman dan Fodiyo, the founder of the local dynasty and a contemporary of Napoleon's and the younger Pitt! His tomb has become a shrine and the holiest ground in West Africa. Of course we took our shoes off; so eager were we in this respect that we removed them unnecessarily at the outer door and had to walk in socks across a thorny courtyard. The tomb itself is about ten feet square and standing about six feet high, the upper part is open to the air and full of bats. The surrounding floor is covered in sand which has come in with the wind and the pilgrims; altogether rather unimpressive but interesting.

I shall probably buy a horse in the very near future. I have had one on loan for some time but it is more like a towel horse than a real one, and this other that I tried today is its master in every way; £4 is the price which seems not unreasonable. He is comfortable and willing and not bad in appearance.

The weather has changed so much that this seems quite a different country to the one I arrived in. The Harmattan wind is blowing with a vengeance; the nights seem better (the temperature actually does drop to about 50°F at times[3]) and in the day I wear my English clothes, tweed coat, pullover and all. The air is full of very fine dust which produces a misty look, with the sun trying to shine through, just like an autumn morning at home. The only difference is the dryness here. It is very difficult to believe that in a couple of months we shall be boiling again but so it will be; everyone speaks of the spring here with awed voices and bated breath.

In February 1937, the personnel of the station changed radically; the Resident and his wife, an ADO and his wife, another ADO, the OC Troops and the well-digging foreman all left. Having almost completed his six months in the Provincial Office Tim wondered what was going to become of him. With any luck he might get sent out to bush for a bit; he was looking forward to it as he knew nothing of the Province itself and it would enable him to save some money and learn the language properly.

In March he was released from the Provincial Office and attached to the Divisional Office with the task of helping to supervise the Native Administration institutions.

I think I told you that the Sultan and his subordinates are salaried officials like ourselves and as far as possible the Native Administration is encouraged to run itself. This is called 'Indirect Rule'. Well as they have done in the generation or so of their existence, they still require careful watching to prevent them in ignorance or guile from running off the rails. As an example of the latter I will mention that the last Native Treasurer, enjoying a salary of £400 p.a. and universal respect, was found to have feathered his nest to the extent of £3000 or so. The Treasury, Police and Prisons are what I help to look after with the result of course that I now spend most of my time in the town about two miles away and not in the station.[4]

I am now in my third house which will probably surprise you until I add that quarters are attached in this country to jobs and not to those who discharge them. It is of permanent material like the last one and rather sparsely furnished. I found some bees had seized their opportunity when there was no tenant to swarm in the wardrobe; there they remain because nobody dare remove them.

I have been visited with a lot of pesky boils which have made walking very painful and games impossible. Most of them have been on my feet. Boils in one's first tour are said to be quite usual and non-recurring. Last week I was compelled to keep to my quarters for three or four days because of yet another boil on my foot. It was therefore natural that when an order came through from the Secretariat asking for a loyal Coronation Address from the Chiefs and Peoples of Northern Nigeria (Sokoto is the senior Sultanate and that is why it was required of us) it was passed on to me to write. So next May when you see in your Telegraph that a particularly loyal message was received from Northern Nigeria you will know who wrote it.

A coded telegram also arrived for which we had not got the code word and this too was given to me to decipher. In the course of a very amusing morning's work I am glad to say that I not only decoded the telegram but correctly deduced the code word from it. This was BLASPHEMING and the principle of the code is as follows: the code-word is written down and after it all the other letters of the alphabet in their correct order and in such a way as to make two equal lines of 13 letters.

BLASPHEMINGCD
FJKOQRTUVWXYZ

In the telegram the lines are interchanged and B would be written instead of F, T instead of E and so on. The method of the code was explained to me and it is of course an easy one to break but at the same time I felt very excited when I started getting it.

I now ride down to the town every morning before breakfast and my horse enjoys cantering the whole way. It is lovely when the sun is just rising and the colours are all at their best, the trees are darkish green and the thatch of the huts a pale mauve which goes rather well with the green. One could almost suspect dew on the grass though of course there is none. At 9 when I canter back the sun is just beginning to get hot and a sun-helmet is required from then until about 5 in the evening. The weather continues to get warmer and when I come back to lunch it is usually about 100°F in the house. This is apparently the merest foretaste of what is to come; the Sultan remarked the other day 'It's not *hot* yet'. However, I don't mind it, such as it's been.

I have heard about all the examinations now and regret to say that I have contrived to fail in law. How I managed to do this I cannot think because, as I told you, the examination is with books and I was quite convinced that I had done well enough to get the 50% required for a pass. I have written to ask for my marks to see on which paper it was that I tripped up or if there was any reason for doing so. I know I wrote very badly and that is a possible explanation I suppose. The Hausa I passed successfully I am glad to say though even there I feel rather dissatisfied because the Agricultural Officer (who himself thought he had done less well than myself, as did the Invigilator and, though I says it what shouldn't, as I did myself) got 265 marks against my 227. Admittedly examinations are queer things but I can't help feeling – no doubt without cause – that *they* don't like Cadets to do too well. However, I am getting much more fluent now that I work in the town all day.

In April Tim received a letter from the Vice Principal of Brasenose College, who told him that he was delighted to hear from another old Brasenose man what a tremendous success he was making of his job. Tim commented that he did not know who the informant was but rather liked his information!

In the same month he had to go to Kwarre, about twelve miles to the north-east of Sokoto, to do an assessment report[5] which, if accepted, would cost the town about £100 p.a. in extra tax because they had not been paying nearly as much as they should. While he was there, the Sultan happened to pass through with some of his council and so Tim asked them to tea:

It was a meal of high comedy: the Sultan and I sat in chairs, the Waziri and the Chief Alkali (Lord Chief Justice) squatted on the floor and their enormous following waited, like wolves, to pick up the crumbs that fell, metaphorically, from our table. The Sultan did not eat very much but drank tea and lime-juice in alternate sips until, tiring of both, he stood the empty glass in the half-empty cup and called for water. The Waziri and the Chief Alkali did not waste their time on liquid but set themselves quietly and methodically to demolish the cake and biscuits. For a time they ran pretty level but the Waziri with a fine spurt raced the Chief Alkali to the last piece of cake that had been cut. The Chief Alkali countered cleverly by taking the rest of the cake and the gleam of crafty triumph that shone in his wall-eye as he did so was easily worth three-quarters of a cake. For a man in the position of Prime Minister, this was a very serious reverse but the Waziri is nothing if not resourceful and he managed to finish very strongly by seizing the moment when everyone else was saying goodbye to empty a tin of my cigarettes into his ample robes. Honour was therefore satisfied and a good day enjoyed by all.

The weather was now at its hottest with temperatures between 112°F–115°F every day; it was usually still at 110°F when he went to play tennis at about 5.30 in the evening and did not come below blood-heat until quite late at night. However, being a perfectly dry heat he found it quite bearable. In May he wrote about the coronation celebrations.

Here we are all recovering from the Coronation which now – thank heavens – is entirely a thing of the past. All the work of organisation fell on us so you can imagine it was anything but a holiday. Proceedings began with the visit of the RAF in two large troop-carriers. They stayed a day and a night and gave joy rides to a limited number of Europeans and Africans. To my great annoyance – especially as most of the dirty work had by a natural process of devolution fallen to my lot – I did not get a flight. The African head of the Hospital was apparently very amusing. He had heard how fast aeroplanes fly and when the machine had climbed ponderously to a couple of hundred feet above Sokoto he looked anxiously down and said 'What town is this? What town is this?', imagining it must at least be Kano or possibly even Khartoum.

The Coronation celebrations proper began in the early morning with a formal function at which the RWAFF presented their arms and shot off their feux de joie and the flag was pulled up and down and everyone saluted several times. When these preliminaries were over the forty-seven District Heads of Sokoto Emirate, each of whom had 20 – 50 hangers-on including always a drummer, a trumpeter and professional praisers and funny men, rode past in procession and saluted the Sultan and the Resident. Everyone of course was wearing his very best and it was all rather colourful and amusing.

In the evening there was a firework display of which I did not see very much because I was in charge of the Commissariat distributing cake, biscuits, ginger beer and lemon squash to the insatiable District Heads. After this, all Europeans repaired to the club where there were cabarets of African singers and dancers. Especially amusing were the professional praisers who recounted the happenings of the day – almost without premeditation – in the monotonous but rather amusing little tunes to which these things are always set.

Next day before breakfast the Europeans played the African clerks in a tennis match and beat them 4–2. The idea was mine and I am glad to say that it went off most successfully. (These clerks all come from the South and it is always rather a problem to know how to fit them into the celebrations.) The DO afterwards gave forty of them, including some wives, breakfast. In the evening the Resident gave a fancy-dress party to the whole station to which I went as a yacht-hand in white trousers, a jersey and a little Hausa cap that looks not unlike an American sailor's.

I am now in my fifth house which was also my first, the Provincial Palace, but it has been done up in the interval and is now quite unrecognisable, being the best house I have yet had. I expect to be in the station for another month and then to get out on tour and with any luck to stay out, off and on, until due for leave. One of the DOs above me has just gone on tour and the other is going on Wednesday so until they come back I shall be in charge of Sokoto Division and its 1.40 million inhabitants.

In June Tim told his aunt that he had had a rather shattering piece of news:

To counteract the seasonal shortage of officers, I am to proceed on leave in December instead of in February. Don't mistake this for good news. It means getting home a couple of months earlier but when you hear the attendant disadvantages I am sure you will agree that it would be much better to wait. First it means that the Sahara trip will (almost undoubtedly) fall through because even if Scott has been served with the same scurvy trick the man who was to take us home will not want to do it at Christmas time. Second it will mean about £50 less in my pocket when I land in England: as you know I was hoping to pay all my debts in my first year and to save money in the last six months but the saving period will now only be four months. Third it will mean a fortnight's shorter leave overall and two winter months – Jan and Feb – instead of two and half summer ones – May, June and the first half of July. Finally: Christmas on the boat. Altogether you can see that whoever it was in the Secretariat who thought it out, it was a pretty fast one that he bowled. Moreover there was no choice about it; the memo read: 'Mr HAS Johnston will proceed' etc. etc. Another thing I forgot to mention is that all my future leaves will be winter ones unless (a) I can secure an extension of a tour of service which, from the nature of things, they would be unlikely to grant or (b) I am invalided home early. My DO here hasn't seen a summer in England for twenty-one years and it doesn't look as if I shall. Now you will understand why I take a pretty black view of what might appear superficially to be good news.

We have had only three lots of rain so far and unless we get more in the near future the position in the North of the Province will be rather serious. The Sultan has prayed for rain – with immediate success – but more is wanted and the next step is to persuade the Scarlet Women of the town to find husbands. If this fails, there is a procession to the prayer-ground in sackcloth and ashes (almost) and this is always successful.

Both my superiors have now returned from tour and – my period in charge of the Division being at an end – I now hope to get out myself. This is the long delayed moment for which I have been waiting. First of all I am going to a town about eighty miles away to do some town-planning and general cleaning up – working in conjunction with an MO – and then I shall go to bush properly in the southern part of the Emirate to supervise collection of tax. With brief intervals for recuperation I hope to remain out for the next six months.

On the second day of his first tour, which lasted a week, Tim decided to send his horse on by land while he took a canoe along the river.

I wished you could have seen me, sitting in a camp-chair in the bow of a little dug-out canoe with my gun and my camera and my Shakespeare, sometimes having a shot at a duck, sometimes pausing to take a photograph and sometimes trying to get by heart the prayer-scene from 'Hamlet' to which, as you know, I have always been rather attached.

The Head of the District to which I went is actually a grandson of the founder of the Sokoto dynasty, Usuman dan Fodiyo, who died in 1817, won his battles at the time that Napoleon won his, and must have been alive when George II was on the throne of England. That is pretty good going you know. And the old boy is as game as you please – he rode about 15 miles with me one day through a particularly searching storm – and greatly liked in the District. We got on very well together and I tell you I am proud to know such a game old chap.

I go out again on Thursday, when tax announcement begins. I shall be making a fairly long circuit, 75 miles by lorry to begin with, then about 150 by horse and another 100 to finish up with in a lorry again. You might imagine me starting from Devizes and driving to Southampton, then riding from there through London to say Leicester and being fetched again from there back to Devizes. It will take 16–20 days I expect and should prove fairly strenuous as the rains are at their height and there is a largish river I have to cross and re-cross as best I can. The DO who did the circuit last year swam it but as his followers refused to attempt it, he had to swim it back again.

In the following letter Tim explained the ins and outs of tax collecting.

I am at the moment in a very remote part of the world about 100 miles south of Sokoto. I am doing the southerly circuit announcing tax for the current year. This probably does not mean very much to you so I will try to explain. It is first decided in Sokoto on what level of adult-male incidence tax will be paid in each district; it is usually between 6/6d and 7/6d. Armed with this knowledge and with elaborate lists of village populations you work out your total for the district – say £3000 – and then summoning all the Village, Hamlet and Ward Heads, together with the more important peasantry of the whole district, you divide it among them, first village by village and then, taking each village separately, hamlet by hamlet.

Supposing for the moment you were announcing the North Wiltshire tax, you would arrive in Devizes and find a crowd of notables, 200–500 strong, with Mr Armin (District Head) waiting to greet you. Although you had ridden over from Bath and had had no breakfast you would get down to work at once dividing your £3000 among ten or fifteen reluctant Village Heads. After prolonged negotiations you finally achieve what you think is rather a neat division. (What of course you don't know is that Churton is getting off light on the pretext of locusts but really because Mr Armin's fourth and favourite wife came from there and that Tilshead, being remote, is also being spared so as not to spoil the market for the private embezzlement in which the Village Head and Mr Armin are accustomed to collaborate and rejoice together.) You then send them away to divide these amounts among their hamlets and yourself retire to your shave and your breakfast.

Afterwards you take each village individually and check its work, altering most of it as often as not. When Market Lavington arrives you ask them if they are all satisfied with the division the Village Head has made. Mrs Hawse (Hamlet-Head of the Sands), as soon as she has overcome her natural reserve and her fear of little Mr Merritt (the rascally Village Head who last year caught her concealing cattle-tax and only agreed to overlook the matter on the condition that she handed the proceeds into his safe-keeping) says, she doesn't think they can pay £7.10.0. Having recourse to your Ready Reckoner you see that it is indeed much too much, representing an adult male incidence of 9/11d as against only 3/6d in Eastcott. You make the necessary adjustments, drawing from the Hamlet Head of Eastcott (who has come mounted on a small and very shaggy pony) an ineffectual protest. You ask three times if anyone else has anything to say before you write in the several amounts in ink, but everyone is apparently satisfied so with a sigh of relief you do so. Just as you are blotting your ink Osman (representing his Hamlet-Head, who has been

3. Crossing a river

too busy to attend himself) is seen to awake from the deep sleep in which he has been sunk and to say that he thinks £6.17.0 is more than they can pay. With an Awful Look you relegate the Wild Man to his native Bornu and (if you are lucky) totter away to a long deferred lunch.

Yesterday was particularly strenuous, beginning with an eighteen-mile ride, then 1$^{1}/_{4}$ hrs work to divide the tax among the villages, then a shave and breakfast about midday and then on again with no lunch or tea until sunset. It is supposed to take no more than a day but if you do it conscientiously and work out all the incidences as I have been doing the day is a pretty full one. However, it is good fun and as the Districts are nearly all two treks apart one gets a day's comparative rest between them.

During the next tour he wrote:

The District Head of Mammande is rather a formidable man, the son of a former Sultan and a strong candidate for the succession. His family – one of the two from which the Sultans are chosen – have a bad record and although this man is efficient and personable I have a feeling that he may be a Bad Man. It is terribly difficult to tell, there is so much string pulling and so many little jealousies and rivalries on the one hand and relationships and connections on the other that one finds the truth very hard to get at. It might be supposed that a man with a grievance would say so without more ado but he doesn't, he is too afraid of what the Village or District Head will do to him afterwards and it is only with the greatest difficulty you can make them speak up. I have with me Isa and Sarkin-Dawaki who are a very trusty couple of assistants. Gwadabawa, where I now am, goes up to the French border and it provides considerable variation, in the south there is the river, in the middle bare rolling hill country and in the north sand-dunes. When I get up there I am going to Birnin-Konni to pay the French DO a visit, it should be rather fun but I believe their hospitality is rather overpowering.

We are just at the end of the rains now and the weather is rather nice. It is too early to start sleeping out again because the dew is very heavy but the early mornings are lovely and some of the country up here might almost be the Rhein.

I had a brush the other day with some of the locals in attempting to settle an old grievance they had against one of their neighbours. I took the side of the solitary neighbour (he may be a scoundrel but they can't prove and won't say what they have against him so he must be regarded as a righteous man) and the opposition became very excited and difficult to handle. They are a Sul-Tuareg tribe who recently immigrated to this country and by way of protest they packed their bags and started to emigrate back to French country. I have just heard that they have come back again and anyway the matter is not settled. I hope Sokoto will not let my solitary neighbour down because it is 50–1 against him. He is right and they are wrong, of that I am sure.

I must tell you this: the other night out shooting I met an old man, who must have been 85–90, tottering home under a load of firewood. I had a little chat with him and made sure that 'they' weren't making him pay tax. As I was bidding him farewell he advised me to go home because 'it was very damp'. The old pet! He was over his ankles in water and wearing hardly anything.

In December Tim wrote to let Aunt Iva know he would be home shortly.

In five days' time I leave Sokoto. Did I tell you that I am being posted to another province next tour? Scott is coming up here and I am going to the Benue. That will be the other Africa, dark forests and ju-jus and Lord knows what. I shall be sorry to leave but they say I shall return to Sokoto for my third tour, e.g. in 1940. I don't think I shall like the Benue so well but it will be interesting and useful experience.

* * * * *

Oturkpo 1938–39

After leave, part of which was spent in Italy, Tim left England in April, this time on the RMS Accra. His next posting was to Oturkpo in the Idoma Division of Benue Province and it must have been quite a culture shock because the Idomas had nothing in common with the Hausas and the Fulani.

I have been posted to the station where Scott spent part of his time but I am glad to say that it is not the one described as the Riverside Inferno. On the contrary it is well situated on a steep escarpment overlooking a sea of bush towards a line of hills in the South. It rains about twice as much as in Sokoto but by compensation is twice as cool. I have got a nice house – with two storeys and furniture – and an attempt at a garden. The personnel of the station is a DO with three ADOs under him (we are expected to spend at least three weeks a month on tour) and one policeman. The DO, Policeman and one ADO have wives and there is a tennis-court, so on the whole my surprise has been wholly pleasant.

I went out on tour almost at once and shall stay out about 3 weeks this time. I have got a touring area of my own about which I will tell you more when I know more myself. It is a very different country to Sokoto; the vegetation varies from thick bush to dense forest and the villages – for protection – are all set in the densest part of the forest. The people are extremely primitive and worship very strange gods; ju-jus and shrines are everywhere. They were only brought under administration in 1923 and five years later they staged quite a handsome rebellion. They were pretty badly beaten up when the rising was suppressed and have subsequently been more docile; at the same time they are always liable to fly off the handle – especially when some old-man says he has found a 'medicine' against bullets or when a malcontent spreads the rumour that the British are going – and need very careful handling and watching. My boys profess to have a very low opinion of them but are secretly rather frightened I think, not without cause because about 40 Hausa traders were massacred in the last flare-up.

The faithful Maiholi Kuku and Usuman were standing in the rain to meet me at Port Harcourt; the steward boy Labbo has succeeded in contracting dysentery, tetanus and bilharzia (one of the worms) all at the same time but is almost recovered and is said to be joining me soon. The post-cards I sent them had been duly treasured up and – believe it or not – Maiholi sure enough produced the Doges Palace and said what a fine house I had!

I am endeavouring to learn the language and if I spend my whole tour here I think I shall manage it all right. If I succeed I shall be one of a select band of about half a dozen who can speak it; it is not a very lovely lingo but is said to be superior to some. There are some German Missionaries in the Division so I hope to get some practice in that too.

I must stop now as a mob has assembled to see me (quite amiable, don't be alarmed).

In his next letter home, Tim reported on the new company which had supplied him with all his kit.

You ask if the O&GT Company did me well or not. On the whole yes; I have only two complaints, both of minor importance. One is that I specified a shaving-mirror with a non-wooden frame and they not only supplied one with a wooden frame but so small that I have to shave on the instalment system; the other that the papers I ordered from them are only now beginning to arrive, seven weeks after sailing. But, as I say, these are small points and considering that I placed all my orders at the eleventh hour they have done very well.

I am still out on tour and shall be for another ten days. I have had two boundary disputes to settle; most tiresome things because the original demarcation was made so long ago that the beacons are either quite or almost invisible and anyway the people were then so imperfectly tamed that they now deny having given their consent and in some cases say they were never consulted. Thereupon they produce some shrine, usually well within another tribe's territory, and say that it marks the traditional boundary between them and this other tribe and further that to run a boundary anywhere but through it would so enrage the indwelling spirit that everyone concerned would die almost instantly. It makes me very homesick for my easy-going and so much more reasonable Hausa. The local difficulties are of course increased by having to talk through interpreters. I thought of learning the local language – Idoma – but half the people in my area talk something else – Egedde – so I am wondering whether it would be worth it. Easy it is not: the word to 'think' – try this on l'onc or the dog – is 'mbgwalalea'. Not a bad beginning you must admit.

You may have seen in the papers that my old friend the Sultan is dead. This came as a frightful shock to me as he had always seemed perfectly fit and was not old, about sixty-five. He was really one of the nicest and best-mannered men that I have ever met and as a ruler he was rather like George V, extremely popular and to be relied upon to say and do the right thing at the right moment.

One of the duties of a District Officer was to act as Magistrate in places within the jurisdiction of the government and to review Native Court cases:

I am now immersed in a second murder case which seems to be even trickier than the first. It will possibly amuse you to hear the facts, such as they are. A small boy – the son of a trader of another tribe – disappeared one day on his way to market and the only answer to such a question in this Division is murder. There was however no corpse and no evidence. I foolishly left the case in local hands – having a lot of work myself – and a large number of people were arrested, but later all but four of them were released. These four then confessed and described how they had done it and why. When told to produce the body and the stolen load they could or would not do so. I sent written instructions that this was essential, and as a result a half-decomposed human head and the stolen load mysteriously appeared from nowhere, although the accused were all under arrest. Obviously very fishy. I therefore sent instructions that the rest of the corpse must be found: a day or two later a half-decomposed corpse appeared in the same mysterious way. A few days previously the whole village had been forced to take a most lethal oath and as a result of it a man came forward and said that it was he who had killed the boy and he named four accomplices. We therefore had two groups, coming from different kindreds, each professing to have committed the murder. The last four accomplices however denied complicity and the man who had confessed therefore named a fresh set of accomplices, two from the first group and two from the second, and modified the rest of his story to meet this new move. The final blow came when the old men admitted that the head that they had surrendered wasn't the head of the boy at all but an old skull doctored with decaying dog to make it small. Moreover a search in one of the suspected compounds revealed four and a half other skulls, of doubtful antiquity, the majority of them with chips in the bone indicating violent deaths. It is all too absurd for words and the culprit is probably someone we don't suspect at all. It is so much like an extravaganza that it is easy to forget that at the bottom of it all there is a brutal and cowardly head-hunting-cum-profit murder. The most ludicrous touch of all was provided by the man who said that he had seen the murder committed but as the murderer had given him 2d to hold his tongue he had of course said nothing. And we still don't know whether to believe him or not: it is quite feasible.

Within a few weeks Tim had settled down happily in his new surroundings.

You will be glad to hear that I am beginning to like this part of the country much better now. Scott greatly exaggerated the hardships of the climate, probably because he was unfit and therefore viewing everything with jaundiced eyes; it is milder in every way than Sokoto. Now that I am getting used to the people I like them much better too; they are rogues and vagabonds of course to a man but are not altogether displeasing. There is no need, by the way, to be nervous, as they are perfectly docile now.

We get a lot of quiet fun each month out of the minutes of the native-courts, some of which are written in English, and an unofficial prose prize is awarded each month. Last month I read in the account of a case of assault: 'So-and-so attacked me and cut off my neck, so I ran to the chief and reported it'. One of the scribes produced an offence which, so far as I know, is not included in any criminal code in the world. It was described as: 'Noise making and playing rubbish in court'; how much more expressive than our expression 'contempt'. So remember Mrs Sturton when they pull you up before the beak never noise-make and above all don't play rubbish in court; it is always punished with the utmost rigour of the law.

In August Tim wrote of another, very complicated, murder case.

I have just had a most strenuous month, one of the most strenuous I can ever remember. You will have gathered from previous letters what a heterogeneous area I have, five languages, eight districts and ten Native Courts. Of these districts I had not, on setting out, visited five and had only spent a few days each in two others so it was my object to do a round of them taking about three weeks. I had only done one, and taken a whole week over it anyway, when the following dramatic telegram was forwarded to me 'Corpse of brother found send detectives'. The detectives needless to say hurried to the spot, retrieved the corpse, which consisted of a skull and two forearm bones, and made four arrests and detained many others for questioning. I have been the detectives, I shall soon be Coroner and at the trial I may be Counsel for the Prosecution so what I shall not know about the case will not be worth knowing.

It will take too long if I attempt to describe how we wormed the information out of an unwilling village, most of whom are friends and relatives of the murderers, so I will just outline the events as I have reconstructed them. 'A' is the murdered man, 'B' his brother who sent the dramatic telegram, X is first murderer, Y is his brother, accessory after the fact, and Z is second murderer, still at liberty. M is the key-witness, cousin to X.

A was not a blood-brother of X and Y but had been adopted into their family and appeared to be living on good terms with them. X and Y however were jealous of him because he was more industrious than they and therefore more wealthy and they were heard to complain that he was not liberal enough with his money. 'A' hears that a rival of his wants to kill him so he determines to go to the fortune teller. An old woman is to take him to one that is highly spoken of but X, hearing of this, goes to the old woman and tells her to mind her own business because X will take A himself. The old woman therefore excuses herself and A, falling into the trap, asks X if he will go with him; X of course agrees. The night before they are to go X borrows rather a handsome knife from a relation of his and Z (second murderer) remembers that he has got to go to another village. Early next morning off they go, A carrying two yams and a chick to present to the fortune-teller and X with the smart knife strapped to his waist. They go to the house of a cousin first in a neighbouring village for a short gossip and then set off down the railway-line towards the fortune-teller's

4. Tim (right) and colleagues 'with the evidence' in Oturkpo

village. Suddenly Z pops out of a side path and says 'I have lost my goat somewhere in this grass; you might help me look for it'. 'Certainly old chap' says X obligingly and A of course helps too. Gradually they work their way into the thick grass away from the line until Z manages to slink up behind A and slip a cord over his head which he instantly draws tight; A is then divested of his clothes (so as not to spoil them) before X dispatches him with his smart knife. The body is buried, Z is paid his fee which may have been £1 and may have been £3 and they go their several ways.

X on his return announces that A has gone on a journey but as he then proceeds to sell-up all A's belongings no-one really believes him. B, in very bad taste, takes his story to Scott last November but there is no corpse at that time and X is able to produce a plausible enough story to avoid arrest. There the matter would have stood had not fate taken a hand.

X at this time began to develop a form of leprosy in which reddish running sores appear on the body; he immediately concluded that it was A's blood finding its way out. He was also troubled with nightmares in which A appeared to him and so he concluded that A's spirit was restless and must be pacified.

A medicine-man was consulted who said that X must dig up the corpse re-bury the skull and fore-arm bones (the effective parts of a skeleton) and bring the rest to him so that he could make a medicine. X with the help of his brother Y does all this one moonless night and the three of them burn and grind these bones to a powder and this powder is put in a calabash and hung up in X's house. The nightmares persist however so X determines to perform a rite over the skull and fore-arm bones; this must be done at night and as he is afraid to go alone and as Y is unwilling to accompany him, he falls back on M, now our key witness.

M is his cousin and senior to himself so X has no hesitation in telling him all about it, as they sit in the dry bed of a stream over the place where the skull is and perform their rites. This in itself was not a mistake because there is so much family solidarity that M would not have dreamt of breathing a word of it to anyone if X had paid him the yams that he had been promised. X's cupidity however got the better of his common-sense and he never made good his promise, so M in a moment of pique (which he has bitterly regretted since) hinted to B where the remains of the corpse might be found. B found it and the rest you know.

It is an interesting case I think from every point of view, legally because it bristles with difficulties connected with the laws governing the admissibility of hearsay evidence and confessions to third parties, evidence of accessories, evidence of accessories' wives and so on; psychologically it is interesting as it contains a shining example of the silly mistake most murderers make; and anthropologically it is interesting as it throws considerable light on the working of their minds and of their social fabric.

All the while, Tim had been trying his best to learn the local language but was finding it much harder than Hausa.

In the last month I have made what I might describe as a real pass at the Idoma language. It is terribly difficult to understand. I can only say that it is like a man with a hare-lip speaking through a gas-mask. I have had my messenger in every evening for an hour between bath and dinner and now I am beginning to understand what he says when speaking slowly and distinctly, though needless to say when an Idoma is speaking fast and indistinctly I don't catch more than 1 word in 10 or 20. However it is beginning to come and in 2 more months I hope to start dispensing with an interpreter. It is an easy language in that it has no depth at all and it is difficult only in that most sounds have two meanings and most meanings two sounds and in that there is an enormous amount of elision. Once I have pierced this hard outer shell the rest should be fairly easy and with any luck I may take my exams at Christmas. If successful I hope to persevere and take the intermediate test next summer; this has only been achieved by the man I told you about who speaks twenty-eight languages. (Did I tell you that he has been known to observe indignantly: 'It is not a gift; it has taken me as much as six weeks' hard work to master a language.')

I am learning entirely by ear because understanding is far more difficult than talking with these languages which have no relation to anything one already knows.

I am going out again in a day or two to hold the inquest on my murdered man and complete the case for the prosecution. The ground-up bone and ashes were pronounced on analysis to be human, probably, but not those of an adult, so that part of the case falls through. I have caught my second murderer however and on the whole am fairly confident. I will let you know more next time.

In September, when Chamberlain went to Munich to negotiate with Hitler the settlement of the Czechoslovakian question, the repercussions were felt as far afield as the dense forests of Benue Province.

I am sorry there has been such a gap in my writing but I am afraid you must blame the crisis for it. You may be interested to hear how it affected us out here.

Well about the 23rd of last month I came into the station from bush to find that a crisis was believed to be taking place in Europe but that no-one knew very much beyond the fact that Chamberlain had flown or was just going to fly to Berlin. This was disturbing but no-one really knew what it was all about so I don't think we lost much sleep. On the 24th we, that is a fellow ADO, his wife and I, went in to the Headquarters of the Province, Makurdi, where the Resident had previously bidden us. When we arrived we found him offering 5–1 on war, next day it was 10–1 and before we left he was quoting 15–1. We didn't do much that week-end except cluster round his wireless and discuss the chances. When Hitler spoke I was given pencil and paper and told to translate and this I managed to do with fair success until mercifully relieved by the announcement of dinner.

Even with the wireless there was a great deal of uncertainty. One day we heard that 'Pintpot' was proclaiming his adherence to the Rome–Berlin axis in theory but was in practice intending to show that the axis had a Differential Gear; next day we heard that Pintpot had definitely thrown in his lot with Hitler. Conversely we heard that one day the USSR was staunchly supporting the French alliance and next day was saying that she hadn't mobilised and knew nothing at all about a crisis. All against Germany would be one thing and Germany and Italy v France and GB would be quite another, so you can imagine how flat a spin we were in.

My own estimate of the odds was 6–4 on war before Pintpot said he would support Hitler and 5–2 on afterwards. If it had broken out I had made up my mind to get home as quickly as possible and join the RAF, because after the wastage of say three months of war that, I am positive, is where we should want the men and, while admitting limitations to the efficiency of aerial warfare, I still think one half trained pilot would then be worth at least one half-trained company of infantry.

Most people out here were quietly confident of our preparedness for war, but I am afraid I remained sceptical, and I must say your story of the 40,000 gas-masks painted the moral for me.

The papers of the crisis still have not arrived, so we are not sure yet who climbed down and how much and whether it isn't going to begin all over again next spring.

So long as Hitler was only putting right the wrongs of Versailles I must say I had a sneaking sympathy for him, but all that has quite gone now and I am afraid he must be classed with Pintpot as being of the genus menace. It is comforting to think that the Germans would have to be very hard up for targets or extremely bad shots before anything fell on Lavington.

Once the crisis had died down, life returned to normal and Tim went out on tour.

The touring here is rather different from Sokoto; there you were liable to go anywhere within the very large area – 25,000 square miles – of the Emirate whereas here you have an area of your own to look after. My particular one is triangular in shape, just about 1000 square miles and carrying a population of about 85,000 persons, chiefly of the criminal classes. I spend at least twenty days every month touring in this area and the balance of my time in Oturkpo.

The DO tells me that he is going to move me from this area to another one and, since this will mean getting away from these five languages to where a fairly uniform Idoma is spoken, I am rather glad. I am still toiling at the language and I am glad to say have just begun to see the light at the other end of the tunnel. Sometimes it seems quite near and sometimes as far away as ever (it is when I can't even tell whether they are talking Idoma or one of their other beastly languages that I begin to feel a little depressed) but barring accidents I shall definitely win through now. I hope I am not transferred elsewhere at the critical moment, it would be annoying to think of my labours going down the drain.

In recent weeks I have been concerned chiefly with tax-collection and this I am glad to say is almost over. You have to chivvy the Idoma a good deal before he pays his three or four shillings.

You will be amused to hear that I have become very keen on gardening and today – Sunday – I have put in three or four hours at it. Unfortunately I started rather late and, being out of the station most of the time and having to send a long way for seeds, the rains are almost over and a lot of my seedlings are still in their boxes.

I took over something of a barren waste and although there is not much to show for my tenure so far I think next season there may be quite a decent blossoming. I am still crassly ignorant of species but the ones I am growing or trying to grow are marigolds of various types, balsam, snap-dragons, dianthus, petunia, nasturtium and phlox.

The house is situated on laterite, a gravelly soil quite useless for a garden, so all our earth has to be brought from elsewhere on a lorry and lowered into beds scooped out for the purpose. I have got a good garden-boy: he looks much more like a gorilla than a human-being but is willing, amiable and quite shrewd. Once or twice a week I get half a dozen prisoners and they are a great help.

Maiholi Kuku by the way is in much better form than last tour and is really cooking very decently. He has found a yeast that suits him and is making as decent bread as I have tasted anywhere in the country. Further, we are on the Railway here and so I can always get fresh butter and now and then a kipper or some English bacon from the Railway cold-storage. And I have also got a Frig. so domestically I am much happier.

In the New Year Tim described how he had spent Christmas.

Our Christmas here was slightly depressing because first Simey, one of the ADOs, and then Mrs were unfit and when there are only four of you anyway it makes it difficult for the others to be hilarious. The Idoma, too, made their customary effort to sabotage the issue by staging a miniature riot on Boxing Day, the underlying belief being that since it was a European holiday they could kill a man and it wouldn't count. The only thing that really suffered was my dinner-party, which had to wait while we pacified them. Having celebrated Christmas with a riot, they welcomed the New Year with a particularly brutal and senseless murder. We were out from 12.30–3.30 a.m. and we found the unfortunate victim lying on his back in his farm, staring up at the stars, with half his chin cut away and two deep wounds in his neck.

This happened on our return from Makurdi, the Provincial Headquarters, where we spent the actual New Year. This is a sort of annual treat and there were lots of parties laid on for us and all enjoyed a good time.

Did I tell you that my murder case looks like falling with a resounding crash to the ground? I mentioned, I think, that the weak link was the connection between the skull and bones and the man that disappeared; I don't know whether I also mentioned that the Pathologist who examined them wrote an extremely slip-shod and ill-expressed report. What he meant to say was 'the bones are those of a human-being of 5'1" or 5'2" and since this is nearer the average height of normal women than of normal men it is more likely to be a woman than a man'. What he actually said was in para. 2 'it is probably a woman' and in para. 3 'if the tribes in these parts are small of stature it is almost certainly a man'. Now Crown Counsel by seizing on para. 2 and ignoring para. 3 has given it as his majestic opinion that this phrase casts an irremovable doubt over the whole case and that it is not even worth prosecuting. This is extremely daunting and I could gladly do that Pathologist an injury; I say his report was slip-shod not only because of the contradictory phrases I have quoted but because of the careless typing and correcting of what would have been an extremely important document in a capital case. I am going to try to fight back but I haven't much hope. I am not just annoyed at losing my scalps or at having a month's work go down the drain but from the little I have told you of this Division you will appreciate that deterrents are pretty badly needed.

A couple of months later Tim was rather pleased to have a change. He would now be looking after the north of the Division whose Districts were much more homogeneous and where only one language, the one he was trying to learn, was spoken.

Trying to master Idoma in the south was like trying to pick up French in the Balkans, but now I hope to get down to it in some earnest.

I spent nearly all February trying to finish off one murder – this I did – and to bring another one to light. I think I mentioned the rather macabre incident of the head. It was first produced, severed and in advanced decomposition, in connection with murder A; subsequently it was stated that it was not a new head but an old one garnished with dead-dog; the Pathologist now states that the head is definitely a new one and my latest theory is that the head really belongs to the B murder and was only put out, as it were, on loan to murder A. I have handed the whole case over to the policeman who arrived at the beginning of the year and was rather thankful to do so. Murder in this country is just too easy.

My pups have grown up into the most revolting little pi-dogs and I have given them all away except one and I think he will follow shortly. The mother I still have and she is a nice old thing.

If the Dictators go on as they are doing now there is almost bound to be a war I think; Hitler is completely unbalanced and Mussolini's plight at home seems to be so serious that he must either gamble for increasingly high stakes or go under. Do you remember I told you last year that a German had bet me 1 BM that Prague would be part of the Reich within 2 years. He wins apparently. The only thing one can really hope for, it seems, is that the Dictators will outdo themselves and fail to fool even their own people. It is not insignificant that when I made my bet all the other listeners, simple souls, took my side on the ground that Prague wasn't and never had been German.

Back in England, a big change was about to occur that would affect Tim deeply. His uncle, the Vicar of Market Lavington, was about to retire which meant that he and Aunt Iva would have to move out of The Vicarage.

What you said in your last letter about leaving the Vicarage made me absolutely miserable. I knew, of course, that it had to come sometime, because you mentioned it once before, and naturally l'onc can't go on running a big parish for ever. But the idea of anyone else living in the Vicarage is simply preposterous and I can't think of it without – well I don't quite know what, but you know what I mean.

All that you say is true, but so much less than the truth. I have never known any other home, or anything approaching one, and when I think of England now I think of Lavington and the Plain, not anywhere else, and in the middle of them the house and everything about it, garden, loft, apple-room, field, kitchen, hall, cannery and all. If I feel like this about it I can't picture what it must be for you. And the Unk, after forty-three years, it really is heart-breaking: I don't know what to say.

There is little news from here. I plod on with Idoma and the more I learn the more I realise how much I underrated it in the first place. For variety it has Cleopatra absolutely cold: there are literally about half a dozen ways of saying any one thing. There are four level tones and three falling tones and each word has one tone per syllable; when elision takes place, which it always does, to the very bone, these tones alter and a tone may jump across from one word to another. The language is written in the phonetic script with tones indicated underneath and apostrophes to show where elision has taken place: the whole looks rather like Russian on blotting paper.

If ever I master Idoma I feel that I shall be able to tell any reasonable language exactly where it gets off. What is so maddening about it is when you say for instance, 'ADUM' and draw a blank; you repeat it in every possible tone combination of which you are capable; and your mentor suddenly says, with the air of a man who knows that only his perspicacity and nimble wits have enabled him to penetrate the fog in which the subject has been shrouded, 'O, you mean ADUM'. That, I may say happens constantly.

I am getting more and more absorbed in gardening. The rains are under way now and so I am at present planting out my seedlings: zinnia, dahlia, balsam, marigold, phlox and nasturtium. In another six weeks I think there ought to be a very good show. Flowering shrubs do well if given enough earth and I have put in a lot of Flamboyant and Pride of Barbados, both very pleasant to the eye. Bougainvillaea too does well, and Coralita, which Maurice probably knows as Honolulu. It is delightful to come back to a garden after a long tour and see how everything has progressed. My boy is as devoted, hard-working and simian as ever, and his salary has consequently been advanced to 12/- p.m. It sounds incredibly little but the poverty of Africa is astonishing. Road labourers get 3d a day and the jobs are sufficiently sought after to enable the headman to make quite a lot on the side in conferring them. My boy, in fact, on his 12/- p.m. is almost a monied man.

The next time Tim wrote, he had been acting as District Officer and they were short-staffed.

The DO – Heath – was invalided home last month and I have been in charge of the Division and will be until another DO, who is expected soon, arrives. Being one's own master is most exhilarating and in a life in which dozens of decisions have to be taken every day it is positively delightful to be able to do so without spoken or mental reservations.

There have only been two of us, another Cadet called Frost and myself, in a Division which should be run by a DO, three ADOs and a Policeman, so we have been extraordinarily busy. Counting my Idoma lessons I have been doing a twelve-hour day as often as not lately; this was partly due to an accumulation of office work and as I have now made that good I hope to be able to let up in the next few days.

There has only been one panic. I settled a chieftainship dispute that has been dragging off and on for a long time and, congratulating myself on its success, went on tour elsewhere. When I was sixty miles away the customary SOS., now almost legendary in this Division, came through to HQ: 'Come quickly, we are shooting each other with guns'. Out where I was I got wind of this and heard to my dismay that Frost, who is new to the Division and was ignorant of the fact that this particular sub-clan had in the past killed soldiers as well as police, had sent five constables, unaccompanied by a messenger, to arrest the ring leader. I came back to HQ at once by lorry, fearing the worst and working out in my head how we could meet different circumstances, but found the Police had just got back and that all was well. I can, however, envisage lots of circumstances which might have made us a head or two and a rifle or two short.

Having broken the back of the tour, Tim was now considering the options for the journey back to England. He thought it would be fun to travel overland to Timbuktu and fly home from there.

I have submitted an application to be allowed to return home through French territory. There is one of those little collapsible canoes in this Province and I think it would be rather fun to make the journey in that. It is very light and it should be possible to do 25 miles a day in it. I should take either Maiholi Kuku or my steward-boy as far as the French border and then exchange him for the small boy, who hails from French country and understands one of the languages spoken there.

Luggage would consist of a mosquito-net and a kettle and possibly, by way of luxury, a bottle of Lea and Perrins sauce, equipment would be a small trawl net and a camera: I am most attracted to the idea and hope that permission will be granted.

The Government are very good and if they approve of the scheme you are given the cost of the normal passage home (£51) to defray the cost of travelling by an extraordinary route.

Needless to say the outbreak of war put paid to his plans.

The war has caused all leave to be cancelled, but it is supposed that it will be restored soon with everyone put back a month or two. I have abandoned all my schemes – naturally – and so I shall probably be home early next year.

At present I am trying to secure my release from the Nigerian Government – for the duration only – and permission to enlist in other than the local forces. My objective being the RAF. Don't think that I have gone belligerent, or anything of that sort; on the contrary, I still regard Germans as amiable, if misguided, creatures. But I don't feel capable of sitting kicking my heels in the tropics as long as the war lasts. For the present, the Idoma has ceased to interest me in the slightest. It is regrettable, but there it is.

We have got a number of German Roman Catholic Missionaries here and they all had to be interned; though now they have been released on parole. We have been quite friendly with them, and so we naturally tried to carry out our orders as tactfully and deprecatingly as possible.

At one time and another I have sat up until 2 a.m. so that one of their number should be met on arrival by a European and not by African Police; made a special journey to the Canteen to try to buy playing cards for them; offered to get them books from our library; performed a number of errands for them and finally lent them £10 out of my own money. For these little services we believed them to be grateful.

You can imagine my feelings therefore when a letter arrived yesterday from the Resident with a list of complaints against what they were pleased to describe as your 'inferior officers' (including myself) alleging that the Fathers had been treated as enemies and made to suffer indignities. The allegations which concerned me were:

> (a) that I had locked up their chapel and prevented the Lady Doctor from praying there,
> (b) that when making an inventory of their belongings, I had offered indignities to their sacred possessions.

I need hardly add that both were completely untrue. We have seen them several times and not a word was breathed to us; it was all done behind our backs. Talk about a generation of vipers!

45

I believe, really, it is ascribable to the pathological determination of the post-war German to indulge in that delectable luxury: self-pity. But still, if those are their ways, the sooner we part company the better.

You wouldn't suppose the war would affect our work here very much, but it has. Every scallywag who is in debt or does not want to pay tax has been going round spreading rumours that the British have lost the war and the Germans are coming to take over the country. In his heart of hearts I am sure the Idoma doesn't believe it, but like his betters he is a wishful thinker (not because he knows anything of Germans but because he is simple-minded enough to believe that he would benefit from a change) and the rumours gain considerable credence: last trek I drew large crowds wherever I went for no other reason but that the people had heard that we had all gone.

I am just back from a very strenuous trek. Rainfall has been exceptionally heavy – 18" last month – and half the bush paths are water-logged: sometimes it is ankle-deep, sometimes knee-deep, sometimes waist-deep and sometimes you have to swim. I was up in the Benue valley where the mosquitoes were awful – just as busy indoors by day as by night. It was quite impossible to avoid being bitten, not once or twice but constantly, and the only thing to do was to take 10–15 grams Quinine a day instead of 5 and hope for the best. So far, I am glad to say, there have been no reactions. On top of it all the grass is now about 8" high and is giving me hay-fever.

I was not sorry to get back to my house and the garden which is looking rather nice. I sowed a lot of grass in the hope of getting a lawn and it has done excellently. At present there are zinnias, balsam, marigold, phlox, canna, dahlia, salvia and nasturtium: all blooming vigorously. From being the Cinderella, my garden has now grown to rival that of the DO, which has been well-cared for for at least five years now. That sounds rather an alarming blast on proper trumpet, but it isn't really: with your garden under my skin, as it were, I should be a poor thing if I couldn't make a good show.

Tim secured his release in November and sailed back to war.

– 2 –

England and Malta 1941–45

Tim joined the RAFVR in July 1940. He started at The De Havilland School of Flying in Hatfield, where he learned to fly Tiger Moths, then in September he was transferred to Grantham to fly Battles. The sorts of things they had to learn, practise and master were steep turns, climbing turns, precautionary landings, forced landings, gliding approach and landing, instrument flying, navigation and cross-country. During October, Tim had a very black day:

> Was sent out to do precautionary landings and forgot my undercart on the second one. Am far from being a methodical person, but I had always observed the drill laid down to prevent negligence of this sort, and normally always had at least two looks to make sure the wheels were safely down. Omitting one, luck had it that I omitted all, and I never dreamt anything was wrong until we fell down on to the prop and nose. Skidded to a standstill in about 50 yards, with the engine dead. Then, ironically enough, the horn which I had failed to hear above the engine when coming in, was blaring deafeningly. I had come in very low over the trees and hedge – about 2' at a guess – and this I suppose had prevented me from taking my usual final look. Not much visible damage, except to the prop, but the engine is probably bent. Good deal of raillery from the boys, though all are willing enough to admit that it might easily have been them.

He went up before the CO on a charge of negligently damaging HM a/c Battle P.6631, admitted frankly that he had no defence and escaped with an admonition: 'Feel I owe HM at least one jerry now.'

When he had some free time, he visited friends and family, and wrote letters. He was always pleased to hear news of Nigeria and when Aunt Iva sent him a cutting about the Sokoto Spitfire, he replied: 'I hope I am nominated pilot: it would be glory indeed to wield against Hitler a weapon bought with the pence of a cheerful, courteous people to whom he would deny even our common humanity.'

In the evenings he went out with his friends. One of them was quite involved with a girl:

> Met Richard's girlfriend and various other girls and had wonderful evening. She is no intellectual, but good-looking and vivacious and quite free from that common feminine suspicion of male good-humour when it verges on the riotous. At times rather envy Richard having someone to hold his hand, but when the mood wears off am always profoundly thankful I haven't; if the affections are not engaged it is, at best, unedifying and, if they are, both exacting and exhausting. As a generalisation I suppose one can say that fighting-efficiency is based on and strengthened by male comradeship, and that female influence is negative.

A couple of weeks later, when he had himself become fond of a girl, he changed his mind:

> Ours must be more or less typical war-time associations with our various girl-friends; nowhere are the affections very closely engaged, but we enjoy each other's company and are determined to make the most of the passing moment. Having been a bit sententious on the 2nd, I suppose it is fitting that I should have to eat my words on the 13th; but still, when all is said and done, they are still essentially male parties with female trimmings: the girls are in no sense a disruptive force.

At the end of November Tim heard that he had got a commission and after taking the Chief Flying Instructor's test, he was told that his assessment had been raised to 'above average'. In the final placings for the whole course he came fourth.

From December to January three of the friends were at Sutton Bridge for training on Hurricanes. Within a week Tim was enthusing:

A week of good flying. Did R/T, practice-homing, pin-pointing, air-to-ground firing, and practice forced-landing. More exciting was formation-flying; went up with Sing (instructor) and a New Zealander. Flying low over a bank of cloud was most exhilarating experience, especially as we were going fairly fast – about 250 mph – and the cloud looked just like snow in the brilliant sunshine. It was, in fact, rather like skiing. We dived down through the cloud and I managed to hold on to Sing. Received a kindly word for this exercise; encouraging, because at Grantham I was considered one of the lame ducks on it. On height-test I found 25,000 feet cold and lonely; shall have to accustom myself to it though. Power-dived down and got 410–20 mph on the clock at about 12,000 feet: must compute it sometime, it cannot be much less than 500 mph, a figure that is so satisfyingly round and large that I couldn't refrain from mentioning it in all my subsequent letters. I am afraid the exhibitionist is strong in most of us. Had no difficulty in pulling out, but experienced shooting pains on way down; hardly surprising, however, since I dropped 15,000 feet in a matter of seconds. Most exciting thing of all was undoubtedly low-flying: slightly frightening – especially the HT cables that kept appearing – but think it is the most exhilarating experience I have ever had. Cruised at just over 200 mph on zero boost and – though it is easy to exaggerate these things – think I must have been down to 6 to 8 feet at times. The more I fly them, the better I like our Hurricanes.

Practising dog-fights was all important and very exhausting:

Fought Sing first, who let me get on his tail and then tried to put me off; however, hung on all right and this seemed to impress him quite a lot. Puffed up with pride, then went to fight Freddie Wilson; soon found that not only was unable to get on his tail, but had work cut out to keep him off mine. Finally, trying to do too much, span at about 3000 feet, pulled out too quickly and span again at 2000 feet, experienced nasty realisation that if the mistake was repeated it would be last I ever made, so let her gather ample speed and found myself straight and level at 500 feet. Climbed back to 8000 feet, with Wilson on tail, and started again; managed to throw him off, but he was getting back again when it was time to pack up. Pride quite deflated. Final fight, in the late evening, with reflector sight showing up like a grill, was against Kelly; flew machine Freddie had fought me in and found it a superb turner, made circles inside Kelly, who hasn't many hours on Hurrys yet. Should like to have had a return match with Freddie, exchanging machines. Found dog-fighting astonishingly hard work: the machine has to be thrown about the sky. Amazing how the Hurry can be flown round a tight turn at less than 100 mph.

At the beginning of February, Tim, Richard and another friend were posted to No 257 Squadron at Coltishall, which was just what they wanted. During that month the weather was mostly indifferent to bad, but they flew whenever possible.

Richard, Ian and I gradually initiated to Squadron duties and finally pronounced operational by day; being better than some at formation flying undoubtedly helped materially. Did my first patrols and gradually got accustomed to quick scrambles, regular instrument check-overs, search formation, and all the other novelties. One day, I noticed my oil pressure was low; watched it and, when it continued to fall, turned for base and throttled back, height then about 6000 feet. Couldn't see aerodrome at first, but luckily picked it out, because moment later there was a detonation in the engine and everything smothered in glycol-fumes, accompanied by violent juddering; difficult to see ground at all, but from glimpses reckoned I would just glide in past the hangars; engine dead by this time, but kept nose down and airspeed up, though had to lean forward and peer to see the indicator; came in by the hangar at 110 mph, lifted a wing over a dispersed aircraft and banged her down on the field with everything retracted; flames coming out of the manifolds, so jumped out quickly. Diagnosed afterwards as a bearing, which had given, and been thrown out through the jacket, releasing all the glycol; exonerated from all blame, in contrast with my last wheels-up landing. Quite unhurt, but morally rather shaken.

In April the three friends completed their night-training and the squadron was re-equipped with Hurricane IIs. Tim's comment was: 'climb and performance at altitude seem much better, and the 4 canon armament should be very powerful'.

By May Tim had a new girlfriend called Berrice. During the next few weeks they saw each other frequently and their romance blossomed:

Did you get in safely the other night? By safely I mean were you able to delude your poor mama into believing it was only half-past eleven; I hope you did. I was told on arrival yesterday that I looked tired but it was adroitly put down to night-fighting.

Towards the end of June, Tim and Richard were speculating about some recent postings. They came to the conclusion that they had been converted into a training squadron, that the finished products were being passed on elsewhere, and that, therefore, they could not expect to survive indefinitely. He told Berrice that it was something they would have to make up their minds to face:

Life seems at its worst to be one long series of good-byes, and I suppose I have had my fair share and more of them, but that brings me small comfort at the thought of this one. We are both going to be pretty unhappy if the worst comes to the worst, but there is nothing that can be done about it and if it comes it comes, and we shall have to make the best of it. But even so I should see you again, sometime, somewhere. I don't mean 'should' but 'shall'.

Berrice must have thought that he was trying to end their relationship because in his next letter he wrote:

I never said anything about things finishing. And what do you mean by 'perhaps it would be just as well'; I'm going to give you some third degree when I see you again! Do you think you ought to pluck up courage and present me to your mama? She doubtless thinks I'm a very bad type (even if she didn't wake up the other night) and introduction will no doubt only confirm that impression, but I think we might try. Anyway, I leave it to you.

In August Tim shot down his first bandit:

Found it difficult to believe aircraft had any occupants, and couldn't help feeling more pleased with the way things had turned out than sorry for them. Poor devils. Richard horribly jealous, as I should have been if he'd got the first.

In September Tim joined 133 Squadron, one of the Eagle squadrons. They were flying Hurricanes to begin with but expected to be given something better when they became operational. He wrote:

The Yanks are a very nice lot indeed and I think I shall get on with them. With a few exceptions they are all very young, not so much actually as in their outlook on life, and they often give me the feeling, just as Africans do, that I am handling children. Only don't tell them I said so! Africans may be crafty, deceitful and addicted to all the vices in the calendar, but they are still for the most part children; similarly these Yanks are tough, hard-boiled and intensely independent, but infants still.

I feel flattered at being given a flight of them, but the responsibility is a heavy one: the number of them who are going to survive depends on the way we train them in the next months or so. At present they all think that the only requisite for a good fighter pilot is the ability to throw his aeroplane all over the sky, preferably upside down. I try to impress on them that vigilance and good shooting are more important, but they don't pay much attention.

There is only one thing I miss and that's the self-deprecation or effacement that most civilised English people possess. Admittedly it is entirely assumed, but it is none the less an endearing quality and so restful compared with American competitiveness. However, that's a small thing and by and large they are an exceptionally nice crowd.

The following month the squadron was sent to Northern Ireland for special training. Before leaving, Tim had proposed to Berrice but he wanted to get the fighting over before they married.

I wish the beastly war would finish. I so very much want to live that it quite frightens me sometimes: I'm afraid I might fail in my duty. I don't think I shall, because I think I have got myself under sufficient control to do what I have to without thinking about it too much, but I'm not naturally a pug, and you never know how you are going to react to any situation until you meet it. That's one of the reasons I want to wait until the end of the war: I'm afraid I might go soft and now that I'm in this thing I have to see it finished. You do see that, don't you? I never even asked you when you would like it to be, which hardly shows me to be very considerate: will you tell me in your next letter? I have always had the idea that the war is going to end next autumn, but if it doesn't I don't know that I should want to wait any longer, in spite of what I have said.

Later he wrote:

I quite agree with you about the futility of waiting too long, but do you mind if it's till next year. I've tried to define my reasons, possibly not very successfully. Do you remember the Normans and Saxons at the battle of Hastings, or rather before it, one side alternately praying and limbering up their sword arms, the other heading for a stupendous hangover. Well it's not that exactly, but it's something like that: I want to fight my way through next summer and have you, if you still want me, waiting for me on the far side, not have you now and fight unwillingly and timidly next summer. This probably doesn't make sense to you, but it is as clear as I can put it. So shall we say next autumn, unless the heavy fighting is over for me earlier than that, in which case it can be as soon as you like.

Throughout the war Tim kept in touch with Maiholi:

I had a letter from my old cook Maiholi a day or two ago, he's a pretty ropey cook but a dear old man, I'm sure you'll like him. He starts as if I was a patriarch: 'Greetings and friendship and respect and fidelity and an asking after your health and that of all your people, young and old, male and female…'

That however is just the local style. I always urge him to pray for me and he finishes: 'May Allah bring you forth safely, may you return to Nigeria, and may we meet each other once more in health and joyfulness. We are praying for you to Allah to the utmost of our endeavour.'

Isn't he an old wizard? Actually I had just written to him myself, telling him among other things about my first victory. I know exactly what he'll do, put on his best robes and his longest turban, go down to the local market and there shoot a most preposterous line. MGM has nothing on him in that respect and he's quite capable of making me a legendary figure before I know where I am.

Meanwhile Berrice had also been undergoing training to be a driver in the ATS and was stationed in North Wales. On his return from Northern Ireland, Tim went to see her but the visit was not a success:

It's useless to pretend that something didn't go rather badly wrong on Wednesday: it has been going round and round and round in my head ever since and I feel we must clear it up before we go any further. So I'm going to tell you what I thought and how I felt, and I hope you will do the same when you reply, and then we may discover how it happened and be able to avoid it in the future. I hope what I'm going to say won't sound as if I'm trying to put the blame on you; if it should, please remember that I quite realise that anything you said or did may have been in response to something I said or did, and the fault therefore my own.

Do you remember at one point I said it wasn't you, and you asked had you changed? Well, that's the feeling I had, on and off, all the evening; you seemed to be rather hard and impersonal and restless, not particularly pleased to see me in the first place, not especially impressed that I had used most of my leave petrol in getting down to see you, and not very sympathetic on leaving me with the prospect of a night in the car on unknown roads. The last two were small enough, goodness knows, and I should never have given them another thought if it wasn't for the first. As it was, it just wasn't you. I felt as if I was taking an actress out at times, you seemed to be so much more concerned about your public, e.g. your original embarrassment and subsequent fear of being in late, than about me.

Then, your saying you didn't think we would ever get married: there could only be three causes, your changing your mind, my changing my mind, or my being killed. I suppose if you thought it was the last that was going to prevent us, you would hardly have mentioned it; that left the first two, and I naturally jumped to the conclusion that you had already changed yours, but hadn't the courage to say so directly. If you think that unreasonable, put yourself in my place and consider what you'd think if I had said the same thing.

The result of all this was that I left that night believing that your feelings for me had changed. I spent the night trying to find my way through those pitch black valleys, losing my road every few miles and finding no-one to ask: on the whole I was thankful for the physical distraction, because my thoughts were in much worse case. Later, when things had fallen into place more, I hoped I was wrong, but I'm still not sure.

This is terribly important: if your feelings have changed, admit it to yourself and me. Even if you are not sure what your feelings are, you must tell me; there is no reproach in that, and I would wait.

There was another thing that worried me: when you said you didn't think you could make me happy I again thought you were feeling your way towards a break; if you think me unreasonable, try it on yourself. An occasional row, however high tempers were, couldn't break up a marriage if the two people really loved each other and felt the same way about the important things of life. That's why you're so aggravating sometimes; you never will tell me your inner thoughts or hopes or ideals and I still only half know you.

And this is where I owe you an explanation. I'm afraid I was very incoherent when trying to tell you something that night and I don't think you fully understood. I will try and amplify so that if you have any doubts it may help you to make up your mind.

What I was trying to say was that I had been lucky in life and that I felt I owed life a debt which, if I lived, I wanted to repay. My only aptitude is for a job like the one I have and I want to do something useful and constructive, not just grub about for money or pleasure. When I said I would give up anything for you except that, I meant that if you were to say that you didn't think you would stand the life or the climate, and that if I wanted to marry you I must get something at home, I should feel that I must choose my job. What I mean is that I should have to choose it, just as much as if you were to say you would only marry me if I got myself a nice safe job on the ground while this war lasts. I am sorry, the suggestion that you would do either is wholly unfair, and I know you wouldn't, but I told you I had never said anything but the truth to you, and when I said I would give up anything for you I had to add that qualification. Moreover I still mean every word of what I said earlier in the evening.

In case you only half know me, perhaps I had better say some more about these things. I told you I was ambitious once: that was about five years ago when I wanted to be top boy at all costs. But I've got over that now, and I only want to be top-boy if I think I should be better at it than anything else, or anyone else, and much more than that I should like to earn the trust and affection of the people I'm looking after. In other words I want to be a good Resident, rather than a thrusting Chief Commissioner.

What is more, if I get back I want to work hard – I have always taken a pretty grim view of people who draw their salaries out of the country and think that because they're homesick, or its hot or something, they are under no obligation to do their jobs. And I'm not terribly sociable and until I know people really well I much prefer not having them around. And I don't like too many parties.

You said you didn't know whether you could make me happy, because you occasionally lost your temper and said violent things: that wouldn't worry me in the least. The only thing that would make me unhappy is if you allowed yourself to be hard and frivolous and pleasure-seeking and self-centred, or rather if you allowed yourself to lead that sort of life, when I know that you really have all the opposite qualities.

You said that you were a very ordinary person and you wouldn't be much help to me; again I wasn't sure whether you were being modest or were feeling your way towards something. Anyway, you know perfectly well it isn't true, you have out-of-the-ordinary qualities, but I know you so little that I still don't know how you want to use them, or whether you want to use them at all.

Please tell me more about yourself. I know it isn't easy, and I have never been able to do it with anyone else, but I have tried to do so with you because I thought it was terribly important that we should know each other through and through, the good, the bad and the indifferent.

I hope nothing I've said will hurt or offend: I've had to write as I have, because I've been trying to thrash this thing out in my head ever since it happened and it still doesn't add up. When you answer please be equally frank and for goodness sake tell me something, I shan't mind how rude it is. And please remember that everything I said earlier that evening still holds, you will always be my one and only now.

Tim then spent Christmas in Holbeach with his family.

I have been very lazy since arrival and have done precisely nothing, but am rather enjoying so doing: being warm, and unworried, and perfectly safe makes rather an engaging change, I find. I read during the day, go for walks with my mama, and we usually play bridge in the evenings. My elder sister – Cynthia – is here too: she is the betwixt-and-between of the family, from my point of view. Alma and I talk exactly the same language, but my brothers – Alan and Maurice, you may as well start learning the names! – I just don't understand from Adam and have nothing in common with. Cynthia lies between the opposing poles.

Harmattan, A Wind of Change

I had a vile journey here from Chester, I know it was foolish to try, but I also knew I shouldn't sleep anyway, so I determined to get as far as I could. Between 12.30 and 8.30 am I think I was only once on the right road and that wasn't for very long. Quite early I found to my horror that I was on the Whitchurch road, driving south instead of east; I got back onto what I thought was the right one, waited half-an-hour at a X-roads until a woman cyclist appeared and confirmed it, and then drove 20 miles without seeing another soul until I came to a town. I need hardly go on, it wasn't Nantwich, but of course Whitchurch. The rest of the night was spent in driving a few miles, realising I was lost again, and sitting down at a cross-roads for someone to put me right again. By and large, and in every sense of the term, I think it was the blackest night I have ever lived through, but not for those reasons.

I hope I didn't say anything in my last letter which will hurt, or be misunderstood; if I did, I'm sorry, it is only because the whole thing is so terribly important that I had to be so direct.

They managed to sort out their misunderstandings and in the New Year Tim wrote:

I feel so thankful we have settled the miserable business. I'm thankful too that you understood what I tried to tell you about my job: you see I realise that there must be quite a difference between that me and the blue-clad line-shooter of the Bell and Castle, and I was afraid that if what I said didn't make sense, then you would never understand that other me. This sounds rather as if I was trying to build up my civilian character into that of a high-minded, hard-working idealist, to whom worldly pleasures meant nothing; that's not what I mean – wouldn't fool you anyway if I pretended it was! – but what I am trying to tell you is that I could never stand this sort of life in peacetime – idle and aimless – and that I can only justify it now because it is dangerous and because it is very, very important to win this bloody war. But when it's all over I want to do something, and something constructive, not just make money for myself or someone else, or persuade people to buy one ropey article rather than another ropey article, or chase after A Good Time and never find it, but to earn people's trust and try to give them health and teach them self-respect. It's the other me and in case you haven't heard about him I am trying to get you acquainted. I hope he doesn't fill you with Alarm and Despondency!

Tim was now stationed at Kirton-in-Lindsey and they had just received some very nice new aircraft (Spitfires). They were still optimistic that the war would end in the autumn and a squadron just back from Russia reckoned the Russians were going to clean the Germans up on their own, whether we did anything to help or not.

Berrice wrote that she had had a bit of a crash and managed to wrap the radiator of her vehicle round the crank case. This prompted Tim to confess to the skeleton in his cupboard:

> I landed a 'Battle' with the wheels still retracted. Aircraft are such beastly expensive things and my bill was:
>
> | | |
> |---|---|
> | To 1 air screw | £ 500 |
> | 1 Merlin | £1000 |
> | | £1500 |
>
> I was put on a charge for that but escaped with 'admonishment'. Actually I felt rather guilty about the whole thing and didn't really feel I had expiated it until last August. For weeks afterwards I used to experience moments of absolute mental anguish each time I touched down, thinking 'My God, have I forgotten them again'.

At the end of the month Tim's squadron was on the move:

> You will probably be wondering why I asked you to ring me at Sutton Bridge and then wasn't there to take the call. I had visions of you waiting ages for your call, only to find a cryptic message at the other end; I am sorry it had to be like that, but things started happening fast yesterday and far too late to let you know.
>
> Well, I suppose I'd better get it said: you see I heard then that I'm going either where your brother is or further, I don't know myself yet. That was why I asked you to ring me here last night: I thought we might be able to arrange to meet before I went, but I'm afraid it will be too late now, by the time you get this I shall be on my way. I would have given anything to have seen you again first, but there it is.
>
> I don't know what's in store for me, and it may be nothing at all, but I have an inkling that what I have been expecting and trying to prepare for is about to begin. Please don't worry about me; whatever should happen and however badly things appear to be going, remember that I *know* I'm coming back to you.

And please wait for me and don't entirely forget me. Please keep on writing to me, because your letters are going to be life's only luxury.

As soon as they were on their way, the CO told them that their destination was Malta, they would be flying to it from the aircraft carrier Eagle and there was certain to be hard fighting ahead. By the middle of March they had reached Gibraltar and Tim was able to write again:

The time we have had here has been rather enjoyable, though I must admit I am impatient to get where we are going. The weather is glorious, rather like last June in England if you remember it and I hope you haven't forgotten. We usually spend the morning pottering about in the town in the sunshine; it is rather fun, much more Spanish than English.

Yesterday we managed, after endless search, to find a restaurant which cooked Spanish food. We went in and ordered a Spanish lunch; all the Spaniards, needless to say, were eating steak and chips. First came a vegetable soup with a round of coarse bread; the table cloths were ragged but clean, and the spoons and forks massive and pock-marked. Then came the principal dish, I think mess is probably the word, rice soaked in a yellow gravy with lumps of meat concealed in it; this proved to be goat and was perfectly eatable, but with the goat there was something which none of us dared taste, we couldn't make up our minds whether it was the stern of a snail or the extremity of an octopus.

While the pilots were amusing themselves eating, drinking and swimming, the ground-crews worked day and night to assemble and test the aircraft, which had arrived in pieces, packed in crates. It took them a week, working in the cramped, sultry conditions of the Eagle's hangar, with only inches to spare between one machine and its neighbour. They had to adjust and test not only the engines, but the R/T, cannons, hydraulics, the electrical and compressed-air systems, oxygen, instruments and everything else. In his published diary,[1] Tim wrote:

We all sensed it was the lull before the storm, and I think most of us, while making the most of the moment, were busy bracing ourselves in spirit for the ordeal which we knew to be just ahead.

The Eagle left Gibraltar with her escort and on the 21st March the pilots were called at 0515. Tim went up to the flight-deck to supervise the stowage of his belongings in his aircraft; they were allowed ten pounds for the flight, which covered bare essentials but no more. He was glad to find just the right amount of wind; if there had been too much it would be too rough for take-off, and if too little it might not be possible at all: the Eagle's flight-deck was only 450 feet long, not much for Spits. After receiving final instructions, they all climbed into their machines, strapped themselves in and began to wait.

> The sea was getting up; occasionally a shower of spray would sweep over the deck and drench the aircraft, but in the cockpits we were snug and dry. The ground-crews stood round to see us off. They had been working intensively for ten days in most difficult conditions, but now their ordeal was over and ours was just beginning.

After some delay, the signal was given and the CO flew down the deck and disappeared under the bow.

> I couldn't see anything from where I was, so watched the expressions of the airmen, and after what seemed a long interval saw them break into smiles, next instant a very small aeroplane staggered into view about half a mile in front of the ship. Heard afterwards that the CO very nearly hit the drink; not surprising, he'd only flown a Spit once before.

When Tim took off he felt a violent eddy, like hitting a slipstream, as the aircraft crossed the bows. After an hour's flying the African coast showed up. They flew past the Galite Island and Pantellaria and then across the long stretch of sea to Malta. They landed safely at Luqa and waited for instructions. The aerodrome was hot and dusty and no one seemed to know what to do with them. Eventually an officer appeared, took them off to lunch and told them that Takali would be their parent aerodrome.

The following day, they were all rather aggrieved to find that the aircraft, which each pilot had regarded as his own, belonged to the island and not to the individual or squadron, but they soon realised that this was a necessity. No. 249 Squadron, after combat and bombing on the ground, had only one aircraft serviceable; they had nine and there were said to be half a dozen Hurricanes. Tim spent some time questioning those who had flown in the island and knew something of the enemy tactics. He was told that before a raid, patrols of 109s circled the island, that the bombers normally came in with close escort at about 15,000 feet, dived to 5000 to drop their bombs, and that their withdrawal was always covered by further patrols operating off the coast. Four days later, a 109 shot a hole in Tim's oil-tank and he had to make an emergency landing.

As the days went by, the aircraft situation became so bad that both squadrons had to be released so that serviceability could be improved. Tim wondered what the Maltese thought at seeing so many pilots on the ground during raids:

> It would be understandable if they showed some surliness when they saw us on the ground and not in the air, and it's to their credit that they never do; they seem to realise that it isn't our fault if we aren't flying, and although we can do little enough, they still retain a pathetic belief in us.

One day in April Tim was returning to Luqa where the aerodrome had just been bombed and he circled round to make certain there were no new craters on it.

> Third time round, as I was approaching the smoke-pall, I saw two 109s dive through it across my bows not more than 300 yards ahead. They were obviously going to shoot up the aerodrome and I felt sure they hadn't spotted me, so I turned hard left and went through the cloud after them. Re-emerged over the field at 50 feet and knew they must be a short distance ahead, but couldn't see them anywhere; was in the act of cursing my oily wind-shield, when suddenly, without warning, there was a vivid flash and I felt rather than heard a tremendous bang. The stick, which had felt taut and sensitive in my hand, seemed to sag and become quite limp; knew at once that the aircraft had been vitally hit and was out of control, knew too that this must be the end...I remember feeling surprised and thinking rather bitterly that my belief that I should survive had been a myth after all. ...But instead of going down, the aircraft began to climb very steeply...there was hope. ...I began to undo my harness and extracted the pin successfully. I'd decided that I couldn't risk being held to the machine by the R/T cable and oxygen-tube as I tried to jump: I should have little speed and there wouldn't be enough centrifugal

force to snap them, so they might tie me to the aircraft and take me down with it. Therefore I had to get rid of my helmet before I began to get out. All I had to do was to loosen one chin-strap and it would come off easily. I fumbled for this strap with my left hand, but I was wearing thick Canadian gloves and had no sense of touch, also I suppose I was preoccupied with keeping the machine under some sort of control.

After a moment's panic he managed to take hold of himself and undo it. His plane was now in level though precarious flight.

Looked at the altimeter and saw 900 feet; that was enough, so pushed the stick hard forward and felt myself rise from the seat and shoot half out of the cockpit; then I was stranded. I was sitting on the starboard wall of the cockpit with my head and shoulders in the open and my legs inside; the chute had caught somewhere and was holding me fast; the aircraft had fallen off in a left-hand spiral dive and the ground looked incredibly close. I tried to shake myself free, but the machine had gathered speed and the slipstream as well as the chute was pinning me down. …I felt trapped and desperate and as a last resort I threw my head and shoulders back as hard as I could in a backward somersault. Free at last. I was turning over and over so fast that the movement seemed to confuse my arms, and when my hand reached for the rip-cord it wasn't where it should have been; I had to make three separate grabs before I found it. As the chute opened the sensation was as if a giant was swinging me round his head by the scruff of the neck.

A few days later he learned that a stick of bombs had burst on the aerodrome as he had flown across it and that his chute had opened at about two hundred feet!

A couple of weeks later, in a fight with 109s, Tim made the mistake of going after one of them knowing that the other was behind him.

Next instant, without warning, bang, bang, bang. I could hear and feel three cannon-shells exploding in the bottom of my machine. I remember instinctively kicking on the rudder after the first explosion and feeling how futile it was as the other two followed in quick succession, and then experiencing that sensation of insignificance and resignation that comes when you are suddenly overtaken by fate; I remember also that I realised that the aircraft was on fire. Then there is a gap in my memory; it can't have lasted more than two or three seconds, and the most likely explanation seems to be that when it was hit the machine did something of its own accord so violent that I was momentarily blacked out. When full consciousness returned, I found myself still in the seat, squirming this way and that against the straps, but making no effort to undo the harness and get out, with a great flame rushing up from the bottom of the cockpit and being drawn past my face by the suction of the slip-stream. My first thought was that this time it was certainly the end and that there must have been some mistake, because I wasn't supposed to die. The fire prevented me from seeing anything outside the aircraft, but I could tell by feel that it was diving very steeply and fast and, after being blacked out for those few moments, I must have imagined I was nearer the ground than I actually was. After the last experience I never thought I should be able to escape this time.

I can remember I noticed a curious smell; I don't know whether it was something burning, or me being burnt; it was not so much unpleasant as entirely strange to me, and it was this, not heat or pain, which was the most forcible physical sensation. I found afterwards that my legs had been peppered by cannon-splinters, but I never felt them at the time. No past life flashed before me, I think things happen too quickly in the air for this to be possible; I only remember that everything was red, that I felt this terrible flame was robbing me of the power to think, and that I knew that if I lost my head it would destroy me. I thought of what was waiting a few hundred or a few thousand feet below, I didn't know which, that terrible crash and burst of flame. In the meantime I'd very deliberately pulled out the locking-pin of the harness; I knew I couldn't afford to fumble with it and remember I shaded my eyes with my left arm and looked down so as to make sure; then half stood in the cockpit, decided there was no time to try to take my helmet off and it would have to be risked, kicked the stick forward as far as I could, felt the helmet and mask parting, and was shot forward into the air. The aircraft was diving so fast that I might have been an arrow and it a tautened bow. I must have passed out at once, I don't even remember pulling the rip-cord and have no memory of the chute opening or of the descent, only hitting the ground, then more oblivion.

I began to come round as the first Tommies arrived; they helped me to unbuckle the chute and soon had me on a stretcher.

I don't know where they took me, I had a cloth over my head and was taking little interest; I remember hearing the sympathetic wailing of a crowd of Maltese and a voice saying: 'Is he dead?' I wanted to say, 'No bloody fear', or something like that, but shirked the effort, it was so much easier to keep absolutely still.

When Tim woke up in hospital his arms and face were buried in bandages. Next morning the colonel came to change his dressings. The bandages and lint were peeled off and he was told to open his eyes if he could; he found he could not. When the lids had been further cleaned it was possible to force them apart.

I looked up to see, in poor focus, a section of distempered wall with two faces in front of it, peering anxiously into mine. That was all I saw, for two minutes every day, for nearly a fortnight; yet, in spite of the pain which accompanied it, this was a treat to which I looked forward.

When all the bandages had come off, he wrote to Berrice:

My face still looks awful, at the bottom a dirty great beard, inextricably tangled up with scabs and bits of dressing that look as if they were put on in the last war, at the top new skin of a delicate shell-pink and no eyebrows and eyelashes! Yesterday an Italian prisoner – a pilot – came in to see us, took one look at me and said something in Italian; I asked the orderly what it was and was told: he says Isn't war terrible! In the next bed there is a 109 pilot, on whom I vent my German, poor wretch.

By the end of May Tim was fit enough for the journey home and from Gibraltar he wrote:

I had a letter the other day from the good Maiholi. The old villain actually claims that they are all praying for me with all their might; I look for the date on his letter and what do I see? May 6th, the day I was shot down! The Northern Nigerian chiefs are all Muslims and in miniature have a court and pomp and ceremony like that. They are all called Emirs except Sokoto (where I was) and he is top-boy and is called Sultan, their chief advisers are called 'Waziri' which of course is the Hausa version of Vizier. The Waziri of Sokoto was a crafty old villain just like the Viziers of fiction, only he was so clever that no-one could ever catch him out.

They were both anxious about seeing each other again after so long. Tim thought he would feel shy and wondered if either of them had changed. Berrice was terrified and certain she would be horribly self-conscious and spoil everything. However, their fears proved groundless and they agreed that their reunion was the best day they had ever had together.

After convalescing with family, Tim was given a staff appointment at HQ, Fighter Command, Uxbridge. On 8th June he was awarded a DFC in recognition of his operations on Malta. Now that his 'Battle of Hastings' was over they started looking to the future and talked about getting married but, with few opportunities to meet, there were more misunderstandings that had to be ironed out. In July Tim wrote:

> I thought it might be a good thing if I wrote some more on the subject we were talking about yesterday. I'm sorry, I hope you didn't think I was being heavy or reproachful about your not having written when I was in hospital, it was the last thing I meant, but in a way I was glad of the opportunity of getting it out, because it had been worrying me a little. I suppose it was there in the back of my mind and when you said you didn't feel anything very strongly, it popped out and confronted me and I began to wonder whether it wasn't true.
>
> I'm sorry to go over all this again if it's distasteful to you, but it's only part of the process of getting to know you, and it's no good your saying that I should do that by now, because you see there are times when you behave in a contradictory and enigmatic way. But it is rather important to get this straight.
>
> The problem is really very simple; I think you can put it like this: if to you Tim is more important than everything else put together, then it will work, if less important then it won't work. You see I've wanted to go to Africa ever since I was about sixteen and I'm interested enough in it not to worry about all the hardships which you inevitably get there, but for you it's rather different. One day I hope you'll feel as I do, but to begin with your only compensation for giving up an easy life is going to be me. That's why I say that if you feel strongly enough about me the loss of the other things won't matter, if you don't they will.
>
> I know I've no right to feel in any doubt about it at all, you've shown me in lots of ways that you do feel just as strongly and are

quite as single minded as I am. If only you'd give me a little more encouragement I promise you I wouldn't but every now and again you know you do blow cold and when it comes it's a pretty chilly blast.

A couple of days later Berrice replied: 'I couldn't sleep last night so I tried to think of something in life more important than you. I didn't succeed!'

They were married on the 3rd October 1942 in a registry office with two witnesses and spent their honeymoon in Cornwall. Naturally Tim wrote to Maiholi with his news and soon received his congratulations:

I had a very nice letter from Maiholi. He says: 'We have heard that you have made a marriage and that we have got our lady-of-the-house. We are extremely glad and hope to see her here in Nigeria before long. Dela [Mrs Maiholi] sends you greetings, she is glad at your marriage and hopes you are well, Amen. Dela also hopes that Allah disposes so that you see her sometimes and says that she will teach her to sew.'

So now you know what you're in for. Isn't he a nice old man? His daughter, a kid of about ten when I last saw her, is to be married in July. He concludes with a plea that when we return we shall bring a 'Ketchen box compelete'!

In June 1943 Tim was appointed commander of No 165 Squadron, a Spitfire unit based at Ibsley.

I am extremely busy but it is good fun trying to make something out of the Squadron – I have got the usual mixture – English, Canadians, a lot of Australians, very keen and well-behaved, a couple of New Zealanders, two Fighting French and two attached Americans. They are a good crowd, extraordinarily keen and eager to learn, and I think we should do well with them. I'm making them take their training very seriously, not only to get more Huns but to avoid unnecessary losses. I don't think I shall ever be red-hot myself, but I do know, and think I can impart, the form.

Six months later, in January 1944, Tim was posted to the staff of No 10 Group HQ, Fighter Command:

You will be sorry/glad to hear that it has been decided by the powers that I have done my time and that I should therefore be taken off operational flying. As things stand at present I am going to Group on Monday next to do a staff job again. You will also be glad/sorry to hear that I am doing my best to get out of it. Please don't think me a heedless or inconsiderate Old Hound for doing so. Having screwed myself up to do this second tour, and having got through the difficult part/half of it, it is natural that I should want to see the job right through. Further, having built the Squadron up into a really first-class fighting unit (that sounds like a line, but is true) I naturally want to lead it on the big day and, equally naturally, feel sure that no one else could do it as well as I.

You will be glad/sorry to hear that at present I am getting nowhere. The powers are as polite as could be, agree that the Squadron is one of the best in the Command, give me full credit for having made it so, acquiesce when I say I ought to lead it, and yet fail to budge an inch from their position. On Monday I am seeing the AOC himself, but haven't very high hopes.

Please don't think I am doing all this without giving you a thought. I know in a way that I should be glad to be taken off, but if you've really worked hard at something you know how you feel about leaving it unfinished. With everything to live for, I realise it is crazy to want to go on sticking my neck out, but there it is. Please don't think hardly of me; I know it will be difficult to understand the underlying motive but it is not, I think, an altogether unworthy one.

After talking to the AOC, Tim wrote:

He was extraordinarily nice, apologised almost abjectly for dragging me from the Squadron and said he had only done so because he had to have someone who could read and write in this job, and I was the only one he could find. He promised to let me go back to operations after 3 months. Please don't feel hardly about this: I know how unreasonable it must sound to you, but I do want to finish what I have started. And air superiority, you know, is a pretty big thing, to which every possible contribution should be made; if it is absolute and complete, as it should be, it is going to have a gigantic moral and national effect and save, in the long run, literally thousands of lives. For this, I think it is worth sticking my neck out just once more. If I had finished my time I shouldn't have wanted to do it, as it is I promise that this will be the last time. Everyone is very complimentary about the success of the Squadron, so with any luck I might get a Wing next time. I must say I should very much like to go back to the same crowd; they were not only an extremely pleasant bunch, but also very expert pilots with whom I felt comfortably safe.

In March, Tim was awarded a Bar to his DFC, its citation saying in part; 'He has devoted the utmost energy and enthusiasm in perfecting his squadron as a fighting unit.' To Berrice he wrote:

I first heard last night. There was a Group party at which I arrived rather late and Keith L. came up and congratulated me; I asked, innocently enough, 'What for?'; 'Oh,' he said, 'I heard you'd got a bar.' 'Not me,' I says, 'must be someone else of the same name.' A slightly embarrassing pause followed! Then other people came up offered their congratulations and I found it was mine after all. As usual, I was the last to hear the news!

Later in the month he joined the HQ staff of the 2nd Tactical Air Force, then being prepared for the Allied invasion of Normandy. In May he returned to operations with a posting to command No 66 Squadron, one of the three Spitfire squadrons which comprised No 132 Wing, 2nd TAF and in June they took part in the D-Day operations.

In September the wing moved on to the Continent and Tim wrote:

The other day I went down to see for myself the shambles which used to be the escape hatch from the Falaise-Argentan pocket. It was one of the most hideous sights I have ever seen. The most hideous in fact; the small horror of a few burnt-out tanks, which I described last time, was nothing compared to it. A whole area was choked with wrecked German transport, corpses, happily underground at the time of our visit, and the carcasses of horses. It was nearly all the result of attack from the air and we all derived a good deal of grim satisfaction to see the reactions to it of the invincible German Army. There was every evidence of panic: transports jammed abreast in narrow lanes, rifles discarded everywhere, likewise steel helmets, trucks driven so hard into trees or the backs of other trucks as to be partially telescoped, horse-drawn transport overturned after the wildest swerves, staff-cars bogged or stranded out in fields in attempting to make detours round the main jams.

The thing which I haven't yet mentioned, but which dominated all else, was the smell of death: it was so over-powering that it clung afterwards to our clothes and I couldn't wear my battle-dress for 36 hours. A scene like that ought to be preserved intact, complete with corpses and smell, to show each younger generation the reality, as opposed to the illusion, of war.

Meanwhile Berrice had had a rather unsettling experience:

A most extraordinary thing happened this afternoon. I had to get petrol so I took one of the clerks with me, on our way back we stopped at the YMCA for tea. We had just settled at a table when an airman came over and talked to us, he sat down and asked me to put my hand on the table as he wanted to tell my fortune! I thought he was being funny but put my hand on the table, this is what he told me. I'm much too generous and I'm foolish because people take advantage of my generosity and never do anything to repay me! The next thing shattered me quite a bit – I'm going to have an infant fairly soon not one but twins!!! Well I'm the next generation in our family for twins so don't be too surprised! I'm stubborn at times and not easily led by other people. I'm too easy-going and don't assert myself enough. I'm erratic. I have a good brain?? but am too lazy to use it to the best advantage. As a rule I like a quiet life but sometimes have a desire to go to parties. I have fits of depression and very often make myself unhappy by imagining morbid things. If I'm fond of people I'm very affectionate but can't be bothered to be nice to people I don't like. I must learn to have a better opinion of myself – who said I'm conceited? In about eighteen months time I shall have an opportunity to do something that will probably change my whole life and I must have the courage and determination to make the best of the opportunity. I love anything beautiful and am inclined to be extravagant. What do you think of this description of me? I think it's fairly good in some ways but not awfully flattering.

Tim replied:

I was interested in your palmist's character sketch and thought it remarkably accurate, so far as it went, in its diagnosis of you. Let me deal with it in detail. Generosity: quite correct, especially the bit about people taking advantage of it (e.g. the Old Hound who owes you £4!). Twins: wouldn't surprise me at all, and I think a good thing – two for the price of one. Stubborn and not easily led:

yes, but qualities I like. Too easy-going and not sufficiently self-assertive: possibly, but doesn't matter since you aren't swayed by others. Erratic and too lazy to use a good brain: I've always said you had a good head and exceptional judgement, but I think he is right in saying that you are rather casual in using them; however, there is time yet. Quiet life but occasional party appreciated: perfectly correct, thank goodness. Fits of depression and tendency to imagine things: that wouldn't be the moods, would it?! Affectionate to some, but off-hand to others you don't like: touchée I think! Should learn to have a better opinion of yourself: true, I would say, of your self-esteem in intellectual and spiritual (but not physical!) matters. Love of beauty and extravagance: both right! I wonder what the opportunity will be that can change your whole life: not divorcing your Old Hound I trust!

He has only touched on a few attributes and hasn't got down to the major qualities at all, but in any case I don't need telling what those are, and I still think you are the only woman in the world.

Shortly afterwards Tim heard from Peter Scott:

c/o Resident, Minna [Nigeria]

My dear Johnny,

I have not heard from you since I wrote about New Year but to judge from the fate of other letters about then you may not have got that one. If so you will be thinking me very ungrateful for the parcels of books you sent. I was very glad of them and very pleased with the selection. Thank you again, very much.

Mother told me you were on the ground again and Berrice was driving a colonel – I hope not the 'Men Only' type of colonel but a nice domesticated one, preferably with daughters of his own and a proper care for Berrice's comfort etc.

I have been luckier lately for I have been DO Abuja since the end of November. This is a very pleasant assignment with a charming house set on a hill 1800 ft. surrounded by grand views of hilly country. I have the Emirates of Abuja and Lapai. The former is the old Habe[2] kingdom driven out of Zaria, the latter a Nupe-ized Fulani Emir with Nupe and semi-Nupe people. Abuja had an Emir of 78 when I arrived but he died in March and now we have one who was at the Higher College, and will make one of the star chiefs. Lapai has a mean, crafty, greedy old scoundrel as Emir. I am out gunning at the moment.

As I write I am on the banks of the Niger at Muye about half way between Baro and Lokoja. It is Lapai's southern tip, a village of Kakanda canoe-men, very nice fellows with their great canoes with square sails that drift all over Niger, Benue, Kaduna, Gurara, Gongola and other rivers. The people have all the sophistication of Kano with the physical advantages that are found only in places better fed than the frozen north. Last night we had a grand dance complete with acrobatics, some boxing and the pantomime of the Youths' Club with DO, Resident, Governor, Boy etc. In the middle a convoy of canoes drifting with the stream took up the drumming and we had echoes from the water. In the village they have about two dozen small cannon they used to arm their canoes with in the old days. Like most Nigerian antiquities they are rusting in the open.

The country is very short of Admin. Officers though a few cadets are coming out. Lagos has absorbed an absurd number of Junior Officers on oil control, tyre control and such-like jobs. The great cry in the country is Post War Development and huge vague schemes are mooted. The fact that unless a vast inquisition into the political condition of every NA is first made every scheme will be built on sand seems to have been overlooked. I am afraid things are going on in this country which we hoped had died out twenty years ago.

I do not hear much from Idoma except that an ADO called Taylor [J.] is in charge. Beck [D.M.H.] is still Resident. Carrow [Cdr J.H.] is still resident Kano and Patterson [Sir John R.] Chief Commissioner. The latter visited Abuja the other day and talked and talked and talked all about nothing at all. Everybody laments the fact that Carrow was not made CC.

Another great cry at the moment is 'Mass attack on illiteracy'. The South thinks this means thousands of well-paid jobs for half-trained teachers, the money to fall from the skies apparently. The North – 99% have not heard of it and 1% looks on it as a help in the battle with the South for which both sides are now lining up. We try to tell people that the phrase if it means anything in Nigeria means an enormous amount of voluntary work and public subscription of cash. Of this latter commodity there is plenty in the pockets of the people. Every obtainable palm kernel, groundnut or beniseed is bought by the M. of Supply. The countryside is lousy with coin and so the Sarakuna [the gentry] reap a rich harvest of corruption and the talakawa [the peasants] do not feel the loss so do not complain to DO's whom now they scarcely ever see. There are very few canteen goods and these very costly so all the cash goes into the markets and prices soar.

By the way I have forgotten to say how pleased I was with 'Tattered Battlements', do make journal keeping a habit and do the same out here. It was excellent.

Very best to Berrice.

Yours, Peter

Tim then forwarded the letter to Berrice with some explanatory notes

I can't quite decide whether or not Peter's letter will give you a good idea of the life and country; on the whole I think one probably has to read between the lines too much, so I will try to amplify it for you.

The house, sounds very pleasant; it is probably a permanent structure. In a good situation, and with a nice garden, it could be made delightful. Drawbacks: it is probably a one-man station; this can sometimes be an advantage though!

Pantomime of the Youths Club. A standard form of local amusement is to do a sketch, parodying European life; they can be quite acid I believe!

NA: Native Administration, or the Govt. of each Emirate or tribe. Peter's stories of corruption and oppression are quite stimulating: nothing used to please me better than to ferret out such things!

In November Tim was finally rested from operations and posted back to the UK in a non-operational post. He wasted no time in seeking his return to Nigeria:

I have had a reply from the Colonial Office, at long last, after I had written a second time. In Whitehall's cold impersonal manner they express neither surprise, joy, dismay, nor any other emotions found in the busy world, but inform me curtly that my case is under consideration and that in the meantime I had better have a medical examination. This reminds me of the welcome given me by the Air Ministry when I wrote from Nigeria, full of patriotic fervour, and offered my services for the war; they replied that, be that as it might, they would in no circumstances pay my passage home. Under the rough exterior there probably palpitates a pump of platinum, but I have never unearthed it!

Berrice was released from the ATS the following May, on her birthday, and Tim from the RAFVR a few weeks later.

— 3 —

Nassarawa 1945–46

Tim and Berrice wasted no time after their demob and sailed for Nigeria at the end of June 1945. Tim, of course, had done the journey twice before but for Berrice it was the beginning of a wonderful adventure.

Mummy dear,

So far the journey has been perfect and I'm thoroughly enjoying every minute.

We left London last Monday and everything worked out very well, we managed to get taxis and porters without trouble and had a comfortable journey.

We are having a very lazy time and seem to spend most of our days eating and sleeping and playing 'Demon'. The first three days were rather dull and cold but since then the sun has been wonderful and Tim and I are looking quite brown and extremely healthy.

The food is very good and the drinks are amazingly cheap, whisky, gin and brandy price 6d!! Beer is the most expensive drink price 7d!

Our cabin is pleasant but small and we are lucky in having our own bathroom.

Tim found one of his friends on the ship and he is taking his wife out for the first time too; they are going to the Gold Coast and are both extremely nice.

This idle life doesn't suit me very well and I will be glad when we reach our destination, the ship is small and it is practically impossible to take any exercise. I would give anything for a good long walk but I suppose the rest will do me a lot of good after three years of madly rushing from one place to another.

Tim sends 'best wishes'.

After a three-day stop at Takoradi, where Berrice observed that the African women seemed to work much harder than the men and was amazed to see them carrying enormous loads on their heads, they sailed again and arrived in Lagos on Saturday the 21st.

Of her first week in Nigeria she wrote:

We arrived in Lagos at 10.30 a.m. but didn't leave the boat until 2.30 p.m. We were met by a man called Lewis but we didn't find him particularly helpful. We spent an hour fussing in the Customs shed and were then taken by him to the Ikoyi Club where we are to stay until Tim's future has been decided. We are living in a small chalet attached to the Club and are very comfortable. On Sunday, Lewis promised to take us swimming but didn't turn up so we had a lazy day at the Club. The food is very good and after rations in England the change is astounding.

On Monday morning, Tim had an interview but was given no clue as to his future. The uncertainty and inactivity is very trying. We were both surprised to see fleets of taxis rushing about, how odd to have taxis in Lagos when in England it is impossible to buy tyres. Tim's friend, Roy Mant, took us sailing on Thursday afternoon. Later, we dined with him and a Miss Cameron and went on to the open-air cinema to see Veronica Lake in 'I Married A Witch'. I was amused to see a lizard squatting on Veronica Lake's face!

Maiholi turned up on Saturday with masses of presents for me from his family. He's a nice old man and seemed overjoyed to see Tim again. He brought a prospective steward boy with him who looked very nice.

At the beginning of the second week Tim and Berrice were on their way north to Kaduna for an interview with His Honour the Chief Commissioner.[1]

On Sunday we had a nasty day packing but were very much looking forward to seeing the last of Lagos. We left early on

Monday morning in a very uncomfortable old train and travelled all day. Owing to the strike now in progress we had to stop for the night in a station. It was very noisy and the mosquitoes were troublesome. We resumed our journey at 6.30 a.m. It was tiring and hot in the train but it was very interesting to see so much of the countryside.

When they reached Kaduna two days later they were relieved to find Peter Scott waiting for them at the station. A couple of days after their arrival, Tim went down with a fever and was taken off to hospital. This caused another problem; Peter was a bachelor and so Berrice could not remain in his house unchaperoned! It took several hours to find her alternative accommodation with a married couple.

Tim was kept in hospital for just over a week. After yet another week, they were still none the wiser as to his future but were back on the train travelling south to Makurdi.

We left Kaduna on Friday at 6.30 a.m. and arrived at Kafanchan at 2 p.m. only to be told that we had to stay there in the train until Sunday afternoon. It was hell! The mosquitoes were very bad; Tim killed forty-two and I had fifty bites. On Saturday the DO's wife asked us over for a more than welcome bath and dinner. It was so nice to get away from the train for a short time. We left Kafanchan at 4 p.m. on Sunday and arrived in Makurdi at 3 a.m. We spent the rest of the night with the Cullens and after breakfast Mrs Cullen took us to the rest house where we are to stay until it has been decided what to do with us.

We found Tim's six-year-old loads and spent a hectic morning unpacking them. The contents were in surprisingly good condition and we even found a brand new gramophone that he had forgotten about.

Five weeks after arriving in Lagos, Tim was told that he was being posted to Nassarawa, a one-man station. In her next letter home, Berrice wrote:

We left Makurdi last Monday at 1 a.m. and had a six hour journey on the train and then a three hour run in a lorry to our new home. The country round here is simply wonderful and our house is a dream! It is a bungalow, white with a thatched roof and glorious tropical creeper flowering on the roof. There is a nice wide veranda round the house and we have all our meals except dinner there. The situation is beautiful, we are on top of a small hill and are surrounded by a valley and have the river on three sides about a mile away. There are ranges of big hills all round and the view is perfect.

The garden is grand and we have oranges, grapefruit and limes in front of the house. We can get butter and milk, chickens priced 6d - 1/3!!, and more fruit and vegetables than we can eat, in other words we are living on the fat of the land and I feel quite ashamed when I think of the rations in England. I'm looking and feeling frightfully well and am putting on weight and I have never been happier in my life.

When we arrived we were met by the Headman of the African town with great pomp, drums beating and trumpets blowing. He and his followers all wore their flowing robes and the most important men wore silk and satin! They are delightful people, very polite and happy with a childish sense of humour.

Tim's office is about 200 yards away and he is there from 7 to 9 a.m. when he comes back for breakfast. Then he works until 3 p.m. After that we have lunch and later we potter in the garden and do odd jobs. So far it has been quite cool and we have been able to work comfortably. The only thing I don't like very much in this country is the long night, it gets dark at 7 p.m. every night of the year and the sun rises at about 6 a.m., but even now I'm getting used to it and soon won't notice it.

I'm busy making curtains and cushion covers; Aunt Charlotte's sewing machine is a blessing, without it I simply couldn't manage.

Tim sends love and says he's taking care of me.

Soon after settling in, they had a trip to the Divisional Headquarters at Keffi, twenty-eight miles away, so that Tim could look around the Native Authority office, the school and the prison.

In the house where they were staying, Berrice noticed a plaque to the memory of Captain Moloney, the British Resident murdered in October 1902. In 1901, the first Governor of Northern Nigeria, Sir Frederick Lugard, had introduced laws abolishing slavery but the Magaji [Headman] of Keffi, who was the representative of the Emir of Zaria, openly flouted them. When Moloney tried to persuade him to stop the trade, the Magaji pulled a pistol from his gown and shot him. The killing of Moloney assumed considerable historical importance because it convinced Lugard that he had to force a showdown with the Sultan of Sokoto and of course it provided him with a good reason for doing so. It therefore became the *casus belli* that led to the campaign of 1903 and the final downfall of the Fulani Empire that had ruled in Northern Nigeria for nearly a hundred years.

In Berrice's next letter home she wrote:

> We ran out of marmalade last week so I decided to make a small quantity with limes. I bunged sugar, fruit and water in a saucepan

5. Berrice during her first tour in Nassarawa

and hoped for the best and it was simply lovely! My first attempt and with no recipe. If I can get any jam jars I will send you some. At the moment we haven't any jars or bottles because everything in this country seems to be sold in tins.

Our garden is beginning to look very nice and the seeds are coming up well, we have one vegetable garden down by the river and one near the house. We've planted some banana trees and hope, if we are still here next year, to have some home-grown bananas.

My recent presents from the local people include four turkeys and about twelve chickens[2] so we have quite a nice little farmyard. Last week we had the Emir of Nassarawa (sort of local ruler of the district) to tea and ten of his chief men. They ate an enormous tea and even stuffed their pockets with cake to take home to their wives! When offered cigarettes they all took a handful instead of one and showed their appreciation with a hearty barrage of belches! I was quite horrified!

I forgot to tell you that I'm called Queen of Laughter so you can see how happy I am. I simply love Africa and the people, they're all so friendly and dignified even when they are carrying enormous loads on their heads.

Soon afterwards a miner came to the Rest House and they invited him over for drinks and dinner. Mr Hunt had been in Nigeria for seven years without leave and, except for his staff, lived completely alone which Berrice considered must have been rather awful for him at times.

He told them a story about the effect of pagan poison. He was in his house one day when an old pagan went past with a bow and arrows. He asked to look at the arrows and whether they were poisoned. The old man told him they were and that the poison killed immediately. Hunt was sceptical, but the man insisted. Hunt had been given a ram, which he had no use for, so he asked if it would be good to eat after it had been shot with an arrow. The old man said it would be all right, so Hunt told him that he could shoot it and if the ram died before he could get to it, he could have it. The man shot from about thirty yards, hitting the ram in the rump, and sure enough it was dead before he reached it!

In October Berrice described a trip to Makurdi.

We started out for Makurdi on Sunday but the lorry broke down at mile 3 so we returned home. On Monday we set off again at

3 p.m. in a lorry with 'God Help Us' painted on the cab, which was very appropriate as it turned out because we broke down every other mile! We arrived in Gudi at 7.30 p.m. just in time to catch the goods train to Makurdi. We managed to make ourselves comfortable on top of our loads and had a record journey arriving at 1 a.m. Major Peebles (Police) took us to our Rest House and we were very thankful to get into bed. In the morning we found we were in the wrong Rest House so we picked up our beds and walked to the next one.

Tim had to see the Resident and we took advantage of the opportunity to catch up on some socialising and shopping. We went first to the Public Works Department store, where we bought a long mirror, an air-gun (£6) and some odd screw-top jars; and then to an auction of elephants' tusks. Two tusks, each weighing 36 lbs, fetched £45 and £50 respectively. Later we heard that the tusks of another elephant killed at Umaisha weighed 68 lbs and 70 lbs.

The lorry that took us back to Nassarawa was christened the 'Red Headed Match'. It averaged 40 mph, which was slightly nerve-racking on such bad roads with goats running about all over the place.

Back home in Nassarawa, Berrice spent her days helping Tim in the office, looking after the flower beds and vegetable garden, making jam and fruit juice, and sewing. In the evenings they would go out with the gun to shoot whatever they could find – rabbits, pheasants and duck – to supplement their usual diet of scrawny chicken.

Tim managed to persuade the staff to attend Adult School in order to learn the 3Rs and Maiholi came back after his first lesson looking very pleased with himself. Berrice thought it was a pretty good show that a man in his seventies was keen to improve his education.

Shortly afterwards they celebrated Salla Babba, the great festival that marks the start of the new Muslim year.

Yesterday the Emir and District Heads came on horseback followed by over a hundred hangers-on. One of the horses had a purple and yellow saddle and its legs had been henna-ed. It was a most impressive spectacle full of pomp and ceremony. We watched some rather unscientific but good-natured boxing. The boxers had only their right hand bound for punching so they could hit and scratch with their left hand. Kicking was allowed too.

Afterwards we invited the Emir and District Heads to tea. It was much less formal than last time and everyone talked and laughed quite naturally. I gave them ice-cream which was a great success and caused many exclamations. Of course, I had to show them the fridge. When it was time to leave, nearly all of them asked for paper so that they could take pieces of cake to their wives who wanted to taste English food.

Today we went to the town to watch some Fulani boys being initiated into manhood. The ceremony started with a queer little dance after which the victim had to stand perfectly still, looking into a mirror, while he was beaten with sticks. If he wanted to be considered a man and gain the right to marry, he had to suffer the blows without flinching at all. The beatings looked pretty vicious but they all survived.

It was very important for District Officers to visit the remote villages in their area to see what the government could do to improve their living standards. Some villages already had a small school and a dispensary but others lacked even a clean water supply and were taking water from stagnant ponds. During the next few months Tim and Berrice spent a lot of time trekking round on their bikes, on horseback or on foot. The inhabitants of many of these villages were very primitive and mostly pagan. Clothing was practically unheard of; the women wore a fresh bunch of leaves fore and aft, or a piece of cloth wrapped round them, and the men a loin cloth or an animal skin thrown over the shoulder.

The best time to travel was very early in the morning, before the sun became too hot, or late in the afternoon, when the temperature was cooling down. When the terrain was too rough for a vehicle, they employed carriers to take all their kit from one place to the next. This consisted of camp beds, bedding, mosquito nets, a table and chairs, lamps, a tin or canvas bath, cooking equipment, a 'chop' (food) box, water, drinks, and of course whisky and soda. There was, by law, a maximum weight for each head load and everything had to be distributed very carefully. The carriers would generally leave in advance, walking through the night, so that everything would be set up and a meal ready when Tim and Berrice arrived at their destination. A junior steward would be left behind to pack up the bedding and bring it on later.

They stayed in Rest Houses that were usually round mud huts with a thatched roof, a beaten mud floor and no doors or windows. The caretaker of a Rest House was called Sarkin Bariki [King of the Barracks]. In places where there was no Rest House they stayed in a *zaure* which was the entrance hut to an African's compound; or a *rumfa* which was a shelter made of elephant-grass zana mats. In the hot season they slept outside with only a mosquito net between them and the stars.

They set out on their first trek in the late afternoon.

We cycled ten miles to Kurudu where we spent the night. In the morning, we left at 6.45 a.m. and cycled another ten miles to the next Rest House at Lokogoma. After breakfast we went into the village and found it was filthy; everyone and everything was coated with dirt. The huts were very small with one-inch thick walls and there were no BGs [WCs].[3] The people are Gwari and I noticed that they carry loads on their backs and not on their heads. The women look exactly like the men.

The following morning we had an extremely pleasant level ride to Gidabuke which took a couple of hours. We visited the town in the evening and found it rather better than Lokogoma with more space between the houses but still no BGs. We saw the dye pits and a very nice little school that stood in its own grounds. In the evening a man with leprosy came to see Tim. I was quite distressed because the leprosy in his feet was so bad he could hardly walk. We have decided that we will have to think of a way to get him to the Abuja Colony which is about a hundred miles away.

Our departure from Gidabuke was delayed because the boys had forgotten to pump up our tyres. We stopped for breakfast with some missionaries working in the area and I must say I thought they should be teaching the pagans Cleanliness rather than Christianity. After an overnight stop at Kuru, we went on to Toto which was only an hour's ride away. The town was fairly large but dirty and dusty and very overcrowded. There seemed to be a complete lack of planning or interest in their way of living. The townsfolk are chiefly Kwottos. Tim was told that a man-eating crocodile has been menacing the town and that it has already devoured four people. In the evening we walked round to find a new site for the dispensary.

On Sunday we left at 6.30 and stopped for breakfast at a Rest House seven miles away. After breakfast Tim went to survey a new road and I continued on with the Forest Guard and the Sanitary Inspector. The distance from Toto to Ugia was seventeen miles and the journey was a hard one with very troublesome flies. On Monday we covered the fifteen miles from Ugia to Umaisha in an hour and three-quarters which was pretty good going. Although it was rather dirty, we were quite impressed with Umaisha because the spacing between the houses and compounds is much better than in most towns. In the evening we went down to the Benue River to look at the canoes we are going to use for our trip to Loko.

When we set off on the river, we decided to have a go ourselves and Tim airily told the canoeists to go on and wait for us a mile upstream. We started paddling but instead of going a mile in the right direction we went fifty yards t'other way! The Africans on the bank thought it was hilarious and were shaking with laughter. We spent the night in Amara and set off again early next morning, this time more successfully. It was a heavenly morning with mist rising from the water, a red sun in the east and the full moon in the west. At Amagede we went to the Canteen and bought 56 lbs of lump sugar. The manager gave me a tin of salmon and six bars of soap. We spent the night on a sandbank and the mosquitoes were particularly voracious. It was also bitterly cold and I caught a chill. In the morning we walked along the sandbank and Tim had a bathe but came out jolly quickly when he was told that there were crocodiles nearby! In Loko we visited the dispensary, where a man who had been mauled by a leopard was being treated and then we returned to Nassarawa by lorry. It's very nice to be home but we enjoyed the trip immensely.

With only three days until Christmas, Berrice had to busy herself with the preparations. They had invited Mr Hunt, but a Mr B. turned up at the Rest House unexpectedly. On Christmas Eve they had them both over for drinks and dinner and Berrice was rather horrified when each drank a dozen or so whiskies. Mr Hunt got rather maudlin while Mr B. talked a lot of nonsense and by the time they got to bed at 2 a.m. she was feeling thoroughly fed up. On Christmas Day she put her foot down about drinking too much and was grateful to a third guest, Mr Okusi, who seemed to have a sobering effect on the other two. She was quite relieved when they all departed on Boxing Day and glad to see the back of them.

On New Year's Eve there was a sports evening:

> The 880 yards provided much amusement because the winner was a prisoner and for the last 220 yards he was cheered or bullied on by a warder who ran with him yelling encouragement! Schoolboys searching for 3d pieces in bowls of flour with their teeth caused the biggest laugh, with their black faces smothered with flour! The slippery goat and slippery pole also went down very well, particularly when the Ma'aji fell off the pole. Tim and I went into the three-legged race and finished about fifth; Maiholi and Maigani teamed up but came to grief! Jolly sporting of the old things to even attempt it. The whole thing was a great success but I think the very small schoolboys should have more races next time.

In the New Year they bought two horses and Berrice felt very nervous not having ridden for many years. Just before their second trek to the north and west of Keffi, she discovered that her horse was covered in enormous ticks that had to be treated with shea-butter and ash.

> We spent the first two nights at Kokwana and went to see the shrine of the 'Holy Man'. In the eighteenth century, a devout Mallam called Ahamadu went to live there and one of his possessions was a long stick that had special properties. In those days, Kokwana was attacked frequently by the people of Ninkoro, a neighbouring village, but Ahamadu always led the townsfolk into battle carrying his stick and the assailants invariably fled. When he died, he was buried just outside the town and his stick was placed lengthways on his grave. That night the people of Ninkoro came to steal the stick but as they seized it there was a terrific flash of fire and it turned into a pillar of stone which was too heavy to move. They did however manage to cut off a piece about two feet long, and this they took back to Ninkoro.
>
> We left Kokwana at 8.30, called at Keffi to get my new bag and continued to Gitata in the NA lorry. In the evening we looked round the town and watched some mat makers working in an underground work-room covered with grass. Next day I typed all morning and made two maps while Tim looked at the site for a new school. Late that evening the carriers set off for Panda but

wouldn't take the horses with them because lions are reputed to live between the two villages. In the morning, Tim rode over and I cycled. First we visited the school and found that the children were incredibly dirty. I suggested that schools should be provided with pots for water and that the children should be made to wash before lessons. The people are Yeskwa and quite timid because, in the old days, they were rounded up and taken away by the slave-raiders. Later, Tim sat in on a divorce case; the bride price was 3 calabashes of beer, 2 tins of salt, 5 tins of locust beans and a cloth worth 4/2d!

We slept outside and I saw the Southern Cross for the first time. In the morning I had a terribly rough, long ride on my bike to Kugwanu. The paths were so bad that I had to walk a third of the way, and Maigani[4] had to carry me over two streams. Much to my annoyance, Tim had a comfortable ride on his horse. The Rest House is situated amongst masses of shady trees and is very nice. We took the horses out for a ride in the evening and I don't feel so nervous now. The countryside is undulating with impressive ranges of hills. We were amazed to find that we were the first visitors for seven years.

I decided to ride my horse to Gunku and found it much easier than cycling especially as the path was very bad and rocky. The people are chiefly Gwari all living in cramped mushroom-like settlements. It is situated half way up a big hill, which was good protection in the days of tribal warfare, but is now most insanitary as the nearest source of clean water is about two miles away and the people are drinking filthy, stagnant water. We visited the school and were pleased to find that the children were fairly clean.

On Thursday, I was back on my bike because my horse is too lazy and slow. Luckily it was a short journey to Kanu where we visited some missionaries and had an early dinner with them. We were both totally unprepared for the lengthy improvised prayers and bible reading! A missionary doctor was staying there and told us that he had treated people with seven different kinds of worm – guinea, tape, hook, bilharzia, jiggers, filaria and tumbo. One patient even had leprosy as well! The mission was established thirty years ago and there are fifty pupils in school, up to Grade IV, but only one teacher. Attendance at the Dispensary is generally fifty a day, but up to three hundred when the Doctor comes. They have a large church and five hundred adherents, half of whom live in the village, the other half coming from the surrounding area.

There is Sunday school for the children and a bible reading class for young people aged between twenty and thirty.

Next day I had an appalling fifteen-mile trek to Karshi which took me nearly four hours. The bush paths were shocking and I spent most of the time scrambling up hills and pushing my bike. I must get a new horse. When we arrived, we found that the people had just decided to move down from the hill, where they have always lived, and were camping in *rumfas*. Very few houses have been built as yet so we helped them plan the lay-out and hope to have a model village complete with school, dispensary and court house. The people have chosen an excellent site, near a good stream, and the District Head is young and progressive. We also decided on a good shady site for a Rest House and have designed it with a large veranda and windows, which are practically non-existent in most Rest Houses.

In the evening we watched some 'Dodo' dancing. Dodos are mythical spirits who represent the ghosts of the deceased. The men dress up in weird and wonderful costumes, many of which are made of straw so they look like scarecrows. Their faces are always masked so that the women and children can't guess their identity. Their most important function is to dance at funerals. Their meetings are held in an area of dense scrub surrounding the ju-ju tree and young men who wish to join the group are given a severe flogging to ensure that they keep their promise never to reveal the identity of the Dodo. After the initiation ceremony they have a feast and late in the night the meeting breaks up with much yelling and shrieking which puts fear into the hearts of the villagers who believe in the myth of the spirits.

For the return journey to Keffi, we were hoping to hitch a ride on the NA lorry but it had broken down so we had to cycle again. Another horse was brought along for inspection. Tim tried it out and liked it because it has a good trot and a much faster walk than my old horse. I'm going to have it and give my old one to the owner in part exchange. I'm sure he will be well looked after.

When they arrived home, they found that their gardener Yaro had caught and killed a snake that had got into the house. After the coolness of Keffi, Nassarawa seemed unbearably hot and they decided to sleep outside. There was always masses to do in the house after they had been away which pleased Berrice because it was much better for 'morale' to have a fully occupied day. When she had first arrived in Nigeria, she had been given some very sound advice by an old hand: 'You will be spending an awful lot of time on your own while your husband is at work or on tour. You must find ways to fill those long hours or you will soon become depressed and then you will want to run back to England. Make sure you keep busy until your husband comes home for lunch. Then, in the afternoon and evening, you can spend time doing things together and the hardships we all have to face out here won't seem half so bad.'

At the end of January they toured round the Afao hills, to the east of Nassarawa.

We set off at 6.15 a.m., on our horses, and had an easy ride to Onda. It is attractive flat country surrounded by hills. The village looked very picturesque hugging the foot of the hills, but as usual it was dirty. Sarkin Onda has a nice little fenced in garden where he grows indigo, henna and corn.

Next we went to Apawo where there was no rest house, but an adequate room made of zana mats. I spent a pleasant day reading while Tim went about his business. In all the villages we have passed through, there are areas in which ju-ju practices are performed. The main ju-ju house is much bigger and better than the ordinary living houses, and is surrounded by circles outlined in stone and containing straw symbols. It is here that offerings are made in the form of chickens and corn. We were the first European visitors for six years.

On Saturday we had a very short journey to Agwada and again we found that no European visitor had been for eight years. The drumming which annoyed us through the night was said to have been mourning drums for the chief's daughter who had died during the day. The Harmattan was thick and the hills looked very mysterious at dawn shrouded in mist with a fringe of trees just visible on the sky-line.

On Sunday we covered the four or so miles to Iggo in record time. The Rest House was terribly small. We looked round the village in the evening and it is quite the dirtiest I have ever seen. We were given a demonstration of pottery making. Potters wheels are not used and the round shape is formed by the potter walking in circles. A wet rag is used to smooth and mould. It takes one day to make a very large pot, standing about three feet in height. No DO had ever visited Iggo before, only one or two missionaries!

The trek to Rafin Gabas was longer and slightly more difficult. There was a very nice miners' Rest House with a few bits of furniture, including a comfortable armchair. We were taken to see the old wolfram mine workings – beastly shafts going 200 feet into the ground. We went in a few feet and found it completely airless and like an oven. Masses of wolfram is still lying about and it seems an awful waste not to extract it from the stone. The country is very bush.

The following day we had an extremely long and rough ride to Bassan Zarangi. Tim was the first DO to visit for thirteen years! In the evening he rode down to the river. I lent Maigani my horse; he hadn't ridden for years and didn't look at all comfortable. Maiholi and the boys were much amused and all joined in a barrage of rude remarks.

The road to Nicholls Camp, one of the mining camps, was very difficult. One carrier got lost in the night; he stopped for a few minutes and then couldn't find the others although they lit fires and shouted. They believe that he went mad for a few hours – certainly looks queer. The boys arrived at 8 a.m. and we were then taken to Udegi in Mr Hunt's lorry. From there we hitched a lift in another lorry and got back to Nassarawa at lunchtime. Sarkin Daji brought a puppy for me to see, he is a nice little thing and can't be compared with the pi-dogs. We gave Sarkin Daji a white shirt in exchange and everybody seemed satisfied.

Between treks, Berrice wrote:

Shortly after we got back from our last trek, we had problems with one of the boys. Twenty-nine shillings, some sugar and some soap went missing and we decided it must be Labo because nothing had ever gone missing before he arrived. The vast majority of boys are extremely trustworthy so we were very disappointed. We paid him for the work he had done and his full salary for next month – £3.15s – and sent him on his way.

The mobile cinema came to town the other day, which was quite a novelty. Most of the newsreels were incomprehensible to the local people but they enjoyed the films about the Royal West African Frontier Force, boxing, athletics and horse racing. Life in England seems to be getting more difficult with food rationing and coal in short supply and Tim and I feel very privileged to be living in a land of milk and honey. We can't understand why

Europeans complain so much when they are far better off in
Nigeria than they would be back home.

We heard today that the man suffering from leprosy,
whom we managed to send to Abuja, has run away. It is very
disheartening because at the Colony he could have lived happily
with good food and a house provided, and also the chance to
learn a trade.

One of the duties of the DO was to be available to the
lowliest people, to listen to their worries and complaints and, if he
thought they were being oppressed or ill-treated, to take appropriate
action. On their next trek Tim was disturbed to find that people
were being prevented from coming to see him.

The carriers were late getting off, the delay being caused by the
usual haggling over loads. The Headman is too young and has
little control. Consequently, we did not get to Kurudu until the
light was fading. In the morning we made an early start and got
to Loko Goma for breakfast. Tim started to unearth some dirty
work and had to reprimand the Ciroma for trying to prevent
people from complaining.

Between Loko and Gidabuke we stopped to look at the new
bridges. Four apprentices from Nassarawa were employed as
labourers with the possibility of gradually working their way up to
bricklaying. Three of them have already given up and the fourth
is threatening to leave. They all say the work is too hard. It is so
typical of the attitude in the north; they are not good workers
and they are not keen to learn, so the southerners come up and
take all the best paid jobs!

In Gidabuke we went to inspect the town to see if there had
been any improvements since our last visit. We were dismayed to
find that it was still disgustingly dirty in spite of their protestations
of willingness to clean up. The same piles of dirt were lying
around and the people living near the school have started dumping
their rubbish in the school compound. Outside the dispensary
there were piles of filthy ulcer dressings and they hadn't bothered
to repair the roof of the waiting room.

In Toto, Tim heard complaints about having to give the Emir
money at Salla time. Two years ago, the Emir started asking each
hamlet for one shilling, last year he asked for two shillings and
this year he wanted five shillings. Tim told him that the increase
was too much and he settled for three shillings. In the evening we

walked over to the dispensary and again found dirty dressings all over the ground. They hadn't even bothered to put them in a pile. Later, some labourers came to Tim and complained that no one had bothered to get them any food, which was a pretty poor show considering they pay for it. At bed time, the boys killed two scorpions in the Rest House and three small snakes in their huts which had fallen out of the roof.

We went on to Rubochi, and that was even worse. We had to stay in an appalling Rest House bang in the middle of the town with people living within six feet of the door. The town was filthy and Tim turned out all the men and women to clean the place up. When they had finished there was a slight improvement. Very few people approached Tim to make complaints and we think they have been warned off by the Ciroma. The people are Gwari; they are quite the dirtiest and laziest people in the Division.

The cleaning up performance had to be repeated in Gwaragwada. There was a considerable amount of bad feeling amongst the workers because some of the villagers skulked in their houses and didn't do a stroke of work. Later three complainants turned up, including the schoolmaster from Gidabuke.

It was only about five miles to Gwambe but the path was very bad; it's so maddening to have to push a bicycle up a hill and then have to push it down the other side. The town is looking very clean, so word has obviously got round that we consider Cleanliness next to Godliness. There were three graves outside the back door of our hut and we had to sleep with our beds two feet away from them. I would have had the jitters in England but here I'm sure the ghosts, if any, would be friendly souls!

On Friday we should have started at 6.15 but a puncture delayed us until 7. The path was the most appalling we have ever used, just like a switchback and until the last three miles we could only cycle about 30 yards at a time; if we didn't get off for a stream, we had to get off for fallen trees across the path. Maigani said it was eleven miles but it turned out to be seventeen. We didn't get to Gidabuke until 10.45.

On Saturday, Sunday and Monday more than a hundred men came to complain to Tim about having to give money to the Dispenser and the Emir.

On Tuesday we waited all day for the lorry but it didn't appear so we looked round the school in the evening. It finally turned up just before midnight. When we got home we were told that a leopard had killed and eaten a calf in our new farm.

Berrice was now expecting her first baby and she went for a check-up to the nearest doctor in Jos. She stayed at Jos Hill Station, a private hotel that was frequently used by government officials for short holidays, and was very impressed with the mod-cons that she did not enjoy at home such as running water, electric lights and a geyser. It was also an opportunity to make new friends and shop in the canteens that were full of lovely material and all kinds of cosmetics and perfume. She enjoyed the much cooler climate of the Plateau and noticed that people lived in the lap of luxury and seemed to know nothing of bush life.

In July Tim met the new Resident, Macdonald, and was able to discuss with him the evidence he had been collecting which proved that the Emir and his Council were corrupt. Macdonald recommended that the Emir be deposed and they hoped that higher authority would agree.

Given the policy of indirect rule in Nigeria, deposition of an Emir was a very serious business. However, it is highly probable that Tim would have been encouraged to root out corruption and oppression after reading a recent article by Mallam Abubakar Imam, the Editor of the Hausa newspaper *Gaskiya*, in which he wrote: '...The main criticism of the present system of Government that we get from people in the Northern Provinces is that the Government leaves open opportunities for oppression and selfishness. Even though it is difficult to prove specific cases and places where these vices are practised, the people cannot feel safe since they know that Government leaves that opportunity open for an oppressive official to do as he pleases. ...In the old days, if an Emir took to being oppressive, selfish and corrupt, his people often revolted against him. Now the British Government has condemned the practice of revolt, even when an Emir misbehaves himself. If complaints such as would have led to a revolt in the old days become manifest, it is the duty of His Excellency the Governor to depose the Emir concerned.'[5]

At the end of the month the Emir called on his way to Kaduna to see the Chief Commissioner and they hoped he would be gone for good. But a few days later he was back again! His Honour had sacked the Council but had not deposed the Emir. As a punishment he was forbidden to use his drums and trumpet for a week. Tim felt let down by the Chief Commissioner for not supporting his efforts to 'clean up' the NA and asked to be transferred from Nassarawa. Berrice was heart-broken because she was sure that they would never have the good fortune to be stationed in such a delightful place again, or be so happy.

Tim was posted to Makurdi,[6] and within a week the Emir was boasting about how he had got rid of the DO and that certain people had better watch their step. The new District Head of Nassarawa – chosen by the Emir in the Resident's presence – had a nice juicy record of crime! The Emir refused to have the Wakili on the Council because, Tim supposed, he was too honest and might divulge some of his murky doings. Berrice's comment in her diary was: 'Why on earth should the Emir be allowed a say in anything after his disgraceful conduct? Why should he or any member of the family, be allowed to remain in office? It all points to the theory that in HH's eyes no Emir can do wrong.[7] How will the Division or people ever improve with such a corrupt family?'

They packed up and stayed in the Rest House for their last few days so that Tim's replacement could move into their house. When Mr and Mrs F. arrived, Mrs F. told Berrice that she didn't like Africa or Africans, and that she didn't like the house either!

In Makurdi, Tim and Berrice quickly settled into their new home and were soon busy making a vegetable garden. A few weeks later, it was time for Berrice to go and stay near the hospital in Jos until the baby was born. Tim had been summoned to Kaduna for an interview with the Chief Commissioner and they travelled up to Kafanchan together to catch their respective trains. As soon as she had settled herself in her compartment, Berrice started writing to him.

> I don't think we shall leave Kafanchan for some time because a man has just got on to repair the lights and fans, my lights are all right so I will be able to knit and read if I want to.
>
> A bunch of prosperous looking Africans have just rolled down in a taxi and are looking for seats on the train, I rather fear

they have designs on my compartment – swarms of children as well as grown-ups.

I have been watching a woman bathing a baby, in a most scientific manner, outside one of the miserable hovels. – We are off and I'm still alone, it is 3 p.m.

We are stopping at the first station – about 10 miles from Kafanchan.

The country is very nice and open; it looks rather like a park, with a few trees scattered about and hills in the distance. Although the sun is shining, there is a big storm a few miles away and the hills are in cloud. There is not much in the way of crops but the guinea corn is good and has big heads; I suppose the rainfall would be heavier here as it is near the plateau.

Second stop: I can see some extraordinary looking pagan youths with plaited hair tied with beads and metal. They are playing little reed pipes outside the missionaries' compartment. The train gets into Jos at 7.30 so I'm sure I won't be too tired. I hope you have managed to keep your compartment to yourself; it is so much nicer to have room to breathe. I have horrid visions of you knocking back cups of tea, fruit salad and cake! I'm frightfully thirsty but must save the water a little longer – the fruit sweets are not at all refreshing, I've eaten nearly half the tin and am thirstier than ever! We're off again.

Third stop: we are now well up in the hills, we've been winding round and round for the last hour. It is nice to see Fulanis and cattle again, big herds all over the place. I have seen several red flowered trees and a number of wild flowers, some rather nice red ones and some washed out looking blue ones. It is strange that there are so few wild flowers in this country.

We passed a range of rocky hills a few minutes ago, and one formation of rocks looked exactly like an out-size partridge waiting to be shot; I looked at it so hard that I was almost certain that I had seen it move its head! Look out for it when you come up.

This railway must have cost a vast amount to build, nearly all the big streams and eroding places have been reinforced with masonry.

The engine driver – or mate – is oiling the wheels with an oil can suitable for a baby Austin! The ticket collector has just been in and is very much inclined to be too friendly. He asked if I had any books to lend him. I froze him out by telling him that I wanted to write a letter. I can't bear these familiar people, it is so difficult not to be thoroughly rude. A wretched old beggar is pestering me now, perhaps he will get some sympathy from the missionaries.

I imagine our climbing has exhausted the engine; it is lapping up water in readiness for the next climb. A goods train is just coming into the station – probably carrying the fat of the land down to Lagos. It has run over a chicken and is causing great concern! I've got a huge tanker full of petrol parked next door, also going to Lagos I should imagine.

Fourth stop 'Hoss': I'm sure we must be almost at the highest point and yet it is only 5.30 and we still have two more hours in the train. I am eating my rolls – quite nice although they are only made of flour and water. The water in the Thermos is still beautifully cold and most refreshing, I'm so glad I brought it.

The train goes surprisingly fast considering the terrific climb. I wonder if you have reached Kaduna yet – I'm longing to get in and have a drink and bath; I feel awfully scruffy and hot. It is a nuisance having to put down the windows at stations.

Fifth stop Kuru: Feel better after a good wash and tidy up; BG spotless compared with the other train. There seems to be a European railway man on board the train, he gets off at each station and has a snoop around. Another European is just getting on.

These people amuse me; they use sugar cane as walking sticks and occasionally have a nibble! – not a bit concerned about the dirt. We've just passed the highest point.

Wednesday

I had a good journey and arrived at 7.30. The Tollemaches were at the station to meet me and were frightfully kind. Gorgeous whisky when we got in – quite the nicest I have ever tasted! I didn't feel a bit tired and got up this morning at 6 a.m. They wanted me to have dinner in bed last night but of course I didn't. The Rest House is very comfortable; nice big springy bed! When I got into bed I found a hot water bottle and 3 blankets!! The bottle was thrown out immediately and the blankets came off one by one until I was left with my dressing gown. Mr Tollemache has fixed a bell to my bed so that I can get in touch with them immediately; he has also provided a whistle in case the bell doesn't work!

When I opened the wardrobe I found the most adorable baby's dress hanging up; Mrs Tollemache has made it for me and it is perfectly sweet and beautifully made. They are terribly kind and I'm sure I shall be very happy and well looked after. They seem to expect you to come up quite soon and I gather they want you to stay here; I'm sure you will enjoy it.

I have just returned from the hospital, everything seems to be all right except that the baby is the wrong way up at the moment. Dr Selby says there is plenty of time for it to turn round. Both the Doctor and Sister think I am very small and asked if I had made a mistake on the dates! So much for my bulge. The Sister is very nice and most helpful, she took me in to see two babies born this week – they looked rather like little tadpoles but had very definite features and looked quite different. They have had five babies born this month – nearly all missionaries. The Tollemaches say that Dr Selby is very good and takes endless trouble, he is an excellent surgeon but unfortunately is too shy to have a good 'bedside manner'.

There is a terrific to-do going on in Jos – a marriage break-up between the Es and Ns, I don't know who they are but the names are familiar. Mrs E is up here now pouring out her sorrows to Mrs T. Mr E has run off to Kenya with Mrs N; they left three days ago and are driving there. Jos seems to specialise in broken marriages.

Although it is much cooler here I still feel hot. The garden looks lovely and is just like a well-kept English garden. The flowers in my room smell wonderful, I wish we could grow nice things in Makurdi.

Lokoja was helpful on the train and is up here now and wants to know when I shall go back to Makurdi. His fare to Kafanchan is 5/6 and I have given him 7/- pocket money, also a ten bob loan for a uniform for his child at school. I think he said his child but I can never understand him very well.

John and Marie Chartres are staying at Hill Station and are coming up for drinks tonight. They have tried their boat but were too terrified to let it go flat out! I expect I shall hear about it tonight. Tomorrow we are having drinks with the Conneys.

Your interview with His Honour is just over I imagine, I hope it wasn't too unpleasant and I hope you made him feel small – miserable little rat! Did you get transport? or did he make you walk? Do write quickly and tell me all about it, I shall be most interested.

Meanwhile in Kaduna Tim was staying with Peter and was also enjoying the much cooler weather compared to Makurdi. About his interview with the Chief Commissioner he wrote:

I had my interview with Rumtus[8] yesterday, two hours of it. He talked and talked and talked; I sat back and stone-walled in my principles. Twice he said 'I think you made your mistake...' so I interjected rather testily 'Really Sir, I cannot agree that cleaning up Nassarawa was a mistake'. Later he said mistake a third time, but quickly corrected it to action. By and large he was as affable as he is capable of being, and was I suppose trying to be conciliatory; I responded by sticking to my guns but without being provocative. I can't give you details because there was no hard and fast repartee as with HE, it was all obscured in his verbal jungle. Two points that he did make were (i) he didn't want me to think he had chosen between me and the Emir, and (ii) that I must realise I was still under his orders; I answered that (i) hadn't occurred to me and (ii) I didn't dispute. We parted in a sort of armed neutrality.

There was not much that Berrice could do while she waited for the baby to arrive apart from a bit of knitting and sewing, so she was delighted to see her friends John and Marie Chartres when they passed through Jos. To Tim she wrote:

Poor old John's trousers were definitely not on speaking terms with his feet, they ended somewhere near his calf! Marie was wearing a dress well above her knees and they looked rather like over-grown children.

They expect to be posted to Makurdi next tour and will be going there sometime next month so look out for them. John thinks the Nassarawa business is disgusting and wonders if you are thinking of getting out of Nigeria! If they are ever posted south they won't stay in Nigeria.

The flies are perfect pests and are almost as bad as the plague we had at Nassarawa. The cattle graze near the house and bring the flies. I haven't seen a mosquito yet, but always wear my boots in case of accidents. It would be a blessing if we could have a weekly DDT spray in Makurdi; it is sprayed on the walls and stays put for a week. It will last for a month or longer if the walls are thoroughly saturated but it is a messy business. Ask Armstrong why we don't have a DDT man in Makurdi; I'm sure people would be more than willing to pay.

There was a horrid murder in Jos just before I came up; a miner was stabbed in his office in broad daylight; it is so awful because his wife has only just had an infant. Jos seems to be a bad place for scandal and tragedy.

Tim returned to Makurdi by train and at Lafia Gilbert Stephenson turned up at the station for a chat. He had heard most of the Nassarawa story and told Tim, 'We want people like you who stand up to the Government'. This made Tim feel a lot better; he might be in bad-odour with the big-shots but he felt sure he had the approval of the majority of officers. To Berrice he wrote:

I have decided to press on with my Hausa: it will give me something to do, and it won't matter if I fail. On the other hand it would be nice to pass, because it would be an effective answer to HH or anyone else who felt inclined to say: 'Of course Johnston is very inexperienced... knows nothing of the country... quite out of touch'. I tried two old Hausa-English papers today, 1922–23 vintage, and reckon I could have passed comfortably, but the later ones may be more difficult.

The other day, by the way, HH wrote a letter to *Gaskiya* and signed it with a nom-de-plume. His Hausa is not much good, and Peter noticed he had come a cropper over the signature. He sent it back with the comment: the significance of the pseudonym 'The Perjured One' escapes me! It was returned neatly altered in red ink.

It was horrid coming back to an empty house, I did feel lonely.

In Jos, Berrice was now living with the Conneys and had been making enquiries about nursery schools in England for the baby. Somebody had recommended one in Crieff:

I will keep the Nursery School address very carefully, it is definitely cheaper than the other places we've heard about; I'm sure we could afford £13.10s. a month because we lead such quiet lives. The thought of staying at home is too awful – I simply couldn't do it so we shall have to afford a Nursery School!

I received a very nice letter from Eleanor Stephenson,[9] she was most amused at the idea of the Expectant Fathers walking up and down the platform discussing the future infants! They decided on names ages ago and I feel we are being very slack but it is a difficult job. Mrs C's little boy is Ian, it is short and sweet and I think would do very well as one name if we have a boy.

I've seen masses of children in Jos; they all look quite fit but seem to get thinner and paler as they get older. The very small ones look amazingly well.

Three new babies have appeared at the hospital this week, they expect one more and then their quota for the month is finished! I don't know how many they expect next month, but I rather think I am the only case.

I'm more than surprised at people's vegetable gardens, Mrs T's is small and an awful mess; the tomatoes are not propped up and spread all over the ground. Mrs C's garden is the size of a postage stamp and practically empty. It is rather extraordinary because vegetables are expensive up here and quite difficult to get at this time of the year.

People are extraordinary, both Mrs T and Mrs C keep absolutely everything under lock and key. Last night Mrs C had to go and measure out a portion of coffee and the same thing happened with marmalade at breakfast. I'm afraid I simply couldn't be bothered and would rather lose a few things than go to so much bother. They both carry round a little bunch of keys attached to their belts, it reminds me of old-fashioned house-keepers with great bunches of keys dangling from the waist. I expect they are much better house-keepers than I am, but not so happy I'm certain. I think it is rather horrid to show the boys so clearly that they are not trusted. It is funny how people with plenty of money count the 'halfpennies'.

Mrs Conney has a perfectly sweet small-boy, he is about thirteen but looks less than ten and is very small. He speaks English very well and is an excellent worker; he served our dinner single-handed and did it beautifully. He is a Hausa boy. We must try to get a young boy next tour, I think it is the best thing to do and it is much nicer to train them into your own habits.

Tim was now working flat out on the annual estimates. He found a lot of mistakes, which was annoying and time-consuming because each mistake had two or three repercussions, so the typist was 'like a one-legged man at a rump-kicking contest'. There had also been a small riot in the town, the Hausa port-labourers against the Tiv. A few heads had been broken and half-a-dozen houses got burnt, but nothing much.

Berrice was feeling rather isolated at the Conney's house, which was seven miles from Jos, and was looking forward to going back to the Tollemache's.

It amazes me to see how slack people are about taking precautions against fever; Mr and Mrs C don't take quinine regularly and Mrs never wears her boots when Mr C is at home even though her legs are full of lumps and bumps!

The women up here seem to expect the boys to do everything. For example, when the flowers are done in the morning the boys carry the vases to the pantry, empty and clean them, fill them up with water and then when the flowers have been arranged they carry the vases back to the various rooms. In fact the boys do all the dirty work while the women look on. No wonder females get bored out here.

I heard an extraordinary story about E and his Fulani wife. When they are travelling he always makes her go third class while he uses first class on the train! Apparently the marriage is not successful and is breaking up; how awful for her, he sounds rather a brute.

I am getting rather worried about the things we ordered from the Army & Navy Stores because I can't have cot pillows and mattresses made until I know the size. If the infant does arrive early I think I have enough clothes for it, but when we emerge from Hospital the poor little beast won't have nearly enough things. I do hope it is a boy.

The new European School in Jos takes boarders, a new dormitory is being built and several children are already weekly boarders. It might be worth remembering for our hound or hounds.

Mrs C told me last night that Ken has only seen their son ten months in ten years, and for two months of that time Ian was at school. It seems dreadful to know so little of your own child and I hope we can come to a better arrangement. Vera left Ian when he was nine months old with her mother, in the care of a nanny. She saw him again when he was twenty-one months and then not until he was four years old. The next time she went home he was 8 and hardly remembered her. Children are a problem in Nigeria and I can't imagine what we shall do. I couldn't bear to stay at home and yet on the other hand it seems all wrong to be away from the child.

Tim managed to track down one of the A&N parcels, containing the Kari-Kot, and had it forwarded to Berrice in Jos:

The other stuff is in a different parcel, and it is at Gudi. I have told S/M Gudi to forward it and the customs papers to you at Jos. To enable you to claim it I now enclose (I) their advice note and (II) the precious invoice. There is £4–6–1 to pay, plus forwarding charges.

Not much news since my last letter. I soon tired of Faulkner's book about riding through Nigeria, but have got another by Hastings that is far more interesting. He came out in 1906 as a DO, and so far I have only got to the end of his first tour in Bauchi. In ten months he spent 270 days on tour (compare that with today) and rode about 3,000 miles.

You remember our discussing the poor treatment of the North compared with the East. Well the figures came out the other day, and very striking they are. What it amounts to is this: where the Northerner pays 10/- tax, the Ibo pays 5/-; where the Northern NAs contribute £100 to Government revenue, the Eastern ones give £50; and where the North gets £50 of Government expenditure, the East gets £100. It is incredible that the Chief Commissioners of the Northern Province haven't been banging the table for years about it. Too engrossed in compost heaps, I suppose. The West is half-way between the two.

The latest rumour about the Harragin Commission report is that we shall all get nominal rises, but allowances will go, income-tax will probably go up, and nobody will be any better off than before.

In November Berrice was back with the Tollemaches.

It is nice to be back with the Ts, although the Cs were most frightfully kind and nice.

I collected a letter from you at the Post Office containing the Export thing. The Customs must make a pretty penny, I shall grudge paying £4 odd for the goods. However, it is nice to know they are on the way. We simply must decide on names, I'm afraid we are being very slack. It is a frightful job and I haven't any suggestions – have you?

I was most interested in the tax figures for North and East. It is a scandal; is it because we are afraid the turbulent Ibos will make trouble if their tax is raised? It makes me furious to think of those upstarts having all the amenities of civilisation while the poor old Northerner has practically nothing. Apparently there has been a lot of trouble in the African hospital here, the Southern nurses and orderlies are taking money from patients and won't do anything for them unless they get a handsome dash. What a pity the Northerners won't wake themselves up a bit and take the trouble to train for the skilled jobs.

In his next letter Tim had some rather good news.

A really extraordinary thing happened yesterday: looking back I can hardly believe that I didn't dream it. At about 11 in the morning I heard Armstrong calling outside the house and went to the balcony. He said 'I've brought Mr Beresford-Stooke to see you'. Now B.S. is Chief Secretary, as big a shot as a Chief Commissioner. I of course thought Armstrong was playing the buffoon, and the words 'Ha-bloody-ha' as usual sprang to my foul old mouth. Luckily I didn't say them, because it was B.S. He was just back from leave, had been landed at Port Harcourt, and was on his way round to Lagos in a coach hitched to a goods-train. He had come to see Macdonald, but finding him away at Gboko, had been shepherded round to me.

He stayed about half an hour, and then I walked back to the station with him. Well, I ask you: if that wasn't Providence I should like to know what it was. The unsuspecting VIP walks into the lion's den.

Anyway, I felt my way at first, but finding him sympathetic – he's a nice old thing – I gave him the works in full. I told him about office-work and estimates, and how the Resident had to ask Kaduna's permission before he could promote a Messenger from £24 to £27 p.a., and how Mr T at Kaduna on £450 p.a. graciously gave that permission, and how DOs had to ask the Resident's permission before they could appoint a Board of Survey to write-off a few battered old head-pans, and how touring was gradually falling off in consequence, and how Bassan Zarengi had seen no European for fourteen years. All the stuff we've talked about in fact. I told him what was needed was a high-powered, small, ruthless Commission, that would sweep all this away at a stroke; to my surprise he said he'd make a note of it and see if anything could be done. I also told him about the dead-wood in the service, and quoted how moral-fibre cases were dealt with in the RAF. Finally I told him about the resignations, and the underlying discontent. No doubt he'll see Rumtus at Kaduna, and no doubt Rumtus will call me a malcontent or a firebrand or something, but Beresford-Stooke told me he started his career with a first-class row with his Commissioner, so he'll probably think no worse of me for that! Anyway, I said pretty well all I had to say, so let's hope one day something may come of it.

Berrice was delighted and replied:

I had your exciting letter about Beresford-Stooke's visit this morning. I think it is absolutely wonderful and am delighted that you were able to say your piece to someone so high up, and sympathetic. Poor old Rumtus, I do hope he hears about the meeting it will give him a headache. What a blessing the Resident was away, if he had been in you probably wouldn't have even seen Beresford-Stooke. Jolly interesting to see if anything is done: do let me know what happens – if anything. You will have a bad name with HH, but it doesn't matter a bit as long as something is done to cut out all the red-tape and petty nonsense. Good show my love, it is time the younger generation aired its views.

The cot arrived yesterday, it is a most handsome thing and will be frightfully useful for you to carry around! Mr T is going to see about the rods for the mosquito net. The cot hasn't got a stand but it doesn't matter because it is small enough to put on a table or chest of drawers. I'm awfully glad I ordered it because I'm sure it will be ideal for the journey home.

Meanwhile, back in Makurdi, Tim had enjoyed the clerks' performance of *Julius Caesar*.

I will begin by saying that it was far better done than ever I thought it would be. Julius Caesar was played by the Met. clerk whom I had caught out the day before palming off an old hired ruin of a bicycle as his own when applying for a permit for a new one! He wore a fez and a sort of Cardinal Wolsey cloak, quite regal if not Roman. The others were in a variety of garments, including some of our camel-hair rugs lent for the occasion. The only really incongruous note was struck by Cimber, whose Gor-Blimey cap made him look as if he was just back from Sandown Park.

The lines were spoken much better than I would have imagined. Some sounded as if they had potatoes in their mouths, but others were very clear. And none of them gabbled them off line by line as I feared they might. Nor was there any prompting. The murder of Caesar was performed with great spirit. Unfortunately there was a lot of bunting suspended over the stage, in which the wildly hacking swords soon became entangled. Some of it got cut down, some wound round people's arms, some round their necks, but they all hacked gamely away, their movements gradually getting slower and slower as they got caught up more and more in the tails.

Berrice had also had a little outing.

I am alone in the house this afternoon as the Ts have gone to the races; I didn't want to go today because I felt most conspicuous when we went to yesterday's race meeting. Actually, I'm not a bit keen on racing and have no interest in betting – I hate putting money on, knowing that I shall never see it again! I won a miserable 5/- on the Hausa sweepstake – 6th prize, the first prize was over £40!!

I only enjoyed one race and that was the one for Hausa owned horses. I wish you could have seen it, it was an absolute riot. Professional jockeys were not allowed in this race; when the horses came out to the paddock and their jockeys mounted everything seemed to be all right. Suddenly there was an angry shout and a man was pulled off his horse because he had been recognised as a pro. Of course that started things moving, he immediately pointed to another jockey and said he was also a pro. Everyone started shouting and arguing and in the end it was discovered that about 15 out of 20 jockeys were pros!! How like the good old Hausas to try to put it across the stewards. They eventually got themselves sorted out and all sorts of odd people were roped in as jockeys. Including one old man with a beard who looked rather like Maiholi!

The end of the race was terribly funny, the proud owner took off his turban and threw it in the air and did a wild little dance, his friends went completely mad and the scene reminded me of the crowd's reactions to the Keffi Ma-aji's fall from the slippery pole!

We went for a drive down the Bauchi road the other evening; most attractive country and heavenly views of hills in the distance. You know I simply love Nigeria, seeing such nice country made me realise just how lucky I am to be out here. I should hate to have to stay in England.

Take very good care of yourself and try not to worry. I'm sure I shall be perfectly all right. I don't want you to have chewed nails and grey hair when you come up!

Towards the end of November Tim had a busy time.

The last two days have been rather hectic, with European visitors and an African Committee. Lenox-Conyngham [DO] was due on Monday, and I had dinner laid on, but he didn't arrive until next morning, so we had it cold for lunch. Then Brown, the Assistant Director of Agriculture, and his wife were passing through here, and the Resident asked me if I'd give them lunch, which I agreed to do; when they arrived however they said, very politely I admit, would I mind if they pushed on. So that lunch went back into the fridge, to be eaten by John and Marie yesterday. In the afternoon and evening, we hired a canoe from near the canteens and went up to the sand-banks just above the bridge, where we had a high tea provided by them. I wish you could have been there, it was really rather pleasant; perhaps we can do something of the sort when you do get back. We lit a fire for hot-coffee and had paw-paw, duck and marmalade tart. Otto thoroughly enjoyed himself, and begged beautifully for the parson's nose. Later the remains of the carcass was dashed to the crew. You know how they sometimes lie propped on an elbow when they eat, heads to the centre of the circle, feet outwards; well, they got down to it like that, and Otto lay down just like them and completed their circle, so that in the half-light you could hardly tell t'other from which. It really was very comic.

The African Committee came here to elect a representative for the Province to the new Kaduna Parliament.[10] Sarkin Loko and Dan Madami came from Nassarawa to Keffi, and S.L. was elected. I had them all up to tea yesterday. Little Dan Madami was rather funny: he contrasted our treatment of them, giving them chairs and so on, with that of their own chiefs. When he went to Zaria and was admitted to the Emir he had to make obeisance three times, once at the door, once in the middle of the room, and once at the throne, and even then as soon as he had the temerity to lift his head a courtier hit him in the nape of the neck to make him drop it again! I asked them whether they thought they could ever unite with the Ibos; they all said with the Yorubas perhaps, with the Ibos never. Most emphatic they were.

I asked them what they thought the Benue bridge cost, actually just over a million. Dan Madami was nearest with £800,000, not a bad guess. One old bush Alkali from Lafia ventured a guess of £500, this was after noticing from our expressions that his first estimate of £5 was on the low side! They were all very interested in this sort of thing, and the Resident has asked me to prepare a brief for them, giving elementary facts and figures about the country. We might toy with it when I come up to Jos. No-one has ever told them these things, as they point out with some asperity.

I have just had a glance at the Harragin report. Our allowances disappear, but instead we go up £200, back-dated to 1.1.46, so we are definitely better off. I am not certain how much we have been getting in allowances but I think not more than £72, perhaps less. The additional salary also counts for pension. Other points are:

(i) no rent, as some feared
(ii) voluntary retirement permitted with gratuity after 10 years; with pension at age 45 at option of either govt. or the officer
(iii) housing to be improved
(iv) free passages for children
(v) 15 months tour recommended for those with 10–20 years service.

Look after yourself and try and put poor old prospective papá out of his agony and suspense.

November 25th arrived but the baby did not.

Well, my love, D-day is here but the infant doesn't seem to know. For the first time I'm beginning to feel thoroughly brassed off; this uncertainty is the limit. Binks, the cat, has beaten me and produced her kittens yesterday morning! She is lucky to be so active after the event – no staying in bed for two weeks!

It is wonderful to know that you will be arriving on the 7th and it is something to look forward to. Your Hausa exams are going to take a long time; I do hope they won't be too beastly. I suppose you will have them in the mornings, and I hope they won't interfere with visiting hours – 4.30 to 6.30 – at the hospital.

I think we shall have to leave the bratling in a nursery school next tour, I couldn't bear to be away from you again, perhaps for a whole tour. Most people seem to leave their babies at home and we must harden our hearts. Anyway I'm sure a baby doesn't really need its mother after it has been weaned.

Nine days later the baby still hadn't arrived and Tim was very anxious.

I have just opened a private telegram from Jos, with shaking hands, still shaking as you can see, feeling sure it was news of you, only to read: 'Grateful bring me 2 bottles Crystal gin. Lenox.[11] Oh dear, oh dear. I did think that was it. Never mind, these things always come in twos, perhaps yours will follow. I feel quite overcome!'

On December 7th, Berrice wrote in her diary:

Doctor arrived at 1.30 a.m., was given chloroform immediately, thank God. Came round just after 2.15 a.m. feeling absolutely wonderful. Baby girl born at 2 a.m., weighing 6 lbs 3 ozs. Didn't realise it was the baby crying but thought it was a kitten. Baby has lots of hair. Mrs T. brought flowers this a.m. Tim wired at Kafanchan. Tim's birthday too!

* * * * *

Many years later Tim described that day to Carolyn in a letter.

Well, it doesn't seem twenty-one years since I was chugging up to Jos by train when the Postmaster at Kafanchan came on board with a telegram which said 'Girl – both doing well'. And then at Jos there was Lenox-Conyngham to ask, after I'd had my first peep at you: 'Well, what's she like? Japanese Admiral?'

Next tour we found ourselves posted to Kafanchan and it was there that you put together your first phrase: 'Ditty-to-do' which we proudly interpreted as 'Pretty red shoes'. After that it was Kaduna, where you went through your patch of looking like Wallace Beary, and then that famous journey home by sea when the deck-steward expressed his admiration first for the left-hook with which you felled another girl who had done something to vex you and later for your lung-power when you found that we had left you immured in the ship's play-pen.

Just before that voyage, Tim was told that his next tour would be in the north-west and he would be stationed at Birnin Kebbi, a place that was considered quite unsuitable for small children. There was nothing for it but to leave Carolyn in England, not at the Nursery School in Crieff but with Tim's sister Alma and her family.

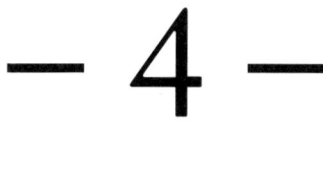

Sokoto – The early 1950s

When they returned to Nigeria Tim was posted not to Birnin Kebbi but to Sokoto, so Carolyn had been left in England unnecessarily.

The city of Sokoto is the home of the Sultan, who is the Sarkin Musulmi or Commander of the Faithful, and it was founded by Shehu Usuman dan Fodiyo's son Muhammadu Bello nearly a hundred years before the British imposed Indirect Rule on Nigeria. The original village of Sokoto, which was the site he chose, had occupied the high ground near the confluence of the Rima and Sokoto Rivers at the point where the Gobir-Kebbi and Adar-Zamfara trade routes intersected. According to tradition, Shehu approved of this site because he thought that corrupting wealth would never come to such a bare and stony plateau.[1]

During the course of his tour there Tim was involved in the Rice Scheme which was financed by the Northern Region Production Development Board. The aim of the scheme was to introduce mechanised ploughing in the *fadama* or floodplain of the rivers and thereby hugely increase the area of production. New areas that had never been worked before were marked out into neat acre plots and ploughed. They were then offered to the farmers who paid a deposit of half the ploughing charge. Unfortunately, the annual floods sometimes descended from the highlands before the farmers had had a chance to sow the rice, or so fast that the young plants were washed away. This meant that the ploughing had to be

107

done again and consequently the farmers had to pay again. Naturally they did not like having to pay twice and in the end many went back to hoeing by hand; that way, if a crop failed, it was only their labour that was lost.[2]

Towards the end of the tour, Berrice flew home early so that she could visit Rome with a friend. Tim wrote:

I was glad to get your letter this morning as I have had no cable. You are a villain: you said you would cable but in such a half-hearted way that I suspected you wouldn't. I have been a forlorn lost dog since you went, and the time, which used to fly past, now limps along at a funeral pace. Anyone would think that after all these years I was still in love with my old woman.

I had a dinner party last night – the mutton was indifferent, Ali forgot to make mint-sauce, the fresh cream had curdled, and the pastry was like vulcanised roofing felt, so the meal was not outstandingly successful.

We had a good game of polo yesterday. In the first chukka Walkiya[3] was very sluggish, apart from an occasional snap at a passing opponent, but in the second he woke up and enabled me to play my best game yet. I actually had three shots at goal and missed them all by three feet, one after running three-quarters the length of the field and one backhand. I wish you'd been there to see me: you would have been proud!

I hope you had a good trip and enjoyed Rome. Write soon and tell me about my daughter.

The promised cable arrived several days later, which was not uncommon in the remote stations where more often than not cables were delivered with the ordinary mail. However, Tim was not mollified:

Your cable arrived this morning at long last. Sent off Monday at 2.45 I notice. You are an old monster: you could easily have telephoned it on Sunday and saved me a bit of worry.

On the whole you have been well out of the last fourteen days. It has been rather bloody, one thing after another. The visiting judge was a nice old thing and no trouble but of course with him in the house I was very much tied up and unable to get on with other things. I had the Sultan, Waziri and Alkali to dinner on his last night and that went off very well thank goodness. I had also polished off several other people to drinks and dinner earlier in the week, so the entertaining duties are being slowly worked off. I feel now that I want a month's peace.

I had a nice little three-day tour over last weekend in Jabo, Dogadaji and Tambawal. I have discovered what I think is a good dam site and am going to send Hanson-Smith [Christopher] to measure it up. The Dange dam is holding water but is not full although we have had a great deal of rain. It is much cooler than last year, too.

Shortly afterwards Tim went out on tour again, this time to Kotorkwashi.

The crops down here are so advanced that the millet is in head and I have had a sharp attack of hay-fever. You would like this country: it is very lush and green, and both Chofa and Kotorkwashi are under big granite domes.

Tonight I hope to see the site of the battlefield where Lieut. Wallace Wright won the V.C. which his second-in-command, Charlie Wells, should have had. You will remember that after Captain Moloney was killed in Keffi, Lugard[4] made no further attempts to conciliate the Fulani but soon afterwards launched an expeditionary force to capture Kano. This was a relatively easy victory since the Emir was away in Sokoto with most of his army. When they received reports that the Kano army was returning, Brig.-Gen. Kemball set out with a column to forestall it.

Meanwhile the Emir had received news that the British had captured his capital and he was flabbergasted by it. After a few days' indecision he determined that he at any rate would carry out the plan that he had unsuccessfully urged on the Sultan. One night, therefore, accompanied only by a small party of women and slaves, he slipped away from his camp in disguise with the intention of emigrating to Arabia. But his road lay through the territory of the Gobir die-hards, who penetrated his disguise, took him prisoner, and later handed him over to the British.

On the morning after the Emir's flight, when news of his disappearance spread abroad, the Kano forces fell into complete confusion. Some of the leaders favoured one course, some another, but none possessed the stature to impose his will on the others. The army therefore broke up into two main groups. The larger body, avoiding Kemball's advancing column, made their way to Kano, where they submitted to the British authorities and laid down their arms. Their leader, the Wambai Abbas, having been chosen by the Electors, was soon afterwards installed by Lugard as the new Emir of Kano.

Meanwhile, the other group, which was led by the Waziri Ahmadu, continued its eastward march with the intention not of avoiding but of seeking battle. It was too far south to meet the main British column, but near Kotorkwashi it ran into a half-company of Mounted Infantry, which was reconnoitring and covering the flank of Kemball's advance. The engagement that followed was a classic of its kind, a contest between modern weapons and disciplined staunchness on the one hand and superior numbers and reckless courage on the other. The Mounted Infantry formed a little square, which had only eleven men on each face, and during the next two hours withstood twelve separate charges. By the narrowest of margins the square held out and when the fighting was over the victors counted sixty-five bodies scattered round it. Among these was that of the Waziri Ahmadu.[5]

Nowadays, the people of Kotorkwashi have an annual ceremony whereby a party of young men from the village have to catch a young griffon from a nest on the rock face and bring it back alive-O. It must be a most hair-raising feat. They go up the rock an easy way and then have to climb down about 100 feet to a tiny ledge along which they make their way to that part of the rock where the birds are nesting. During the last seven years two men have fallen and been killed. These are regarded as bastards: otherwise, they say, the ju-ju would have looked after them.

Meanwhile Berrice had returned to England and had travelled down to Burley to stay with Tim's sister and be reunited with her daughter who was now three-and-a-half. Although Alma had continually tried to remind Carolyn of her parents, she was really too young to understand and was calling Alma 'Mamma' and her uncle 'Daddy'. Over the months her cousins, Susan and Peter, became very attached to their new 'little sister' and were confused about who she really belonged to. When Berrice appeared and it was clear she was going to take Carolyn away, Susan told her: 'You horrid woman, you can't take her away, that's mean'. When the moment of departure came, Susan was kept out of the way and Carolyn sobbed uncontrollably.

Many thanks for the snaps of the children. I must say I thought our daughter made a sweet little Mad-Hatter. Very daunting for

Alma when the judge had never read *Alice*. I suppose I shall have to admire them when I get home but seen from afar the pig-tails and parting in the middle are not very becoming.

Mike Counsell has arrived and today he took over. He stayed with me for two days before moving into the house. He seems very amiable and not too proud to lean pretty heavily on me. I feel sure we shall get along all right. He has a Humber Hawk and I don't think he will tour much, at any rate not off the motor-roads. Generally he gives the impression of being not too sure of himself (he even said: 'I suppose I am supposed to take over from you' when we were signing the documents), and relieved to find that I am a reasonable sort of person on whose support he can count.

Cutie Muffett has also arrived and I had them round for a drink. She didn't talk much; David, as usual, most of the time. Mrs Sharwood-Smith was the only Nigerian at their wedding apparently, but it went off all right. The Barlow-Pooles were in Sokoto today and had a drink with me before lunch and tea afterwards. Lucie said the house was quite different without you and asked specially to be remembered. Richard came in to buy tyres, having run through seven coming back on the Kamba-Bunza road.

With Counsell here the work has been a bit easier. I have finished the confidential reports but we are still struggling with estimates and a budget that won't balance. However, the worst is past.

I am getting down to my Hausa as much as I can. I want to add 1000 new words to my vocabulary and so far have added about 130. It's dull work. The other day I asked Jibbo how 'tangaran' (crockery) was pronounced. He told me and then volunteered that another name was 'fadi-ka-mutu'.[6] With these he swept out with the tea-tray. There was a crash and the cup toppled off, fadi'd and mutu'd.

Tim then went off to visit Hamma'ali, twelve miles north-east of Sokoto.

The carriers set off after I'd had an early lunch. Just as we were ready to follow it started pouring with rain, and we had to ride off in the storm – poor old Wambai with no raincoat. The Sokoto River is in full spate and has cut the embankment beyond the bridge. There is a thirty-yard gap there with water rushing through so we had to be ferried over and the horses led round.

This all took time and as a result we didn't reach Hamma'ali until about 7. I was looking forward to a nice hot bath but arrived to find a miserable little *zaure*, Jibbo making the bed in a jumble of loads, and Ali trying unsuccessfully to make a fire with some damp firewood. No hot-water. However, I rubbed myself down with a rough towel, changed into dry clothes, had a nice big whisky, and felt better. In the morning I surveyed a good dam site – 200 yards long and 10–12 ft high.

Some promotions have just come through. Frank Humphreys and Foxy Cole to Resident. They were at the top of the list of SDOs, and Frank's elevation is understandable – but Foxy! They will have to give him a Province now: Kabba I hope. Nothing for Waddle Weatherhead which is surprising and will be disappointing for him. I shall be amused to hear Peter's views on this. I must say cautious mediocrity seems to be the touchstone for promotion!

Richard Barlow-Poole has just written in from Argungu about the rice-scheme. Rather a critical letter (in a decorous way) implying that we have bitten off more than we can chew and wouldn't it have been a good thing if they'd been consulted and so on. A lot in it, I think, but Waddle won't like it.

On Tuesday I am going off to bush again, which will bring the number of Districts I've visited to 35 out of 47: the other 12 I shall hope to do in September. That should make me the greatest living expert on Sokoto Division and may help to bring us back here (as opposed to Birnin Kebbi) next tour.

I'm feeling very end-of-tourish and am much looking forward to October.

His next letter was all about the fascinating life of a gentleman he had met in Tureta.

I had a good trip to Talata Mafara, and to Tureta which is down the turning that you pass at mile 35 or thereabouts on the Gusau road. The District Head of Tureta, Sarkin Burmi, is an engaging but eccentric old gentleman. I looked in the District Note Book to see what my predecessors had said about him. The first entry was far from promising: '1934. An unfortunate appointment. It was known that he had no previous acquaintance with district affairs but there was no indication that he would be almost completely lacking in all the qualities which a District Head should possess.' Two years afterwards another report said that he was late with his tax and that his accounts were full of errors. Later District Officers described him variously as poor, shabby, weak, lazy, and incapable.

Compared to most of the grandees of Sokoto who set much store by dignity and presence and therefore spend a lot of money on clothes and take great pains with the appearance that they present to the world, Sarkin Burmi was certainly shabby when I met him. His trousers hung in an exaggerated bag from his hips, his gown was grubby, and his turban was coming unravelled and hanging round his neck in loose and rather greasy coils. My messenger told me that a year or two before he had caused a mild sensation when his office had fallen down and he had made his household, including his own family, turn out to rebuild it.

We did our work together and in the afternoon he came to my lodgings (for the Rest House had also fallen down) to drink tea. In the meantime he had sent me some milk of very superior quality which was entirely free of the usual dirt and adulteration. Over tea I thanked him for this and he startled me by saying that he always did the milking himself. This remark, coming from an elderly member of an intensely conservative aristocracy with strict notions of decorum, was as surprising as if it had emanated from a bishop or a duchess. He told me that as a boy of seven he had been captured in the great sack of Tureta in 1893, carried off into slavery, and his whole youth had been spent in herding animals as a slave to a family of Tuaregs on the confines of the desert. 'And so you see' he concluded 'I look after my animals myself and if a distinguished personage like yourself honours my district with a visit I do not dream of entrusting the milking to any of my servants who are careless and slipshod but always insist on doing it myself.' He was over twenty years in captivity before his master set him free, and all he could remember was that his home-town was called Tureta and that it lay to the west. So he wandered along until he struck it. This is the gist of his story:

Abdulbaki, as he was called, was seven years old when Tureta was attacked and he was taken captive to a place called Cikaji. He was there for two years before his father Almusdafa learnt where he was and sent some of his men to ransom him.

Unfortunately the ransom money was twenty thousand cowries short and Abdulbaki's master Dantata refused to hand him over until they had paid the full amount.

Now before all this happened, Almusdafa's friends used to say: 'Dangaladima, that boy is going to be Sarkin Burmi one day. But alas! only when he has passed through a world of troubles.' Before they set off again with the balance of the money, Almusdafa's men were told that it would be propitious for them to set out on the seventh day of the month. Now Abdulbaki's uncle Maigunya had not forgotten the prophecy and so he said that he would go too. But he told the others that they would have to follow along behind because *he* had been advised that the second of the month was the propitious day for him.

On arrival at Cikaji he found Abdulbaki's master and hatched a plot with him that would benefit them both. When the others arrived, Dantata took the rest of the ransom money from them and then told them that unfortunately Abdulbaki had died a couple of days previously. He then took them to see the false grave and the men shed a few tears and returned home.

When they had gone, Abdulbaki was brought out of his hiding place and sold to some Tuareg traders who took him off into the back of beyond to a place called Dadin Kowa.

His new master, Bubakar, wanted to try him out to see whether he was lucky or unlucky with animals. So he gave him an old ewe and told him he could do what he wanted with it. Within a short time his ewe had two lambs and then the three were multiplied and became ten. From the offspring of this one ewe his herd grew and grew until he had fifty sheep.

Many years later Bubakar asked Abdulbaki if he thought he would be able to find his way home. When he said no, Bubakar told him that he was setting him free anyway but that if he decided to go he must not take anything with him. Abdulbaki said nothing.

Next morning he took the animals out to graze as usual but in the early afternoon he came back in a very black mood. He told his master that he had decided to go and so saying he picked up his quiver and water-bottle, strapped them on, and walked out. But Bubakar overtook him, seized him by the right arm, and shouted for help. At this Hammado appeared and seized his left arm with both his hands. They were standing there like that when his quiver slipped and fell to the ground, so they both released him in order that he could bend down and pick it up. Naturally Abdulbaki was very agitated but he had his *layar zana*[7] charm with him and so, as he stooped down, he was able to vanish from their sight.

After slipping away from them he made his way to the house of his friend Tanko who used to brew the poison which he put on his arrowheads. He told him what had happened and asked him for some provisions for his journey. Tanko was very angry that Abdulbaki had not been allowed to take his flock with him and took him to Tessawa to see the Chief. The Chief listened to the story and sent them straight to the French Commandant. Tanko explained the whole story again and without further ado the Commandant sent a constable to recover the herd.

Shortly afterwards Abdulbaki found a party of Udi shepherds who were going south to Hausaland and he arranged to join them and drive his animals with theirs. Now Abdulbaki and the Udi shepherds did not trust one another and eventually parted company. Abdulbaki kept on asking his way to Hausaland and, after passing through Fara, Dambo, Bakura and Binasa, at length he came to Tureta.

When he arrived in the town, he made his way to the Chief's house, and sent in a message. His animals filled the square and people soon came running out to stare at him. Then he heard one of them say: 'Good Heavens, if I hadn't known that he was dead, I might have taken that young shepherd for Almusdafa's boy Abdulbaki.'

In the midst of this commotion his mother and two elder sisters appeared, having come to see the animals which they had been told a Ba'ude[8] had brought into the town. His mother recognised him at once and she rushed up, flung her arms round him and cried: 'Here's little Abdulbaki come back – they said he was dead but I knew that it wasn't true.' After this there was great shouting and rejoicing.[9]

Now you could be forgiven for doubting the truth of this story because all the episodes can be found in folk-tales of great antiquity. There is the prophecy that one day the lad will inherit the family title and become ruler of the town. There is the wicked uncle who is ambitious to succeed himself. There is the raid in which the boy is carried off into slavery. There is the attempt at ransom that is frustrated by the trick of a false grave. There is the acquisition in captivity of a large flock. There is the escape by means of *layar zana*, the charm of invisibility. There is the triumphal homecoming. And finally, there is the fulfilment of the prophecy and the succession of the hero as chief of the town. The strange thing is not simply that his story happens to be true, but that he has lived on to see aeroplanes and listen to the radio!

When Councillors from Sokoto in their embroidered, scented robes visit him they are inclined to look askance at a house where the livestock seem to enjoy rights of use at least equal to those of the human beings. Likewise DOs on tour, grappling in his chaotic office with books which never balance, or seeking in vain for records which have been devoured by white ants, have despaired and tended to dismiss him in exasperation as unfit for his office. With the people of Tureta, however, he is deservedly popular. They admire him for being just and upright. They like his easy-going, fatherly régime. They have even come to accept the rather plebeian ways he got into as a slave because in his unworldliness they recognise true piety. For me he epitomises a great deal in the character of the Hausa people: their piety, their kindliness, their refusal to take themselves too seriously, their strength of character, and above all the patient fortitude with which they confront whatever calamities fate may send them. He is a truly remarkable man.

Back in Sokoto, Tim heard news from Kaduna that when the new constitution came into effect a bigger and better secretariat would be needed, and that there were likely to be about four new Resident's jobs created for the boys. To Berrice he wrote:

If this leaves me as DO Sokoto I shall be well content. At any rate I think the Resident will give me a good reference: he dropped in to tea today and said it was years since they had had a DO who got about and saw things for himself as your infamous old husband tries to do. I hope we do come back here: I have so many irons in the fire that I shall hate to see someone else leaving them all to go cold.

Wee Anne was at the club the other night, a little bit tight and very forward. I was subjected to a barrage of melting looks and fluttered eyelids, and even asked to dance. No doubt you'll be relieved to hear that I declined.

I'm afraid there have been exceptional floods in both rivers. The breach in the Sokoto embankment is twice what it was and the Rima embankment was swallowed almost throughout its whole length. The rice crop in Sokoto, both tractor ploughed and hand cultivated, is an almost complete washout. When I crossed, it was by canoe over an unbroken sheet of water in the Rima *fadama* except where the bridges were about two feet clear of the flood. There are rumours that the Argungu rice has also had it. Naturally this is a very nasty knock for the Rice Scheme: I am glad it was Waddle and not I who pressed so hard for twelve new D7 tractors and 25,000 acres next year. The farmers, as I expected, are associating the disaster with the machines and are beginning to mutter 'Take the things away'.

I hope you are doing some cooking while at home, Mrs J. I am getting awfully tired of Ali's food: it all seems to taste the same and occasionally he serves up some dreadful messes. The other day my supper was cauliflower cheese without the cheese, just a sodden mass in a tin dish. And he only has two soups. Things have been worse recently because the UAC strike has meant no cold-store stuff for a month now. It may be a sign of approaching senility but I do feel sometimes that it would be nice to eat well out here for a change.

I hope you and Miss J are both well. I think you ought to discourage her from calling all her uncles daddy.

Tim's next tour was of the north-west circuit.

I had an enjoyable and worthwhile tour and penetrated to where even Giles had not been. In fact Binji and Tangaza had not been visited by a DO for at least eight years, possibly longer. Pretty disgraceful I think. At Surame I saw the ruins of the town built by Muhammadu Kanta.

Now according to tradition, Kanta's father came to Hausaland from the east in the fifteenth century and settled in Katsina. In due course he was appointed head of his village and given the title of Magaji. He married a Hausa woman and she bore him two sons of whom the elder was Kanta.

As a boy, Kanta showed exceptional strength and skill in boxing, wrestling, and all the pastimes of youth. As a young man, however, he was headstrong and turbulent and was often in trouble with his elders. Consequently, when his father died, he was not chosen to succeed him. The loss of his father's office and title was a severe blow to his pride and caused him to leave the village and go out into the world to seek his fortune.

He went west across Gobir and Zamfara, which were then the most westerly of the Hausa States, and did not stop until he was beyond the Rima. He settled in a remote village called

Surame and before long was joined there by a number of former companions and kindred spirits.

At that time Surame was in the territory of the Sarkin Burmi who found Kanta and his followers so unruly and obstreperous that he determined to teach them a lesson. He therefore led a small party of armed men against them with the idea of bringing them to heel. But instead of submitting, Kanta and his companions turned out to fight. In the skirmish which followed Sarkin Burmi's henchmen were all killed or overpowered and Sarkin Burmi, it is said, was strangled by Kanta's own hands. After this fight, Kanta's followers hailed him as their king.

The valley of the Rima River where they had established themselves was between the Hausa States in the east and the Songhai Empire in the west. When Askia the Great marched into Hausaland in 1513, Kanta enlisted under him and by the time the campaign was over he had become a man of some importance.

Two years after subjugating Hausaland, Askia led his army against the desert State of Air and again Kanta marched with him. The expedition was successful but when the booty was divided, Kanta was not satisfied with his share and renounced his allegiance. Askia then sent an army to crush the rebellion but Kanta defeated it and preserved the independence which he had declared. This victory marked the birth of Kebbi, the last of the Hausa States to come into being.

Kanta ruled Kebbi for thirty-five years and raised it from nothing to be the greatest power in Hausaland. He subdued all his neighbours and made them pay tribute to him instead of to Bornu or Songhai. To the north he conquered Asben and Air, to the south Nupe and Borgu, to the east Zamfara and Zazzau, and to the west Arewa and Zaberma. His dominions extended from the Niger to the Sahara and he holds a unique place in the history of Hausaland because he was the only Hausa who ever showed imperial ambitions and was successful in realising them.[10]

In all, Kanta built three capitals, one of which was Surame. As part of the palace in Surame, Kanta constructed a *sirati* across a dry moat. If when trying a case he was doubtful whether a man was innocent or guilty he would order him to cross it. Those who crossed successfully were pronounced innocent and set free. Those who did not, fell to the sharpened stakes, red-hot embers, or wild beasts which were waiting below and were deemed to have been guilty. The *sirati* in Muslim theology is the bridge, narrow as the edge of a sword, which all must cross after death and from which the wicked fall into the gulfs of everlasting fire. Kanta's earthly *sirati* was a neat device for giving an air of Muslim respectability to the old pagan practice of trial by ordeal.

Surame is deserted now but the ruins of the city walls, of the palace, and even of the *sirati* can still be seen. If we come back to Sokoto next tour I will take you there.

Tim then went off to the Zamfara Valley.

It was thirteen years all but a day since I last went round and it was interesting to see these places again. Some I remembered very well and some I had almost entirely forgotten. The greatest hardship was a night in a dog-infested town called Gayeri. At 2.30 a.m. I could stand it no longer, not having had a wink of sleep, and I had Sarkin Bariki roused and Wambai and the Village Head and the District Head and the Messenger and half the town. An hour and a half of pandemonium followed while dogs were caught and removed, and at about four o'clock I went off to sleep, only to be roused two hours later of course. I was angry, especially as I had originally been wakened, just when I was dropping off, by a porter from the town arguing and shouting. Apart from this the trip was very enjoyable.

At Gummi I met the Canadian Missionary and his wife. They told me a thing or two about the local NA officials. The Alkali taking bribes, the Sanitary Inspector taking bribes, the police taking bribes, the veterinary mallams taking bribes. The mosquitoes were very bad there and in addition nearly everyone has bilharzia. For good measure they have occasional dysentery and last year a very severe measles epidemic. Quite a spa in fact. Now here's an intriguing story I was told about a man-eating lion that lived in the bush between the Zamfara Valley and the Dead River in the time of Sultan Hassan.[11] It killed and devoured several men who tried to cross the bush on the track between Tureta and Anka and the people of the district became so frightened of it that they refused to follow this path, even in daytime, unless they were in large parties. This is how it goes:

One day, an old man called Dasuki came to Tureta on his way from Denge, where he lived, to Anka. In Tureta he was warned about the man-eater and advised to wait until a party of travellers had assembled so that he could make the crossing with

119

them. He was in a hurry, however, and said that he could not wait for a party to assemble but must set out without delay.

Now the old man was blind and had a boy to lead him on the road. On the following morning, therefore, he and the boy set off together from Tureta but in order not to frighten the lad the blind man said nothing about the man-eater.

When they had travelled a long way and were deep in the heart of the bush the boy saw something on the track ahead of them, which made him stop. 'What is it, my boy' asked the old man 'why do you stop?'

'There is something on the path ahead of us' said the boy who had never seen a lion before.

'Is it a man or an animal?' asked the old man.

'It is an animal' said the boy.

'Perhaps it is a donkey which has strayed' said the old man.

'No' said the boy. 'It is as big as a donkey and yet it is not a donkey.'

'Is it then a wild animal?' asked the blind man.

'I don't know' said the boy. 'It is bigger than a hyena and it has a long tail with a tuft at the end of it and it has now started to come towards us.'

'My boy' said the old man 'look about you quickly and see whether there is a tree close at hand which you can climb.'

'Yes' said the boy. 'There is one right beside us here.'

'Then climb into it at once' said the old man.

'But you, Baba' said the boy 'what are you going to do?'

'I am old and cannot climb' said the blind man 'and so I must stay here and wait the judgement of God. Now hurry, boy, hurry.'

So the boy did as the old man told him and climbed into the tree. No sooner had he done so than the lion charged and sprang on the old man and carried him off a little distance into the bush where he put him down and devoured him.

When the lion had gone, the boy ran back to the town and told the District Head about the old man's death. He then consulted with the District Head of Anka and they made proclamations in the Sultan's name saying that no one was to use the track between the two places until the lion had been killed.

For the people of Anka and Tureta the ban was no hardship as none of them wanted to venture into the bush while the lion was still at large. But with the packmen it was different. They came from other parts of Sokoto and in the dry-season they earned their livelihood by driving pack-asses down to the Zamfara Valley and buying corn where it was cheap and bringing it back to Sokoto market where they sold it at a profit. For them the ban on crossing this belt of bush meant either going a long way round or waiting they knew not how long.

Soon after the order was made a party of them came into Anka from the south. Their asses were laden with corn and they wanted to press on to Sokoto but they were told that because of the lion the road had been closed and that they must not leave until permission was given. A day passed and then another and then a third and there were no further reports of the lion being seen, much less of its attacking anybody.

After a week of arguing whether they should wait or take the detour, a man called Dan Alewa said: 'Now listen, all of you, if we go round by Talata Mafara or Gummi we shall lose another three days on top of the seven which we have already wasted here. Now you all know that a man cannot escape his fate. If it is ordained that one of us is to be killed by this lion it will not help him to go round by Gummi or Talata Mafara because the lion will have gone there before him and will kill him just the same. What I say therefore is let us waste no more time but forget the lion and take the Tureta road tomorrow.'

These arguments satisfied the other packmen and so early next morning they loaded their animals and without saying anything to the District Head they slipped out of the town and set off for Tureta. For a time all went well and they neither saw nor heard anything of the lion. But when they were deep in the bush that divides the two valleys there was a sudden commotion from the rear of the column with sounds of shouting and screaming and cursing. This caused a general panic and the animals stampeded and shed their packs and the men climbed trees or rushed wildly into the bush to hide.

When the packmen had recovered from their terror, they picked up their fallen packs and rounded up their scattered animals and hurried on to the next village. There they took stock and found that out of all their number only one man was missing and that he was none other than Dan Alewa who had persuaded them the day before to take the road.

Those who had been nearest to the missing man then told how they had heard a growl and had looked round to see him lying on the ground with the lion standing over him and how the lion had then seized him in its jaws and carried him off into the bush.

When the news of the packman's death spread abroad the pious said: '*kaddara ce* – it was fate and he was ordained to meet his death through the lion.' However, when pressed about Dan Alewa's place in the column, those in the know admitted that the other packmen prudently insisted that he should occupy the position of tail-end Charlie because 'It was his idea, wasn't it?'[12]

By now Tim's leave was only a couple of weeks away and his last hurdle was the Hausa exam.

My Hausa exam is fixed for tomorrow week. I am going to visit Maredun and Bungudu (where the big bridge is on the Gusau Road) on the way to Kano, and Gusau and Shinkafe on the way back so as to polish off my touring. This will leave two Districts un-visited, not one as I had hoped, but it can't be helped. At present I am having a last burst of swatting and then I shall knock off three days before the exam to let the dust settle. I failed in my object of learning 1000 new words but I have reached 850. One of the exercises is to tell a fairy-story: I hope I am offered 'The Pied Piper' which goes easily into Hausa; I shall be furious if it's something silly like the 'Three Bears'.

I was gratified but rather shaken by a conversation that I had recently with the Sardauna. He has just been to Lagos for Legislative Council and was telling me about it. He went on to describe how they had met HE and Foot [Chief Secretary] and Pleass [Governor, Eastern Nigeria] at a cocktail party and how he had told them what progress was being made in Sokoto and how he had given me most of the credit and how HE had seemed to know me well and had repeated my initials. No doubt Sardauna made it sound afterwards a bit better than it actually was but anyway he seems to have put in a word in high places for us. Then came his bombshell. 'I told HE' he went on, 'that if we were allowed to choose our Resident we should choose you'. I felt rather uncomfortable and didn't know what to do so I turned it into a joke and said 'You'd better not let Mr W. hear you saying that' to which Sardauna replied 'Well, it's true', so I quickly changed the subject. It was an improper thing for the Sardauna to say to me and put me in a very awkward position.

Lucie Barlow-Poole asked especially to be remembered to you. She opined that you were one of those English people whom it is difficult to get to know but that you had 'a very lovable disposition' as she put it. So there's a little bouquet for you too Mrs J.

A week later Tim travelled home in a Hermes.

* * * * *

Birnin Kebbi

On his return to Nigeria with Berrice and Carolyn, Tim was posted to Birnin Kebbi, the very place that had been considered unsuitable for children the previous tour! There followed several happy years during which there was only one short separation.

Birnin Kebbi was the administrative headquarters of the Gwandu Division of Sokoto Province and the Emir and his Council were very progressive and keen to see their area developed. Before the war, Nigeria had had to pay its own way but in 1944 the Colonial Development and Welfare Act provided £55 million, of which £23 million would come from the British taxpayer, to be spent over a ten-year period. The development plan included the provision of pipe-borne water for all towns of 5000+ inhabitants and a water point with pure water for every 500 people. There were to be dozens more hospitals built and millions spent on health, education, farming and irrigation schemes, veterinary services, trunk roads and link roads, embankments and bridges, and new markets. It was a time of great optimism; at last there was enough money to make a real difference.

There was a very small European community in Birnin Kebbi, consisting mostly of development workers, and Carolyn was the only European child.

While they were stationed there lions started attacking the herds of cattle. Every year during the dry season, when the flood plain of the Sokoto River was dry, tens of thousand of cattle migrated to it because of its lakes and rich pasture. Normally there was no game for miles around but in this particular year seven or eight lions left the great uninhabited expanse of bush between the Zamfara and Ka Rivers, and entered the lower valley of the

Sokoto. There they preyed on cattle by night and by day lay up in the dense thickets of thorn which were to be found all over the flood plain. The Fulani cattle herders were a fearless and extraordinarily tough race who in normal circumstances were perfectly capable of looking after themselves and their beasts. Far from being intimidated by lions they preferred to tackle them armed not with bows and arrows or spears but only with the long staffs which they carried to control their cattle. They believed that a lion, which was not used to being outfaced and defied, would hesitate to charge home against a man so armed if he stood his ground. In addition they had a charming theory of their own that the lion, being king of the beasts, had to think of his dignity and dared not put himself in a position where, if his charge miscarried, he might be beaten like a cur.

But the Fulani herdsmen were for once defeated by the boldness and cunning of these lions and were unable to protect their cattle. After suffering some losses they appealed to the Native Authority for help. The Emir and Council discussed the problem with Tim and their first plan was to invite Europeans to come down from Sokoto and sit up for the lions. Three did so but without getting a shot and in the meantime more cattle were taken. They therefore decided to call in the local hunters and offer a reward of £10 for each lion killed.

One legacy from the past, which the Hausas still possessed and employed, was their knowledge of vegetable poisons. These were among the most deadly in the world and fell into two broad categories, those which attacked the blood-stream and those which paralysed the nervous system, and the Hausas were familiar with both kinds. In war and in hunting big game they relied on the strength of their poisons and not on the penetrating power of their arrows. Consequently their bows were short and light like their arrows, which were often made from the dried stems of reeds or elephant grass. They seldom shot at long ranges and normally raised their bows and flicked arrows out of them in a single swift motion.

The first hunter to respond soon earned £20 and departed satisfied. The second was a Hausa in middle age who was known by the name of Kibiya or Arrow. Though lean and grizzled, he had a deceptively mild manner and could easily have been taken for a potter or leather-worker rather than a professional hunter. The killing of two lions had made the others more cautious and it was some time before Kibiya was able to locate the places where they drank and lay up in relation to their usual hunting ground. He had hoped to be able to sit up for them as the other hunter had done but the *fadama* is almost bare of trees and this proved to be impossible. He therefore decided that he would have to follow the lions into the thorn thicket after their next kill and this is what in fact he did. The

6. Tim on Walkiya

thorn, which is a dull dark green in colour, grows to a height of eight to ten feet. It does not entirely cover the ground but sprawls about untidily in a maze of clumps between which there are some clear lanes, some paths hemmed in and obstructed by overhanging or trailing brambles, and not a few blind alleys. To follow a lion into such a place would be suicide for any man who was not a hunter of consummate skill. When he went in on the morning after the kill, Kibiya was armed only with his bow and quiver of poisoned arrows. He took nothing else with him, not even a knife. At the start he had no idea which part of the thicket the lion whose spoor he had picked up had retreated to nor indeed where the others might be concealed. His first task was therefore to locate his lion without betraying himself. He hoped that after its meal it might be asleep but he could not count on this. Advancing with infinite stealth and caution he needed several hours to find the particular thicket in which it lay hidden. His next problem was to approach closer from a direction in which the lion could neither scent him nor, if it was awake, see him. This manoeuvre required more time. Finally he had to find a spot from which to get an unobstructed shot. At last he found himself in position in such a spot at a range of about twenty-five yards on the lion's quarter. It was a full-grown male and though lying down was

7. Tim (left) with Peter Scott in Birnin Kebbi

not asleep. Everything now depended on his aim and the potency of his poison, which was one that attacked the nervous system and caused almost immediate paralysis followed by early death. He raised his bow and flicked his ready little arrow into the lion's flank. The lion sprang to its feet with its tail erect, gave a great roar, and charged blindly to its front.

'And how far did it get?' Tim asked. Kibiya considered the question and then, knowing nothing of yards and feet, said 'From about here to that tree' (a distance of about fifty feet). Tim must have looked rather incredulous because Kibiya added '*Ai, zaki ba ya jimrin dafi*', meaning lions have no resistance to poison. While telling his story he remained perfectly impassive and showed not the slightest trace of boastfulness or even elation at his success. Similarly, when he detected Tim's doubt he displayed no resentment but politely explained a point that he could not be expected to appreciate. 'And how long did the lion take to die?' Tim asked as he handed Kibiya his reward. 'Not long' he said, 'perhaps five or ten minutes'. Quiet and unassuming as ever, he took his money and departed.

Kibiya, like every other Hausa hunter, carried charms sewn up in a little leather envelope and Tim was sure that these had helped to give him courage when he was tracking down the lion.

8. Berrice and Carolyn looking over the garden and *fadama* in Birnin Kebbi

Life in Birnin Kebbi was very basic. There was no electricity or running water and the loo was an EC rather than a WC that was emptied every day through a little door in the outside wall by the *mai-bucketi* or bearer of the bucket. There was no swimming pool either so Tim, Berrice and Carolyn took to swimming in a natural pool near the river. Unfortunately, it soon became evident that they had all picked up bilharzia, which is caused by parasitic worms that spend their life partly in water snails, where the larvae develop, and partly in humans where they mature and reproduce.

Towards the end of that year, Tim was posted back to Sokoto as Senior District Officer.

* * * * *

Sokoto again

Soon after they had moved in, the Resident, Waddle Weatherhead, went round to their house with an invitation. To his wife, Sylvia, he wrote: 'I went and asked Berrice (Tim's on tour) to lunch but she said she had never left Caroline. She thereupon asked C. if she

9. Carolyn and friend Iggy in Birnin Kebbi

would have lunch with the boys looking after her and she said "No" she would come to lunch too. So Berrice said it was no good. C. had not slept till 10.30 last night; but she hoped some day she would be able to leave her. She has apparently reduced her parents to a state of abject slavery. It must be very bad for her character.'[13]

About a week later Waddle told Sylvia that he had had a dinner party for ten people including Tim and Berrice 'who actually left Caroline'. Not long after that he complained, 'Tim and Berrice never drop in. I have to go and look for them if I want to see them.' Unfortunately, Tim and Berrice were not very good at socialising and it took them a while to get to know people and feel comfortable with them. Berrice, who was very beautiful, found it particularly difficult and because she was so reserved she came to be known in Sokoto as 'the ice queen'.

As a result of the new Macpherson Constitution that provided a form of parliamentary government in each of the three regions and at the centre, elections were going to be held throughout the country. The new House of Assembly was to have ninety members chosen by indirect elections through a series of electoral colleges from village to Provincial level. Richard Barlow-Poole described the process in his area: 'Each one hundred electors choose one representative, then representatives in one village area choose some of their number to go to a District College; all those thereby chosen then choose some of their number to go to the Electoral College of Argungu. Then these in the same way choose some representatives to go to Sokoto; and there at the Provincial Council are chosen the men who will sit in the House of Assembly at Kaduna'.[14]

In September, Tim was involved in the first elections held in Sokoto Province, about which Waddle wrote: 'I went down to see them accompanied by the Sardauna and Tim. We went first to Rijiya Dorowa. There are more southerners there than elsewhere. The election was due to start at 4 p.m. and by that time approximately 130% of the electorate were there. First the youths of under 21 were eliminated, then the rival candidates stood apart with their supporters and two from each side were given the right to raise objections to electors in the other party on the grounds of non-payment of tax, or residence outside the ward. Then the count

10. Tim, Berrice, Carolyn and the noble Aunt Charlotte on the Sokoto River

started. Tim and Madawakin Sokoto stood facing each other and the electors were counted as they passed between them – it was rather like Oranges and Lemons – and checked off in tens on Madawaki's rosary. The southern candidate got in by ten votes. This was, of course, only the first round of the primaries.'[15]

The following June 1952, Waddle became Resident Kano and Tim was promoted to Resident Sokoto, which meant moving from the SDO's house to the Residency. Sir Bryan Sharwood-Smith, who was now Lieutenant Governor, had described the Residency in his day: 'The setting was superb. It was surrounded on all sides by open woodland and overlooked the famous gardens, a bird-watcher's paradise of shady alleyways and open lawns. Almost overhanging one end of the Residency stood a giant baobab, hollow with age, which plainly should be felled. But local opinion stubbornly resisted any such suggestion. The tree, we were told, had from time immemorial been the home of *djinns*. They must on no account be disturbed. The tree was almost certainly also the home of a pair of spitting cobras, for the Gardens abounded with them. I agreed to spare the tree for the present, and the djinns, out of gratitude, must have protected us for the snakes never gave any trouble.'[16]

Unfortunately, the baobab became so unsafe that Tim had to have it cut down. By then, the cobras had multiplied and five slithered out as their dwelling was destroyed! The *djinns* did not complain and must have found accommodation elsewhere.

In Hausaland there was a fraternity whose members not only claimed the ability to make themselves invisible at will but affirmed that those who were fully initiated into their mysteries had special powers over the whole animal kingdom. These were the Gardawa and in Sokoto they were sufficiently numerous to have a chief of their own appointed by the Sultan. They earned their living mainly by entertaining and, though they also went in for drumming, dancing and minstrelsy, their real speciality was snake charming.

Among the poisonous snakes of Hausaland the most common are the cobra family and the viper family. When a snake appears in a story it is always one of two varieties of cobra, *gamshaka* or *kumurai*. The former is the ordinary hooded cobra and the latter the black spitting cobra. These snakes grow to a length of seven feet and have a girth as thick as a man's arm. The spitting cobra invariably aims at the eyes of its victim and is said to be accurate up to a range of about twelve feet. If the venom is washed out of the eyes at once no harm ensues but if this is not done the sight may be destroyed. Another member of the cobra family, though it has no hood, is called *tsadaraki*. It is the fastest mover of all the local snakes and can easily outpace a man. Among the vipers the puff adder, bloated and sluggish, is perhaps the most loathsome though the smaller *kebubuwa* and *gajera* are no less deadly. The puff adders have the peculiarity of being able to flick themselves over and strike backwards and when they do this their movement is extremely quick and often catches their victims off their guard. The poison of the viper family attacks the nervous system whereas that of the cobras acts on the blood.

During most of the year snakes live in holes in buildings, trees, ants' nests, or indeed any place that is dry and secure. During the hot weather, however, they forsake these homes and seek damp cool places in the open. They mate during the rains and afterwards the male and female separate. The female does not brood her eggs but stays near them until the young are ready to hatch out. Young snakes begin life with their fangs and poison sacks complete and can fend for themselves from the start. All snakes can swim and the bigger ones can and often do climb trees in search of food. Though they like warmth they detest very hot sun and become bad-tempered and dangerous if left in it too long.

The Gardawa had an extraordinary way with snakes which in a scientific age was difficult to explain or comprehend. Tim had first met their then chief, Sarkin Gardi Balaraba, in 1937 when he was still quite a young man. He and his men were drumming for a big labour gang who were eradicating weeds from the common around Sokoto City when the men disturbed a large black spitting cobra. They fell back and shouted for Sarkin Gardi who caught it without any difficulty in his bare hands and stuffed it away in the leather satchel which he always carried slung under his armpit. The snake was unquestionably wild and dangerous and this fact convinced Tim that there was nothing bogus about Sarkin Gardi's powers. His family had been members of the fraternity for generations and he himself grew up into it and never knew any other life.

By 1952 Sokoto had cold tap water but hot water for the bath still had to be heated in kerosene tins in the cookhouse. Water for drinking was always boiled and filtered. Electricity had been switched on officially by the Sultan that year but not everyone was connected and only a few had the benefit of electric fans in temperatures that could reach 50°C in the hot season.

Tim's role as Resident was to develop the Native Administration and to ensure that its funds were spent appropriately to improve conditions for the common people. Sole NAs were abolished and replaced by a Chief-in-Council to make them more democratic. Naturally there was quite a lot of opposition from chiefs afraid of losing their power, but the right of ordinary people to make their views known in local government was thereby established.[17] Although the Resident had considerable powers of intervention, he could only *advise* the Sultan who was ultimately responsible for hiring and firing the staff. The Resident was also the chief representative of the central government, and he was responsible for keeping the peace. With few government police, he had to rely on the NA police who were not as well trained but had extensive local knowledge. The real peace-keepers were in fact the Village Heads who knew exactly what was going on in their domain.

The Northern Region was still a long way behind the Eastern and Western Regions educationally and there were not enough suitably qualified Northerners for the higher posts. This meant that

11. Berrice in Sokoto in the early 1950s

the better educated Ibos from the East and Yorubas from the West headed north to fill the gaps. The Northern leaders were trained administrators who wanted to get on with the job of developing their region and they had little interest in politics. Their Eastern and Western counterparts, on the other hand, were much more politically minded and were keen to press for self-government. In March 1953, when all were assembled in Lagos for the budget meeting, a motion was tabled that the House should accept self-government by 1956 as 'the primary political objective'. The Northern leaders did not feel they would be ready to take over from the British so soon and the Sardauna moved an amendment to replace '1956' with 'as soon as practicable'. As a result they were jeered when they left the House and had to endure many insults from crowds of Ibos and Yorubas. This incident soured relations so much that, for a short time, the North considered breaking with the East and West and going it alone. The greatest obstacle to this was the fact that the Region was landlocked and they were afraid that the East and West would make it difficult for them to transport their goods to the seaports for export. No one then realised that airfreight would become the norm in the not very distant future. In the end they reluctantly decided that they must remain part of Nigeria. They were determined, however, not to employ any more southerners and to ensure that jobs in the North went firstly to Northerners, and then to expats or other West Africans. A few weeks later there were serious riots between Northerners and Southerners in Kano and thirty-six people were killed.

During the summer a conference was called in London and, after much bargaining, it was agreed that Nigeria would become a federation and each region would have almost complete autonomy. The Sardauna would become the first Premier of the North, and the three Lieutenant-Governors would thenceforth be called Governors under the Governor-General of the Federation.[18]

In July, Berrice who was expecting another baby went to Kaduna for the birth and it was with some frustration that she wrote to Tim to let him know she had arrived safely.

> The telephone business was a complete shambles tonight. The female operator of the Catering Rest House switchboard had never heard of Sokoto and I had to tell her again and again

that I really did want to put a call through to Sokoto and nowhere else.

I hope daughter is behaving. Tell her I will write the next letter to her. She has a very clear voice on the telephone and I could hear her most distinctly.

The dining room is a great improvement on the old one but it's a pity there are no fans. The rest of the main building is being re-built and there are lumps of cement and wood shavings all over the place. The CRH seems to be full of men who have nothing to do except booze!

I saw a Minister's house last night; it appeared to be the same size as Buckingham Palace. I think it's absolutely wicked that they should have such enormous expensive houses. The Health Sister has been visiting all the Ministers' houses and compounds. The only clean house was the Sardauna's; all the others were absolutely filthy with the BGs blocked up and children spending pennies all over the floors. One wife was even found starting a fire for her cooking pots in the middle of a beautiful parquet floor! None of the wives seem to know how to use the BGs or bathrooms.[19]

Meanwhile Tim had been hearing how the British took Sokoto in 1903.

12. Sarkin Gardi and his snakes

I have been learning more about the Battle of Sokoto from Mallam Nagwamatse, who was a small boy at the time, and from the Majasirdi who was a slave and is now a member of the Sultan's household. First Mallam Nagwamatse's story:

The British appeared before Sokoto on the Saturday afternoon while the Sultan's forces were mustering on the common south of the City. Neither side was ready for battle but some minor skirmishes nevertheless took place and there were a few casualties.

One of those who was killed on this day was the Shamaki, a slave of the Waziri Buhari. He rode out alone and made a single-handed attack on the British force from which he knew he would never return.

For those in the City that night there was little sleep. The streets were full of the men who had come in from the neighbouring districts and all were sharpening their weapons and making ready for the battle which they knew would take place next day.

Amongst this throng the Majidadi Babdarai, another slave of the Waziri's, was searching for his friend the Shamaki. When news was brought to him that the Shamaki had already been killed he was thunderstruck. 'To think' he kept repeating over and over again 'to think that Shamaki should have preceded me to God!'

The Majidadi spent the rest of the night in prayer. Before dawn he performed the ceremonial ablutions and put on a new gown.

In the morning, when the line of battle had been drawn up on the common south of the city, the Majidadi waited until he saw that the enemy were advancing. Then he rode up to the Sultan and demanded the *goron yaki*, or kola-nuts of war, which signified that he intended to seek death in the battle. They were given to him and then, with his squire running before him on foot, he rode out alone against the British.

As he set off to cover the open ground that separated the two armies the Majidadi ordered his squire to return because he wished to spare him. But the squire refused to leave him. 'God give you long life' he said 'I have always run ahead of you and I'm going to keep on – even if it's into the next world.'

And so they went forward together until they were destroyed by the machine-guns.[20]

As you know, according to Muslim beliefs, warriors who find death in a war fought in defence of their faith will enter paradise.

Apparently it was the custom for those who had steeled themselves to seek this kind of death to demand the *goron yaki*, the kola-nuts of battle, as a way of proclaiming their intentions. The Shamaki and the Majidadi sacrificed their lives deliberately in a hopeless gesture of defiance, and it is a good example of the fanatical resolution which slaves often displayed in their masters' causes. The main battle was swift because the Sultan's feudal cavalry stood no chance whatsoever against the British machine-guns and artillery. This is what happened the following day as told by the Majasirdi:

On the Sunday we formed up again on the common with the line of battle covering the City and facing the south where the British had camped for the night. Our forces were divided into three divisions. On the right the Marafa Maiturare was in command and on the left Sarkin Rabah Ibrahim. The Sultan himself was in command of the centre and he took up his position at the foot of a fan-palm tree which then stood on the common. Beside him the Sa'i of Kilgori set up his standard.

Except for the fan-palm where the Sultan took up his stand, the common was as flat and bare as it is today. Beyond the common was farmland with *gawo* trees dotted about all over it. That is where the enemy were, on the other side of the valley, and because of the trees we could not see them at all clearly.

13. The children of Sokoto at a birthday party

When the British started firing, the Sultan sent five of us slaves to reconnoitre, Sarkin Dawaki and Sarkin Rakuma and Gulbi and Tirai and myself. There was so much smoke from the guns, and so much dust kicked up by the horses and men, that we could hardly see the enemy at all. Moreover, as we drew nearer to them, the noise of the machine-guns and rifles was so loud that our horses became unmanageable and we could not make them go on. They were not used to that kind of fighting and swerved away to the left so that we found ourselves on Sarkin Rabah's front.

It was some time before I could make my way back to the Sultan's headquarters and when I at last got there he had already gone. But I heard afterwards what had happened. The Marafa was an experienced soldier and he had soon seen that our horsemen could not fight against guns. He had therefore galloped over to the Sultan and urged him to abandon the battle. What he had actually said was: 'Don't let the torch go out while you are holding it.' By this he had meant that if the Sultan persisted he would be risking the destruction of Sokoto and Shehu's line.

But the Sultan had not welcomed this advice and had said angrily: 'Do you think that this is my first battle? Leave it to me, will you.' The Marafa had then remounted his horse but it had immediately been shot under him. He had mounted another but that too had been brought down. Finally, he himself had been hit in the shoulder.

Meanwhile the fire round the Sultan had been growing hotter. Shells had been falling all round the palm-tree and the Sa'i Umaru and his standard-bearers had all been mown down by the machine-guns. At this the Waziri Buhari had spoken up. 'God give you long life' he had said to the Sultan 'from now on the blood of all those who are killed will be on your head.' Attahiru had still been unwilling to quit but when he had heard this he had let his slaves lead his horse away.

By the time that I got back to where the Sultan had had his headquarters he and his bodyguard had gone. But the dead were lying thick round the fan-palm and among them I found my own father.[21]

When I said I was sorry his father had been killed in the battle, he replied: 'Why do you say that you are sorry? Were his days not fulfilled?' That really sums up the faith and resignation of these people.

When she wrote again, Berrice had had the opportunity to see inside one of the ministerial palaces.

Bruce Greatbatch took me for a very nice drive this evening and showed me the sights of Kaduna. It is an absolute rabbit warren and I was completely lost most of the time. Even Bruce still gets lost. We visited the Sardauna's new house and went over it. It's a lovely place but all the internal woodwork, such as cupboard doors, is very rough. We didn't go through to the walled-in compound because his wives were there.

There are some very odd Europeans in Kaduna. Yesterday morning I heard: 'What the bloody hell are you doing to that blasted car', I looked out of the window and saw a perfectly harmless looking African dusting a car and, as far as I could see, doing no harm at all. And this morning, two people were very rude to one of the Stewards when he asked them what they wanted for breakfast. They said they had been waiting to be served for fifteen minutes and would report him. It was quite untrue and they certainly hadn't been in the dining room more than five minutes.

The Sardauna was touring Zaria a short time ago and was horrified by the neglect of Southern Zaria. All the people down there complained that no DO ever visited them and that nothing was done for them. On his return, the Sardauna went straight to HH and said Mr HASJ must become Resident Zaria. I gather Sardauna wants you to be in all the Provinces that are not making much headway! By the way he is absolutely delighted with his photograph and shows it to everyone.

At about this time Tim's secretary went on leave and she warned Peggy Watt, who took over from her, 'He's a tremendous worker himself, and I've never had to do so much for anyone else.'[22]

Berrice gave birth to Robin, on the 23rd July and a few days later Tim received a letter of congratulations from Sir Bryan and a personal word about his report: 'I have just written your confidential report. It is an extremely good one but there is an item on the debit side, i.e. that you can be a little too uncomprising [sic] and that there are sometimes a slight tendency to rigidity of outlook. Everybody has a debit as well as a credit side and the credit in your case is very heavily weighted. Before I go on leave I should like to express appreciation of the way in which you have handled Sokoto this tour.

You know my feelings with regard to the Province and I am very particular to whom I entrust it. KP Maddocks should be coming back North towards the end of the year but I do not think that after such a heavy tour you should extend to wait for him. You have got to the point when you have got to consider yourself a little and there is no object in burning yourself up to the limit before you go on leave.'

– 5 –

Kano – The mid-1950s

While they were on leave, Tim and Berrice bought their first house, 'Four Winds', which was situated on the hill overlooking Westward Ho! in North Devon. It was a large house with a lovely garden and they were looking forward to inviting all the relatives who had been so kind to them over the years. Having a base in England was a big expense to take on since it meant having to run two homes, but they planned to cover some of the costs by letting it. Colonial Officers' pay did not compare favourably with the private sector and it was rumoured that a certain ADO who resigned from government with a salary of about £750 received about £1750 from the oil company which he then joined.[1]

When they returned to Nigeria Tim was posted to Kano, where Waddle Weatherhead was still Resident.

Kano had always been the terminus for the Saharan caravans which brought cotton goods and other treasures from North Africa and returned with leather goods and groundnuts (and slaves, before slavery was abolished). Now it was the commercial capital of the north where all the big trading firms had their headquarters, and where the fabulously wealthy merchants, known as the 'Merchant Princes', had their homes. It was a hierarchical society and soon Tim and Berrice would be living in the 'top layer' having to entertain the bosses of the top companies such as UAC and John Holt. In those days rank was all important and there was a huge gulf between

Residents and their wives and junior officers. That is how it was, and it was all understood and accepted.[2]

The old city of Kano was surrounded by a wall that was penetrated by *kofas* or gates. When the British had attacked it in 1903, the outer face of the wall was almost sheer and was protected by a double ditch which was choked, over much of its length, with an impenetrable growth of thorn. However, with the Emir and half his army away in Sokoto and the Hausa population remaining passive, neither helping nor hindering the remaining Fulani troops, it had been relatively easy for them to blow in one of the gates and put a storming party through it.

To the east of the old city were the commercial area, the Syrian and Lebanese quarter, and the Sabon Gari, or New Town, where all the southerners lived. A little further to the south was the European suburb called Nassarawa.

The population around Kano was growing fast and had reached about 500 people to the square mile in the Home Districts. While touring around, Tim was constantly struck by the fact that the 'bush' had vanished under the pressure of population and that virtually the only empty spaces which could now be found consisted of eroded or worn-out farmland. All the people with whom he discussed the question agreed that it was becoming increasingly difficult for either Fulanis or Hausas to keep cattle in these districts. There had been a recent experiment in anti-erosion work that had produced very encouraging results and Tim believed that the solution to the problem lay in this direction. His idea was that the Native Authority should take possession of a number of areas that had been abandoned by farmers and reverted to inferior scrub and, after rehabilitation, should convert them into Grazing Reserves. Over the course of the year Kano NA took over an area of 160 acres of worn-out farmland, ploughed out the scrub which had covered it, and planted a succulent grass. The experiment was highly encouraging and the improvement achieved was great enough to suggest that it would be possible to rehabilitate the thousands of acres of similar wasteland that were to be found in all parts of the Province.

On the political front, Federal Elections took place that year. According to the Kano Divisional Intelligence Summary,[3] the standard of debate at the meetings of the Northern Peoples' Congress in the run-up to polling had been abysmal, no use whatever being made of the laboriously collected facts and figures of progress. Instead, all their efforts were concentrated on whipping up religious and racial prejudice by alleging that if the Northern Elements' Progressive Union and their friends the National Council of Nigeria and the Cameroons won, the Ibos would seize all power and mosques would be turned into churches.

In Kano City, the NPC gained thirty seats and the NEPU–NCNC alliance twenty-five. The NEPU leaders, finding themselves beaten, then fell back on a policy of provoking violence in the hope of discrediting the elections and of building up their own reputation as a martyred minority. But their methods were too crude to give them any chance of success. In the following fortnight they suffered five convictions for brawling at an election booth, five for disorderly conduct, one for cutting a political opponent's throat and one for laying false information with the police. In addition, five were awaiting trial for wounding a boy with a machete, four for throwing stones and injuring a woman, six for axing a political opponent, and five for beating up a Sanitary Inspector and burning some huts.

The day after the axing and throat-cutting incidents, Mallam Aminu Kano, the NEPU leader, wrote to the Resident enquiring what steps he proposed to take to curb the fresh outbreak of lawlessness. The newspaper *The Comet* followed up with an article alleging that the real aggressors were the two victims! A Reconciliation Committee was convened but the independent members concluded that reconciliation was useless since neither side kept its promises, and suggested that the only remedy lay in persuading His Excellency to ban NEPU.

Mallam Aminu Kano had also been vociferous against Europeans. In an article in *The Comet* entitled IT IS THE EUROPEANS WHO HAVE DEGRADED OUR RELIGION AND SELF-RESPECT, he wrote: '... Our great enemies are the Europeans who have imposed an oppressive rule upon us. They have confused our affairs and caused our religion and our self-respect to be slighted. They have made mischief of all kinds; they have devised means of despoiling the wealth of the country; they have left us in poverty and the hardship of finding our daily bread ... Between us and the Europeans there can be no harmony, let alone loyalty, because we do not admit that they ever conquered us. When did they conquer us? Where did they conquer us? Whom did they conquer? We admit that they tricked the Sultan Umoru and deceived him into signing a document he did not understand. We men of modern outlook are bursting with indignation at the wicked deception which the thieving English practised on the Sultan...'[4]

Such was the atmosphere that prevailed in Kano; a few firebrands were endeavouring to whip up public feeling to further their own ends while the ordinary man in the street was left perplexed and troubled by their behaviour.

In 1955 Waddle Weatherhead was posted to the Plateau and Tim became Resident. Carolyn, who had been attending the Kano Convent School, was due to start prep school in Dorset at the beginning of the summer term and Berrice took her back to England in April. It was the start of another long separation because Tim was not due leave for four and a half months. Living apart was hard enough but, as Resident, he was expected to do a great deal of entertaining and now he would have to manage on his own. Nigeria was developing apace and there was a constant stream of visitors to Kano who had to be met at the airport and looked after for the duration of their stay.

> It was very nice to get back from tour today and find your letter. I must say I dislike very much having to entrust you all to one aircraft and I watched you out of sight over Panisau blister with some anxiety. I was relieved to hear that you had had a good journey and been met on arrival by the noble aunts.
>
> I have just come back from three days in the bush. On the second night it tried to rain without much success, just enough to compel me to go inside and suffocate. It has been hotter since you went but I think the rains can't be far off now. I went down to the pool this evening and the water felt hot, rather as it does from our tap when the sun has been all day on the tank.
>
> Sir Frederick Bellamy turned out to be a nice old boy. I missed my game of tennis meeting him and had to see him off next evening when I had forty miles to go in the opposite direction. These two visits to the airport brought the total (excluding seeing you off) to six in twelve days.

The new Chief Justice, Sir Algernon Browne, is coming here next week for two days. He is to stay in the Governor's Lodge but have most of his meals here. Peter Achimugu, the Minister, is here all this week and I am giving a dinner party for him on Friday and asking, among others, the Dikkos and Bukar Shaib.

Tomorrow I am off on tour again, this time to Ringim. Last time I went I told Miss P. to wire the Civil Secretary and the Governor's Office. What she actually did was to send the following telegram: 'Governor Kaduna – Please note that I shall be on tour April 20–23 – Resident'. Sharwood needed quite a lot of pacifying before he saw the humour of it.

How slowly the time goes: only six days out of about 132.

Maiholi had also been missing the Uwargida (mother of the house) and had dictated his own letter: 'I am very glad to quote these few lines, and will be grateful to hear your safely arrival at home with childrens. I am praying God daily to take you home safely. And when returning may God bring you back safely. Our wives are very sorry for your absent. We all well with master. And begging God to help me to last master up to the time which he will left Nigeria to England. I close with best regards. Forget me not. Your lovely cook, Baba Maiholi X (his mark).'

The hot season was nearly over and everyone was impatient for the cooling rains to arrive. From Ringim Tim wrote:

Yesterday and today it has been trying to rain but so far without much success. Last night there was a roaring wind and a lot of dust and this afternoon there was a short shower. It is cooler, however, and rain must have fallen nearby. All the scorpions have taken the hint and emerged from their holes: Shehu has killed four here and I one.

All today I have been watching two grasshoppers, sitting on my umbrella in close embrace and oblivious of the world. Except for an occasional shiver of ecstasy they show no sign of life. She is a fat old party, at least twice his size, but he seems to think the world of her. How nice to be a grasshopper and hop off to 'Four Winds' and into the arms of my mate. Four months to go still, unfortunately.

I wonder how you will get on tomorrow taking Carolyn to school. I expect she will be very good. How much of a fortune did you have to spend on her outfit?

At about this time the Sardauna and the Emir of Kano went on a trip to Tripoli, Cairo and Saudi Arabia to see for themselves what arrangements were in place for the reception and accommodation of Pilgrims.

> The Emir [Alhaji Muhammadu Sanusi] and Premier returned yesterday and of course we had to go and meet them. Dick Greswell's plane to Kaduna failed to get off so he stayed the night here and told me all about their journey. The Emir got through about £500 during the fifteen days and the Sardauna a mere £250. In Saudi Arabia they saw severed hands (cut off for theft) dangling in the streets and were shown photographs of the public beheading of murderers. Although King Saud has acquired a taste for coal-black concubines, the Arabs as a whole were apparently rather off-hand and supercilious. They kept them cooling their heels for an hour at Jeddah airport before anyone attended to them (much indignation over this) and then detained their baggage for another three hours after that. This stung the Emir into saying that they had evidently got their self-government prematurely. An Arabian dinner still consists of fat mutton served up in about seven different ways but the ceremonial belch of appreciation has apparently gone out of fashion. Unaware of this, the Sardauna was loosing off great reverberating rafter-shakers with the utmost complacency and earning (without noticing it) many sly and disdainful looks down long aquiline nebs.

Tim was beginning to make plans for the Residency garden and had already brought the prisoners in to strip off the old loose surface on the tennis court. After several days without mail, he was pleased to receive two letters at once. In one of them Berrice asked for his help in composing a letter to the Governor's wife who wanted her to get involved with the Girl Guides. A Resident's wife was traditionally expected not only to be the perfect hostess, but also to perform other social duties such as presiding over the Girl Guides and Red Cross. Handicapped by her shyness and intimidated by women she believed to be better educated than herself, Berrice felt unable to cope. Tim was considered very young to be a Senior Resident, and Berrice was eight years his junior so the burden of being a 'senior wife' was even greater. Tim replied:

> I will deal first with Lady S-S and get her over. I should reply as follows:

Dear Lady S-S

Thank you for your letter of –. There are a number of reasons why I did not take over the Girl Guides in Kano from Sylvia Weatherhead. The main one is personal. I am not naturally a very sociable person, nor have I any aptitude for work of this sort. Some people I know can take it in their stride but I am afraid I am not one of them. To me it would have been a disproportionately heavy burden. As it was, I found entertaining and looking after my family very exhausting. I felt, moreover, that there were many other people in Kano capable of doing the job better than I could. Finally there was the consideration that I should be in England until February next year. I have thought the matter over again but have reached the same conclusion, namely that I cannot take on social work as well as manage the entertaining and look after my husband and family. (And so, dear Lady S-S, kindly stop badgering me.)

That should do, I think.

I am glad you had a good journey down to 'Four Winds' and installed yourself without difficulty. It is very annoying that the tenants left the house in such a mess but, if you have succeeded in getting the carpet clean, then it seems that all the casualties were minor ones. Remember that we have been very lucky to have had the house occupied all the winter and £5.5 a week coming in. We can easily pick up new decanters and tumblers.

I've had rather a fiendish week here with dinner parties on three successive nights. Now I'm hoping for a good rest from parties.

In May Tim drove down to Jos for the Residents' Conference. The direct dry-season road[5] was cut which meant having to go via Bauchi or Zaria, 350–400 miles either way. He decided to go by one route and come back by the other.

Here I am in Jos. A month today since you went. It does seem a long weary time. Let's try to avoid such long separations in future: a couple of months is not too bad but four and a half seem endless. I do pine for you, you know, and it does seem a waste of our lives.

Foxy Cole is apparently disappointed at not getting the Plateau. He is in a most odd mood, not holding forth as much as usual but breaking in pretty regularly either to prophesy doom or to make remarks beginning 'Of course I'm finished but you mark my words...'. Last night we all went to a cocktail party and Foxy got rather tight. Afterwards when we were talking shop he attacked me rather offensively as an Emirates man who didn't know what the Middle Belt was thinking etc. etc. It did not worry me because the others present were obviously on my side. At the same time Rosie Cole (known as the Cosy Roll) mortally offended Mrs Gunn by saying to her face that she was a foreigner whom all Africans would regard in a different light to an Englishwoman. Apart from this, we all got on very well together.

Our conference breaks up tomorrow and I am getting away as soon as I can. Two years ago we had a very easy time but this time they have worked us rather hard. No lie-ins for the last three days. Still, it has been a break from the daily round of Kano.

Soon after Tim got back to Kano Nicky McClintock, his new SDO, arrived. Many years later Nicky described his first meeting with Tim and the Emir: '[The Emir] was now seated with Tim Johnston in the drawing room in the Residency and his council were being ushered in. First the Madaki, the senior councillor, aged about forty perhaps he was a saint-like person, a man of the highest principles, who would certainly have been a member of the government if he had not chosen to stay at home and devote his life to Kano instead. The Waziri, the Lord Chancellor as it were, old and wrinkled, learned in Muslim law but understanding very little of the modern world. The Sarkin Shanu, a kinsman of the Madaki and responsible for Kano City; loyal and hardworking, he would always try hard to keep up and to understand the new ideas which were flowing in. Ja'idanawa, in charge of agriculture, forestry and veterinary; Mutawali, the Works Department; Alhaji Alassan Dantata, a fabulously wealthy Kano trader with interests as far afield as Sierra Leone. One by one they were introduced, some twelve of them in number. Yes, this was surely a day of good omen they told me, for had I not arrived on Empire Day, the 24th of May, the day on which the rains traditionally started in Kano.'[6]

He later went on to describe his daily meetings with Tim when they would discuss what needed to be done: 'Every morning after breakfast I would go down to the Residency, and there for half an hour Tim Johnston and I would exchange our news and views. What were the engagements for today? He would be off on tour to Gaya district tomorrow, and he would be out until Thursday. I must not leave Kano in his absence. This was a standing order, that one or other of us must always be in Kano at all times. Derek Mountain was going on leave; who would be sent to us to replace him, and was there a house for him? There seemed to be some trouble over the new railway spur to the abattoir which was to be built outside the Kofar Mara; I had better look into it. And the NEPU... were kicking up a fuss about those houses which were being demolished to make way for a new road. It had been stupid of the Public Works Department to choose that line in the first place, and then to insist upon it when it was obvious that trouble would follow, but the harm had been done now. Did I know who the native authority were going to suggest as the new district head of Birnin Kudu? Tim hoped it was not going to be Mallam Musa, who was well connected but a fool and had put up such a black last year. The money was now available for the new girls' school which the Education Department was so keen on; I ought to convene a site board. The department wanted the school to be inside the walls of Kano, probably somewhere on the western edge, but all sorts of interests would be involved here and it would be as well to have a quiet word with the Madaki and others before we started looking at any land just there.

'The work of clearing the bush in Ningi to the south of our province in order to prevent the spread of tsetse fly was coming along well, and it would soon be across the border and into Kano province; I would like to go down there to contact the people in charge of this work and see that our district and village authorities were properly briefed about it. Mr Adlai Stevenson and a party of American congressmen would be arriving on Friday; I had better arrange for them to be received by the Emir the following morning, and then we might take them out to see the new dam at Kuwasa, and perhaps the village weaving enterprise at Minjibir as well. There was a recently convicted murderer in the prison. I had interviewed him this morning and would be writing my report on the case for the Governor-General's Privy Council, but it seemed that after he had committed the murder he had escaped across the border into French territory and had been handed back to us by the French authorities without any formal extradition proceedings. Ought I to mention this in my report? The Adult Education campaign seemed to be having very disappointing results in Kazaure Emirate; the old emir up there was known to be unsympathetic, and I would like to spend a few days in Kazaure and give it a push. There had been an appeal for help from the far end of Gwaram district which was said to be overrun by lions. We were only half-way through the financial year, and yet the Native Authority had already exhausted the amount provided in the estimates for road maintenance and had submitted an AISE (Application to Incur Supplementary Expenditure). What had gone wrong?

'The problems were infinite in their variety. In Kano we never knew what the day would bring forth; it might be an air crash or other emergency at the airport; all too often it was a death among our small European community and their children; it was once a total escape of water from our only reservoir. But we could never get away from the constant threat of politics. In the last five years Nigeria had come a long way along the road to independence and by now the political pattern was well established.'[7]

At the beginning of the year several Northerners had been honoured by the Queen in the New Year's List and Tim wrote to tell Berrice that the Governor was going to make the presentations.

HE is now coming up for three nights not one as we had hoped. On Saturday morning he is giving the Emir his CMG; in the evening there will be another ceremony for Sarkin Bai and myself [OBE] followed by a reception in the Residency. On Sunday he is going to spend the night at Kazaure so that he can give the Emir the Queen's Medal next morning and on Monday he returns to Kano and departs in the Austin. I can see that it is going to be a fiendish week. The only consolation is that Lady S-S and Angela are not coming. For myself I am rather thankful to be getting my gong here and not at the Palace but I am sorry that Carolyn will miss seeing the Queen.

For the Emir's investiture we are all riding in procession from the Nassarawa Gate to the Palace. I hope to God none of the horses bolt or fight.

You were wise to steer clear of the Red Cross. There has just been an awful quarrel between Mrs M and Jack Davies with the result that Jack has resigned. The general opinion is that Mrs M is intolerably bossy. She has now been offered £110 p.a. to take over the Fagge Dispensary. I don't think this is unreasonable but all the other MOO say it is too much and are up in arms. What I think is rather steep is that she wants to work a 5-hour day and knock off at 1 p.m.

There has just been another list of promotions. Foxy has become a Senior Resident so my Cedric has now got his rights. Having got them let us hope he will retire but I expect he'll hang on for more pension.

After the presentation Tim wrote:

Well, we are through the fiendish week and all went well. The presentation of the Emir's CMG took place first. The Emir and his horses and camels and helmets and mail met us at Kofar Nassarawa and we climbed on our horses and rode in procession to the Palace. HE was in his blues, frock-coat, cocked hat, plumes, mounted on the Emir's white horse, an impressive figure. The crowd loved it and were more animated and cheerful than I have ever seen them. HE was so loaded with gold-braid that people were saying 'Ashe, Mai-wandon karfi ya samo wandon zinariya'. [Ironpants has taken to golden pants.][8] All the horses behaved and no-one fell off. In the central square there was a very big crowd. Early on it had been beautifully sunny but just before the ceremony began it clouded over and became very threatening. We just got through the programme when the wind and dust came, followed shortly afterwards by the rain. The Union Jack was upside-down but not many people noticed that and on the whole the thing was voted a success. At any rate we didn't have Bauchi's chapter of accidents. There Bruce Greatbatch, receiving his MBE, found he had forgotten to bring his helmet. Then when HE pinned the medal on he pinned his glove in with it at the first attempt and at the second affixed it firmly to the flesh on Bruce's chest. The climax came when Hopkins, Acting Resident, sat in his chair and the chair collapsed. Picking himself up, he realised that his braces buttons had all parted and he had to shuffle off the platform with his hands in his pockets holding up his trousers. Almost too good to be true.

The rest of HE's visit went off all right without any hitches. We stopped to shoot on the way up to Kazaure: I had two shots and got one bird. HE missed with four shots and then afterwards shamelessly claimed one of Patterson's. We had quite a good little ceremony there and then returned to Kano and thankfully saw him off. He was very affable all the time but it is nice to get these things over.

Seven weeks today and the 50 up tomorrow. I am glad that you are missing me and longing for me but I'm sure that it is not more than I am missing and longing for you. These separations are such a waste of life. Don't leave me for as long as this again: I can't bear it. If a djinn were to say to me that I could be in 'Four Winds' tomorrow provided that I gave up the last three months of my life I should take the offer like a shot. I suppose this time we owed it to Carolyn and Robin but I hope you won't want to do it again.

In June it was reported from Lagos that a party of four, travelling by car from Kenya to Britain via Kano and Agades, had lost their way in the Sahara. Two had perished from thirst but Miss Barbara Duthy, aged thirty, and Peter Barnes, aged eighteen, had survived the ordeal.

Kano is full of reporters dredging up the Saharan survivors' story. The man from the 'Mail' and the man from the 'Express' are apparently very disgruntled at what they describe as lack of co-operation from the British administration. They bombarded Bill Ford with all sorts of questions such as 'Do you consider five gallons of water enough for the desert crossing?' and then got annoyed with Bill because he would not answer. I am going to see them later this morning to smooth, if I can, their ruffled plumes. If I fail you will no doubt see your poor old husband denounced in banner headlines. Master Barnes and Miss Duthy are still in Kano staying with the Trevitts and thoroughly enjoying the publicity. What puzzles me is how, after the lorry had rescued them, they managed to part company again.

An official French report later stated: 'A few days after the car left Agades an Algerian lorry driver found Mr Cooper, half naked, dying of thirst beside the track, 36 miles from In-Guezzam. The driver gave him water and Mr Cooper recovered sufficiently to tell him that his car was stranded a few kilometres away, with his three companions on board. The Algerian soon found the car, the occupants of which were in a serious condition. After repairing the car, the driver took Miss Duthy with him and told the others to follow him and not let the lorry out of their sight, but at midday on May 12 the car disappeared. The Algerian circled the area for some time in a vain search until his own vehicle broke down and he and Miss Duthy got a lift into Agades with a passing Swiss motorist. A search party set out, and 24 hours later the car was discovered, half buried in sand. Mr Cooper had died the previous day in a final effort to drive back on to the desert track. The naked body of Miss Taylor was lying a few yards from the car. Peter Barnes was alive but unconscious. The travellers had drunk the water in the radiator. They were finally stranded when their petrol ran out.'[9] The incident caused quite a stir and the press were trying to milk it for all it was worth. Tim continued the story:

> The two reporters were an odd couple. The man from the 'Mail' was youngish and really their air correspondent. Rather a bogus one I suspect because my mention of the RAF evoked no spark and he seemed to know far less about the Bristol Wayfarer's troubles than I did. The man from the Express was a middle-aged, bald, and I suspect renegade Irishman. They were chiefly angry with Bill Ford because he had declined to tell them anything, partly because he didn't know much himself. The reporters thought that this was obstruction of the worst sort, interfering with the liberty of the press. I mollified them somewhat with beer yesterday and a visit to the Emir today but they are still threatening to blast us in their columns. I tried to convince them that the tragedy took place a long way away and had little to do with us but they wouldn't have it and kept saying how helpful the French had been and how obstructive the British. Of course I think Bill was wrong in refusing to tell them that Miss D. was staying with the Trevitts but he says that he wanted to avoid exposing the Trevitts to tiresome infestations of journalists. Well, well, you had better look out and see what they say about us.

Later in the month Tim went off on tour and his next letter was from Malammaduri.

> I knew this tour was going to be difficult if it rained much and it has rained hard every second day. Consequently it has been awful.
> We set off at noon on Thursday, one and a half hours later than I had intended, but I thought we should get in to Hadejia between five and six. I went in Adamu's car with the loads in the lorry. The road proved to be awful. It is all sunken and we had to keep turning off into the bush wherever the depth of water or

the presence of clay made progress impossible. Even so we got bogged once and the lorry once. It took us an hour to extricate the lorry. In the end it was 8 p.m. before we got to Hadejia, all very tired. Then came the final straw. Adamu did not know the way through the town and did not ask and soon got lost. Old Nuhu[10] pretended to know the way, flapped about like a decapitated bird, and got even more lost. At this point, when we were within half a mile of our destination, the engine stalled and refused to start. Adamu said he thought we must have run out of petrol. In the end, after a large crowd had collected, the engine came back to life but only after we had spent half-an-hour messing about in the town. By this time Maconachie, having given us up, was having supper in his dressing gown and looked rather embarrassed at our sudden appearance. After one and a half bottles of beer I went to bed believing that I should sleep beautifully but not a bit of it, I lay awake until well after two. I can bear the hardships of the day fairly philosophically but I must say I do hate being unable to sleep.

Maconachie is waiting for his cable, already overdue, to say that he is a father. I like him very much and he is doing well.

Martin Maconachie had copied to Tim a letter he had written to the Provincial Education Officer explaining that since they had built a number of new primary schools in Hadejia and Gumel Emirates and only one new middle school – the latter being the PEO's responsibility – there was now a serious mismatch between the number of children qualifying for middle school and the number of places available. Tim and Martin agreed that the PEO, in his first few months in the job and with a young family, was a reluctant tourer. Tim therefore decided to visit all the schools in the next two days and discuss the problem with the Headmasters and the Emirs. He said he would do this on his own and Martin was to stay in Hadejia awaiting news from England. In due course, on his return to Kano, Tim wrote to the PEO with an analysis of the problem and tactfully suggested various temporary and permanent solutions.[11]

For several months a Commission, headed by Gorsuch, had been looking into and revising the salaries and conditions of service of expatriate and African civil servants and its report was awaited by all with hopeful expectation. Rumours were circulating that he had recommended a £400 increase for Puisne Judges, with the likelihood of a similar rise for Senior Residents, and increases in children's allowances. Not long afterwards Tim learned some more concrete details about how the Report was going to affect them.

> Gordon Wilson was here yesterday and he says that Gorsuch has recommended Senior Residents going from £2240 to £2400, not to £2640 as I hoped. Residents advance from £2075 to £2200. These are the smallest increases recommended for anyone, only about 7–8%. He has gone on to say that Permanent Secretaries are underpaid and to propose raising them from the status of SDOs to that of Senior Residents. This is going to make a lot of blood boil in the Provinces. It has completely destroyed my faith in Gorsuch: the man must be an ass to make such a proposal. Rumour now says that he is anti-administration and there seems some ground for believing this. At present Puisne Judges and Senior Residents are on the same level: he wants to put the PJs on £2640 and the SRs on £2400. This too I think a monstrous suggestion. The report has evoked a great deal of criticism and I think Government will have to improve on his suggestions if they are to avoid much discontent in the service.

Other sources of discontent in the North were the much harsher living conditions compared to the East or West, and the poor communications. Even though there had been progress in many areas, dental treatment, European shops, libraries and cinemas were available only in the big towns like Kaduna, Kano and Zaria. Officers in remote stations were usually many miles away from the nearest doctor and often completely cut off by floods or broken bridges. Children, whose condition could deteriorate very quickly, were particularly vulnerable in the event of an illness or emergency.

In the Administration, although the North was beginning to catch up with the East and West, there were few Northerners capable of doing anything beyond ordinary routine work so everything else was the responsibility of the expatriate. Furthermore, some of the politically conscious junior Northern civil servants felt that appointments and promotions should be a matter of personal patronage, and the determination of the Administration to keep the Civil Service clean often resulted in bitter complaints that white officialdom was deliberately blocking their path to promotion.[12]

Most of the senior officers had known their ministers and leading politicians for a long time and there was mutual appreciation and affection, but even so there had been several incidents of ministers' discourtesy and one or two of downright rudeness and humiliation.[13] Certain ministers wanted to regard the Permanent Secretaries as potential political subordinates and it was hard to make them understand that PermSecs were members of the Public Service and could not be employed politically.[14] In a rapidly changing world this was probably inevitable but quite distressing for officers who could see the dangers and had only the best interests of the region at heart.

At the end of July Carolyn broke up from school.

Thank you for your letter with news of Carolyn's report. It was not very good but not too bad either. I told you I thought she had a gift for arithmetic. You had better warn her now that she will have to do some reading and writing and spelling with me in September: if we can improve these she should be all right. What effect has school had on her temperament?

I gather that nothing is being done in Kaduna about Gorsuch's scurvy treatment of the administration. Waddle, who is invincibly modest, merely said that if he got £200 a month he thought he was being adequately paid. I have entered a dignified protest.

I am beginning to feel very tired and end of tourish. Playing tennis today I found I had no energy at all and I'm beginning to wonder how I shall get through the next month. It is going to be a perfectly bloody month anyway. Oliver and his wife come tomorrow for the polo tournament. But before they arrive I have to be up at 5 (Sunday of course) to meet Michael S-S. On Monday (public holiday of course) I must get up again at dawn to meet the Maddocks [Civil Secretary, Kaduna]. Later in the day a retired Air Commodore [North Carter] arrives who is going to take over the Provincial Office and as he is new to the country I shall have to put him up too. On Wednesday Niven [Rex] arrives, looking for a bed as usual. On Thursday the Emir, Premier and Co return from Mecca and I shall be at the airport again. On Saturday I have to give a cocktail party as the culmination of the Polo Week. This will be the second in nine days because I had to give one for the Es' farewell. Then next week Peter is coming. And so it goes on. The climax is that the Imperial Defence College party is arriving here the day before I fly.

By the way, when I was in Kaduna Sylvia [Weatherhead] told me that there had been talk there about Peter and some African girl in his office but I know no details.

I can't tell you how I'm looking forward to leave. I feel really depressed and sick of everything and everyone here. Not long now but I wish the time would pass more quickly. I'm longing to see you.

Tim managed to get away on leave at the end of August in time for the last three weeks of Carolyn's summer holiday. The weather in England was still good and they had a happy time at 'Four Winds' with trips down to the beach most days and plenty of surfing.

By the time Carolyn broke up for the Christmas holidays Tim had already returned to Kano and Berrice was worried about her latest report. Having missed out on the infant years of education, she was lagging behind her age group and had been kept down.

I was so pleased to hear from you when I got back last night after collecting Carolyn from school. It is good news about the Queen's forthcoming visit to Nigeria. I am already beginning to feel sick at the prospect and shall probably faint with fright on the day. Have you heard how many Governors are coming to Kano, I suppose we shall have to turn out anyway?

I managed to have a few words alone with Miss Clark and told her we were disturbed to hear that Carolyn was so backward and needed coaching in tables as well as reading and spelling. She said we were not to worry because she is really doing very well!! But Miss Roberts has very high standards and expects the children to not only know multiplication tables but also money tables and other weird tables which appear to be Miss R's own invention. I asked whether Carolyn would be going up and Miss Clark said Miss R. hadn't yet decided. She seemed to think that she would probably stay in 2b another term and then go straight up to the third form skipping 2a. I again mentioned that we thought she felt out of things and Miss Clark said that if Miss R. decided to keep her down another term, she was sure it was the right thing. I must say I don't understand it, except that I've come to the conclusion that Miss Clark is a bit scared of Miss Roberts.

Miss R's comments are: Carolyn's spelling is her only drawback. She so often puts forth very little effort due to colds and catarrh – if these could be attended to life would be so much easier for her and her work would be outstanding.

Personally I feel at sixes and sevens about the whole business: in one breath they say Carolyn is pretty hopeless and in the next that she could be outstanding if something could be done about her colds. What do you think about it all?

Fees are going up by 5 guineas a term. Carolyn seems well and much happier. Also seems very fond of Miss Clark and Matron – great hugs and kisses all round.

Tim's first job when he got back to Kano was to write the Annual Report on the Province. With plentiful rainfall it had been an excellent year for crops and the farmers were feeling prosperous. In the villages, much good work had been done to improve life for the villagers with new reading rooms, offices and court houses being built, and six more primary schools had been opened. However, it was still a struggle to persuade parents to allow their daughters to go to school and to encourage children to continue with secondary education. In the Adult Education campaign, strenuous efforts had been made to improve results but there was everywhere a formidable mass of inertia that needed to be overcome. If a class was opened during the rains people said they could not attend because they were busy on their farms; if it was opened during the dry-season they said they could not attend because they were occupied with their trading expeditions.

Serious crime in the Emirate had increased slightly although homicides had decreased by nearly a third. In Kano City the number of burglaries had been halved by the exertions of a new mobile patrol, but the activities of political extremists had given the police more work than either crime or traffic. On several occasions prompt intervention in ugly situations had prevented serious trouble from developing.

In the Administration, Tim had introduced a new system of correspondence whereby the Resident no longer addressed DOs but wrote to the Native Authorities through them. The object was to bring home to the NAs their responsibilities in every field of local government and compel them to undertake more work themselves.

In the past, work had tended to grind to a halt whenever administrative staff had been short and there was no supervision. With this new system, they were now expected to frame replies and institute action where necessary without having to be prompted to do so by a DO.

To conclude his report Tim wrote:

> A country moving towards self-government reaches a point where the current of events takes control and begins to hurry it towards its destination. In the grip of these forces the ship of state, like a canoe attempting the passage of the Grand Canyon, is swept along willy nilly and is powerless to turn aside or hold back. The most the crew can then do is to keep her head to the stream, make everything shipshape, try to anticipate hidden dangers, and trust in Providence. During the past year the tug of this current has been perceptible in Kano and the roar of the approaching rapids has sometimes been clearly heard. With this sound in their ears, the great majority of the servants of Government and the Native Authorities have worked at their tasks with their old industry and with a new and growing sense of urgency. Africans and Europeans alike have devoted themselves manfully to their duties, have helped one another in their difficulties, and without regard for colour or creed have done all in their power to prepare the Province for the ordeals which undoubtedly lie ahead.[15]

Tim spent Christmas with Peter Scott and then, in order to escape the New Year festivities, went off on tour for a few days. In his last letter before Berrice joined him, there was more news about the preparations for the Queen's visit, and Tim was busy organising the refurbishment of the Residency in her honour.

> A very happy New Year to you all.
>
> I don't know what to make of Miss Clark's account of Carolyn. I suppose the idea is that if she has a really thorough grounding she will be able to hold her own afterwards. Her report was quite good certainly but Miss Clark gives us no idea how far she is behind other girls of her age and what prospects she has of catching up. I am glad she is happy anyway, even if not brilliant.
>
> I found out a bit more about The Royal Visit. The household officers are apparently very nice and helpful. The Queen has a maid called Bobo whom everyone stands in awe of; she is the kind that has to be placated.

For the drawing room I have ordered a new glass-fronted book-case and new picture frames. I really think we shall have to have a new sofa as well. I think we need some ornaments for the top of the bookcase: what about one of your nice glass paper weights? I have chosen electric light brackets in gilt: is that all right? Upstairs Skipper is going to try to improve the floors by laying down 4 ft. squares of ply-wood surrounded by 3" battens of some light wood. He says it will remain flush and take polish. I have now handed over our bedroom and taken refuge in the little room beyond it. The house is still a shambles but they will try to get things straight before you come.

Here is some information about HM's preferences. Clock in sitting room. Writing table with small table beside it for Red Boxes. Malvern and tonic water, ginger pop, Heinz tomato juice, Gordon's gin, Vat 69 whisky, fresh orange juice. Small cutlery. Cooper's marmalade. I will look after all this. What you had better think of is a 5 lb. electric iron for Bobo. On second thoughts you had better deal with the clock as well.

Maiholi has now completed over sixty years in European service. He is in good form and has just invested (at my expense) in a chef's hat in honour of HM's visit.

The main celebrations in the North were held in Kaduna with a great Durbar consisting of two thousand horsemen and several thousand followers, the contingents representing every Province. Some of those from the more distant parts had been on the road for four weeks before reaching Kaduna. About a third of the horsemen and a fifth of the pedestrians had had to pass through Kano Province where Ken Vorley was the officer in charge of organising provisions for them, a mammoth task. Fifteen miles was considered the optimum distance for each day's travel so staging posts had to be established at each of these distances at which supplies of food were placed for horses and people. Each person had a printed card indicating the number of staging posts in the Province at which he would be staying, depending on the route he had to follow. When the staging post was a District Headquarters the visitors made their arrival as a sort of celebration, rising in their saddles and waving their swords and all accompanied by the local musicians.

Tim travelled down to Kaduna to see the Durbar with Pam McClintock since Berrice could not leave Robin and Nicky had to remain in charge of Kano while Tim was absent, a rule that could not be relaxed. After the procession of all the contingents passed the Queen, the climax of the Durbar was the Ja'afi, which was: 'the traditional salute given to any high dignitary, a headlong charge by a line of horsemen who rein their horses suddenly back upon their haunches only the barest yard or two in front of him, and salute with their spears shaken in the air above their heads. For those who do not know what to expect, it takes a lot of nerve to face. On this occasion it had been arranged that three waves of horsemen would charge in succession towards the dais on which the Queen was seated, but would halt at the broad white line drawn on the ground a safe few yards before it.

'However, when this was rehearsed a few days beforehand the Premier, the Sardauna of Sokoto, was rather disappointed; he thought it rather tame, and so he sent for the Emir of Fika and asked him to lead the final wave. He could not have chosen better, and on the day he was superb. For him there was to be no stopping at the broad white line, he was across it at the gallop and up the first few steps of the dais too before he halted and reined back. Then, erect in his stirrups and with flashing eyes he shook his spear at the dais and flung it quivering into the ground at the horse's feet. This he did a second, and yet a third time, before he finally wheeled his horse around and rode magnificently away.'[16]

Tim then returned to Kano where the Queen was to spend her last day and he was quite relieved when the visit was over.

The Queen came here on February 16th. She was due to arrive by air at 2.15 p.m. and I had to accompany the Governor, Premier, and Emir of Kano in order to meet her. Her Argonaut, the 'Atlanta', arrived dead on time and she and the Duke emerged at once. They were met by the Governor and Premier and escorted along seventy-five yards of red carpet to the royal pavilion where the rest of us were waiting. We were presented and bowed and shook hands.

On the other side of the pavilion, which was decorated in blue and silver, the girls and mistresses of the Kano Girls School and Women's Training College were waiting to greet the Queen. As she moved over towards them, HM asked what the temperature was. The question was relayed down through the Governor and others until some underling was sent flying off to the Airport Buildings to find out. Cdr. Parker observed sotto voce that a confident 101° would have served just as well. The Queen then received a bouquet from a very small black girl and walked round among the others and spoke to a few of them. In the meantime her Rolls (built for the late M. Gulbenkian) drew up quietly behind her. As she stepped in a panting messenger arrived with the news that the shade temperature was 99.2°.

The procession then set off with a Police car in the lead, HM following, and the Governor, Premier, Emir and myself behind. The royal car was an open one and the sun was exceedingly hot but fortunately the pace was slow enough for the Queen to hoist her parasol which Lady Euston had as usual forgotten but which Perkins the detective had rescued from the aircraft. As soon as we reached the crowds the speed was reduced to 8 mph. This gave them an excellent view and they all cheered and waved most loyally. The distance is 5 miles and it took us over half an hour to cover the ground. As we approached the Residency I heard a voice say 'There goes Daddy' and caught a glimpse of Robin being held up by a kind friend who was looking after him. Needless to say, he was far more interested in the array of cars than in any of the mortals sitting in them.

At the Residency Berrice was waiting in the porch and was presented by Lady Sharwood-Smith. The Queen by this time was looking rather tired, as well she might be, and she and the Duke went straight up to their rooms. HM's room we were very proud of. It had cream Indian carpet and rugs, cream furniture (brought out originally for the Prince of Wales in 1925 but repainted and looking like new), blue curtains with a classical design, blue bedspreads, and, setting off all the other colours, a brand-new mosquito-net as white as a bridal veil and deep red cushion covers. An air-conditioner was working so the temperature in the room was ten degrees cooler than outside. We heard afterwards that HM had been very pleased with the room and it even earned a word of praise from Miss Macdonald, the Queen's dresser.

The next item on the programme was the Queen's visit to the Emir's palace and the state drive through the City. For this we all changed into uniform and I had to leave first so as to be with the Emir when the royal party arrived. There were huge crowds lining the streets and filling the central square. In the Emir's outer courtyard there were about 500 invited guests but the inner court was empty except for dogarai (the Emir's uniformed henchmen), the press, and a jester. The Emir and I waited here and soon from the noises of the crowd outside we knew that the procession was approaching. When they arrived I saluted and then the Emir and I again shook hands with the Queen and the Duke. The Governor and the members of the household, meanwhile, were tumbling out of their cars and hurrying up. The Emir led the way to a third inner courtyard where the members of his council were lined up and these were presented. From there we went to the main council chamber, a room about 30 ft. square and 20 ft. high built entirely of mud, like the rest of the palace, and decorated inside with shining black and gold mica. After this HM went in to another building to see the Emir's wives and children while the Duke and the rest of us waited in the garden court where a loyal gardener had picked out 'God save the Queen' in a little plant that looks like dwarf box. After ten minutes the Emir came out and asked if he might take HM further into the harem and the Governor said of course, if she wants to go. The Duke meanwhile was talking to the Emirs of Hadejia, Gumel and Kazaure who thus got an unusually long innings. When the Queen finally emerged, the whole party continued the tour of the palace. The Emir had done it very well: all the rooms were covered in eastern rugs and carpets, some of them very good ones which he bought in Hejaz last year, and all the mica wall decorations had been newly furbished. At one point there were a series of black and white drawings which were supposed to represent the Queen and the Duke but in which the Queen was made to look like a luscious eastern beauty. The Duke stopped to ask who had done them and the Emir said (as if it was the most natural thing in the world) that the artist was one of the prisoners from the gaol. At the end of the tour of the palace HM and HRH both signed the Emir's visitors book and HM thanked him and presented him with a signed photograph.

We then returned to the inner courtyard where there was a display of various graphs, charts and diagrams showing how rapidly we were advancing in every conceivable direction. The ones dealing with Kano Emirate were explained by the Madaki, the chief councillor, whom I had taken over the course a day or two before. The vaccination graph showed a spectacular rise to 1954 and then a slight drop in 1955. I had told the Madaki that the Duke was sure to pounce on this and had carefully briefed him with the explanation for the slight setback, which lay in the re-organisation of the system and the re-training of the staff. Sure enough when we got to this graph the Duke seized on the fall and asked the reason for it. Without batting an eyelid, the Madaki blandly explained that the fall was illusory because the last figure was for a half-year only and really represented a substantial advance. At the end of the graphs and diagrams there was a class of adults, sitting under a tree and being taught to read and write. When we reached them they were looking at three syllables on the blackboard and chanting in unison 'Ha-ra-ji, ha-ra-ji, har-ra-ji'. The Duke asked what the word meant and was told tax. At this he slapped his thigh, roared with laughter, and said: 'Well, can you beat that? You teach them to read and the very first word the poor devils have to master is tax'.

After this we piled back into our cars to continue the state drive through the City. By this time it was after six and much cooler. The procession turned out of the palace and drove through immense crowds to the mosque, hospital, and Mata Gate. Even the half-mile between the gate and the suburb of Fagge was densely packed. Some of the press reports were exaggerated but there were certainly five thousand horsemen and about a quarter

14. Sir Ahmadu Bello, Sardauna of Sokoto, Premier of Northern Nigeria

Tim, the Emir of Kano, + Governor Genl

of a million spectators. The northerners are undemonstrative people so there was no cheering but HM had been warned about that and did not expect it. On the other hand all those with flags waved them vigorously and the crowds were very cheerful, orderly and good-tempered. They only broke through the cordons at one point and that was after the Queen had passed so she did not notice it.

By the time we got back to the Residency it was dusk. The Queen and Duke went straight upstairs and the rest of us dispersed to our lodgings to change out of uniform. I was the first one back and joined Berrice in the drawing room. She had been in the house all the afternoon supervising things and seeing that the royal staff had all they needed. We were sitting talking when we heard someone at the door and a voice said 'May we come in?' and HM and HRH walked into the room. The Queen sat in the corner of one of the settees and asked us to sit down too. I was on her left and Berrice on the other side between her and the Duke. No-one else was there and we had them to ourselves for five or ten minutes until the Governor and the members of the household began reassembling. We talked about the events of the afternoon and they both seemed very pleased at the size of the crowds and the friendly reception they had had.

When the procession was about to leave the Emir's palace there had been some confusion round the Emir's car while the staff-bearer was piled in. The Queen and the Duke had noticed all this and they spoke and laughed about it, especially about the man who kept trying to shut the car door on the staff of office. The Queen then mentioned the harem and said how odd it was to find a brand new refrigerator standing in the middle of an old mud room. At this the Duke pointed out that if you came to think of it a refrigerator was just as incongruous in Windsor Castle (what he actually said was 'at home in Windsor') as it was in Kano. The Queen then said she supposed that the women were not treated as equals. I said that in theory it was so but in practice most of the women more than held their own. The Duke roared with laughter at this as if I had said something very witty and I am sure that this subject must be one of their private jokes.

At this point we asked if they would like a drink. The Queen refused but the Duke said he would have a squash. All the drinks were on a side table and as I got up to get it for him he came over to take it. I poured out his squash (Idris is what they both fancy) and then found that there was no opener for the soda-water. I was about to ring but found I couldn't because the bell was wound round the arm of the settee and therefore practically in HM's lap. The duke said 'let me get it' but of course I darted out myself. All the boys were out at the back listening for the bell and in the dining room all I could find was a very ancient and rusty opener whose handle had broken off half way. So as not to waste time calling boys I grabbed this and, holding it after the manner of one playing Up Jenkins, gave the Duke his drink.

Soon afterwards HE and the members of the royal household started filtering back and our monopoly was over. The Queen did not seem a bit tired and was in fact amazingly animated. We think that she and the Duke must have enjoyed a nice little sleep during the afternoon, not only because they were so fresh in the evening but because their bedside literature appeared to be untouched. For uplift we had put out an historical note on Kano Emirate written by me, for homework the two latest copies of the 'Times' which they could not then have seen, and for light reading a collection of the 'Times' Fourth Leaders and a book called 'The Twelfth' about a keen shot who finds himself turned into a grouse and having to face a barrage of his friends. As even the 'Timeses' had not been opened we think it a reasonable deduction that what they both did was to get their heads down. Be that as it may, they were certainly both in very good form in the evening. Probably another reason was that they felt the tour was over and they were really on their way home. The Duke, I noticed, treated Sir Michael Adeane and Capt. Steele-Perkins in exactly the easy bantering way that a young CO might treat an elderly rather punctilious Adjutant and a fussy conscientious medical officer. Relations with the members of the household, in fact, were extraordinarily friendly and familiar and we noticed that even Blount, a junior and recent recruit, was addressed by the Queen as Christopher.

At this stage the Duke asked who those people were in the caravan. There were in Kano at the time a party of South Africans in two huge motor caravans and I thought he must have spotted them. No-one else answered so I said I thought they were South Africans. He looked rather surprised and said in an incredulous voice 'What, on CAMELS?' There was a general laugh at this, of course, and I had to explain the misunderstanding and tell him that the camel drivers were slaves of the Tuaregs called Buzus. This name seemed to amuse him too. Later on I could not resist telling him about the Madaki and the graph. He roared with laughter again and said: 'The man ought to have been a soldier'.

By this time everyone had assembled and it was time to go. The Queen got up and called Berrice and me over to her. She then thanked us very nicely for the arrangements we had made for her comfort and said she wanted to present us with a photograph of herself and the Duke. This was then handed over to Berrice, framed in black and bearing both their signatures. Berrice curtseyed and I bowed and we both managed to get out some thanks for the honour.

For the drive to the airport it was quite dark but the royal Rolls has special lighting and this was turned on to illuminate them sitting in the back. All the Europeans who turned out to see them off remarked on how particularly nice the Queen looked and how animated she was. The general verdict, in fact, was that her pictures never did her justice and that she was much more beautiful than they made her look. Personally I think that she is very like her pictures but that they seldom bring out her lovely complexion. Furthermore photographers seldom catch her full smile which is very wide and happy. In our drawing room she was so relaxed that she was not only flashing this out but, as we observed with humble amusement, she was also resting her feet by easing off the heel of one of her shoes.

At the airport we went up one by one in the royal pavilion to say good-bye. When my turn came the Queen again thanked me for all the arrangements for the visit and Berrice and me for having made them both so comfortable in the house. The Governor and Premier then escorted the Queen and the Duke back along the 75 yards of red carpet to the Argonaut. Even when she was inside the aircraft the Queen remained at one of the ports and continued to wave until out of sight. This was characteristic of her great conscientiousness. As for us, we were both sorry to see her go and also profoundly thankful that there had been no hitch to stop her going.

Berrice had been terrified but she had managed not to faint!

Just before 3 p.m. I stood in the porch with Lady Sharwood-Smith to await their arrival. At exactly 3 p.m. they arrived and as they stepped out of the car Lady S-S presented me and I curtsied and shook hands with them both. I was somewhat surprised when they both said 'How do you do'; I don't know why it seemed odd for royalty to say that but it did.

I took them into the house and asked the Queen if she would like to go straight up to her bedroom. She said she would so I took them up and of course curtsied again when I left them.

Tea was taken up to them in their room by the Sergeant Footman and at 5 p.m. we and members of the royal household assembled in the hall. A few minutes later the Duke, dressed in white naval uniform came down the stairs and disconcerted me by dashing straight up to me and asking 'is the promised drink ready'. I was completely taken aback and murmured that I didn't know he had been promised a drink. With that he smiled and rushed into the dining room and helped himself to a squash. While he was in the dining room the Queen came down and then they all got into their cars to start the drive to the Emir's Palace and the City.

They returned at 6.30 p.m. and I (alone this time) waited to welcome them in the porch. The Queen was charming to the Sgt. Footman who rushed forward to take her parasol and bag. He had been in the procession to the City and the Queen, when she saw him, said 'Hello Pearce how did you manage to get back so quickly?' with a lovely smile.

They went straight upstairs because the Duke wanted to change out of uniform. Just after 7 p.m. Tim and I were sitting alone in the drawing room when we heard footsteps and a voice asking 'May we come in please' and in walked the Duke followed by the Queen. We all sat down and looking back on it it was just like a most improbable dream for us to be chatting so easily with them.

I can't tell you how lovely the Queen is and I just couldn't take my eyes off her. She wasn't a bit tired and was most animated. She was very thrilled with everything she had seen and told us that there was so much to look at that she just didn't know where to look. While she was talking, she looked and behaved like a very charming girl of 17 and all the time she was talking she was slipping her feet out of her shoes. She didn't change her clothes at all and looked beautifully fresh in a pale blue and grey printed cotton dress: it had the low hip line and a big off the shoulder collar. Her hat was very small and made of pale blue feathers. Her shoes were white with a tiny diamond buckle. She has a lovely figure and a most beautiful complexion and colouring. Her photographs don't do her justice.

The Duke was very easy to talk to and seemed most interested in everything. While he was talking he fiddled with an ashtray which eventually crashed to the ground.

A few minutes before 7.30 the Governor, Lady Sharwood-Smith and members of the royal household joined us and when the Queen got up from the sofa she thanked us most delightfully for making them so comfortable and presented us with a framed photograph signed by them both as a momento of their visit.

I said 'good-bye' to them in the porch and Tim joined the procession up to the airport. Everything went off beautifully and it is something I shall remember all my life.

The Queen's Dresser Miss Macdonald (who is said to be a dragon of a woman) gave us great praise for all our arrangements and said everything was perfect.

In her description, Berrice missed out an incident that nearly ended in disaster. She had told the household staff that whatever Her Majesty wanted she should have. Just after she had shown the Queen to her room, she met the head steward coming up the stairs with a tray. On it was a loaf of bread, a bread knife, some butter and a large cucumber. 'What are you doing?' asked Berrice. 'The Queen say she want cucumber sandwiches,' replied the steward![17]

After the excitement of the royal visit everyone slipped back into their normal routines. Later in the year regional elections were held and although no trouble had been expected in the rural areas, two minor riots took place during the primaries. Both disturbances were caused by the supporters of NEPU and the police had to intervene to calm the situation. There were also serious tensions between the main political parties before the Kano City Council elections.[18]

There was real concern in the administration about the political unrest and the Governor asked Tim to produce a paper on 'The Impact of Democracy on Northern Nigeria':

The Protectorate of Northern Nigeria was declared in 1900 and direct British control established throughout the Region in 1903 but it was not until 1947 that northerners experienced their first election. Since then, events have moved with such extraordinary

169

rapidity that self-government and independence are already in sight after less than one decade and may well be attained before another one has passed. With the Constitutional Conference about to begin, we can therefore be said to have reached a half-way house where we should pause and see whether, on our present bearing, we are in fact making good the course we have set ourselves.

First of all a word of caution is necessary. The north is too large a territory and its people too diverse for generalisations about it to be universally valid. This study deals primarily with the Muslim areas of the north which contain the majority but not the whole of the population of the Region. The inhabitants of these areas, however, possess such a preponderance in numbers and such weight and authority that it is likely that their uniform culture will gradually assimilate the diverse cultures of their lesser neighbours. It is therefore hardly too much to say that what they think today the rest of the Region will be thinking tomorrow.

In the hundred years which the Sokoto Empire lasted the Fulani imposed on the Hausa a strict and narrow form of Islam and, for their part, absorbed the language and most of the customs of the Hausa. Nevertheless they did not succeed in welding the two tribes into one people. This fact was constantly noted in Lord Lugard's early reports and accounted for the ease with which his tiny columns overthrew a large empire. After over fifty years of British rule, the gulf between the two tribes still remains and, with the advent of politics, has recently acquired a new significance.

The Hausa are an enigmatic people, their origins shrouded in mystery and their language the only unclassified one in Africa. Anyone who knows them well would agree that they have two sides to their character. As Dr. Jekyll they are friendly, sensible, loyal, biddable and easy-going; a lovable people who do not take life too seriously and have the great virtues of humour and good manners. As Mr. Hyde, however, they have a pronounced streak of rebelliousness and anarchism. This was first noted in 1903 during the short interval of confusion between the overthrow of Sokoto and the final defeat of the Sultan Attahiru and the diehards at Burmi. Lord Lugard, quoting Dr. Cargill, first Resident Kano, wrote as follows about the behaviour of the people at this time: 'The Hausa peasantry are not all intelligent traders; many are of low brutal stamp... Slaves deserted their masters and, with many of the idle or criminal classes, went about personating soldiers and looting and robbing. They did not desire our rule or Fulani rule, but no rule at all.'

Three years later the same spirit was seen at Satiru. In the brief month which elapsed between the victory of the Mahdists over the Mounted Infantry and their subsequent annihilation by British reinforcements, Satiru grew from an insignificant village to a town with an estimated population of 10,000. While the Fulani stood firm by our side, the Hausa flocked to join the rebels, many no doubt moved by religious motives, many others certainly attracted by the prospect of booty and a release from taxation and the other trammels of authority. More recently this spirit of lawlessness appeared again in the Kano Riots of 1953 when the Hausa mob not only rose on the Saturday but, after order had once been restored, again broke loose on the Monday with even worse excesses. Since then, the City has never been really free from the threat of violence. Finally in 1956, during the Regional Elections, subversion spread for the first time to the villages and caused three disturbances. These were not very serious in themselves but they all had one significant thing in common. They were not directed against the British or against a rival political party or even against Fulani rule: they were simply aimed at constituted authority. To anyone capable of reading the signs, these were portents.

Such then, were the dominant factors in the background when democracy first came to be put into practice in the north: a ruling caste which after a century and a half had failed to create a single people, a subject tribe usually docile but having a strong streak of lawlessness and, on both sides, genuine fervour for a narrow and rigid form of Islam. On to this society democracy burst like a river in spate, first with the Richards Constitution of 1947, then with the Revision of 1949 and the appointment of Ministers, next with the creation of the Federation in 1954 and finally with the prospect of early self-government. During this period NPC has emerged as the dominant political party and NEPU as the main opposition. The political warfare of these two parties has now thrust itself right into the foreground and has, at any rate in Kano Province where it has been most severe, made the ordinary man wonder where his society is heading.

In politics it was NEPU that first took the gloves off and introduced the sweeping attacks on all constituted authority and the personal vilification of opponents which has so bewildered the average northerner. The most important of NEPU's leaders, including M. Aminu Kano himself, are Fulani but the rank and file are for the most part Hausa. Certainly the party has owed much of its past success to the clever exploitation of the ancient dislike of the subject Hausas for their Fulani overlords. In Kano City, for example, the NEPU strongholds are the Hausa quarters while in the districts it is significant that NEPU's main successes have been won in old Hausa towns like Babeji and Getse. The tribal influence, however, is by no means the only one and age, occupation, environment and education all appear to play their part. In Kano today the portrait of a typical member of the party would show a young townsman in his early twenties, a petty trader or craftsman, living by his wits rather than his industry, literate but lacking in real education, the owner of a bicycle but not a house, probably unmarried and possibly estranged from his father. In the northern society of the past such a smart-alick would count for nothing. It is precisely because he now counts for a good deal in the conditions which we have created that northerners have begun to wonder where we are leading them.

Why, it may be asked, has such a young man, who is clearly not a high product of his society, nor even representative of it, now assumed importance? The answer is that it is because he is prepared to play politics for all he is worth, without reserve or scruple. His leaders have taught him that, under liberal British laws, he can go to what by local standards are extraordinary lengths not only in abuse of his political opponents but in defiance to authority. He has also discovered from experience that this is good sport and not attended by serious risks for those who have a little cunning.

The public who watch and listen to these young men fall into two groups. The minority, the dismissed and disgruntled, the misguided idealists and sub-conscious anarchists, applaud their daring and echo their views. The vast majority, however, reared in a tradition which demands obedience to the righteous ruler and acceptance of the unrighteous, are perplexed and shocked that such behaviour should be permitted. They finally conclude that it is tolerated because the British, for obscure reasons of their own, are secret supporters of the firebrands. 'Lalle turawa sun daure masu gindi'. This belief, which may seem extravagant to us, is in fact very widely held.

The danger of all this is not that NEPU may win a few seats, or even a majority, but that they may give parliamentary democracy such an odious name that it will be swept away as soon as the British relinquish power. I have recently heard a leading Chief and a leading commoner say exactly the same thing, namely that when the British leave the political parties will not last the night. If the parties go, parliamentary democracy as we understand it, goes too. It is not a native growth and its continued acceptance after our departure is at best doubtful. So far it has established itself with only a small minority and even among them there are some who have welcomed it not so much as a way of life but as an instrument of power. To the majority, at any rate in Kano, party politics is something alien which stirs up strife, sets subjects against rulers and sons against fathers and is leading the country heaven knows where. When I asked the distinguished commoner mentioned above whether he attached no value to the liberties of speech and association his blunt answer was: 'No, not at the price we are having to pay for them.'

Genuine parliamentary democracy is bound to lead a precarious life in any immature and backward country but in Northern Nigeria it is likely to be assailed by more than the ordinary perils. The two most formidable ones are a reaction towards primitive Islam and a counter-attack by the forces of tradition to recover their lost or threatened authority. If these two influences were to unite after British authority was withdrawn, as is quite possible, democracy would need to be much stronger than it is now to withstand their combined assault. But if democracy were submerged by Islamic reaction, the ferment of an awakened peasantry and proletariat would still continue underground. The danger of insurrection would tend to make the rulers oppressive and this in turn would tempt the people to seek freedom through revolt. In short, if democracy were to fail, it would probably be replaced at first by a repressive theocracy which in due course might well go down before a communist-inspired revolution.

If these premises are accepted it appears that we are on a lee shore and that, though our course is set to weather the point, we are in fact likely to go on the rocks. In such conditions it is better to go about and beat out to sea than hold blindly on hoping for a more favourable wind. That is what I think we should now do and I venture to suggest how it might be attempted.

First let us consider the fundamentals among our ideals which we hope to see preserved in this country after we have gone. To my mind they are:

Religious liberty and toleration;
The rule of law;
The liberty of the subject within the law;
The political supremacy within the constitution of a freely elected parliament.

The first and second of these principles are at present accepted but would almost certainly be early casualties if the forces of reaction were to prevail. It is the third and fourth, however, which are the critical ones and by them the other two will stand or fall.

The liberty of the subject, which we defend as our most precious possession, is coming to mean to the majority of northerners the freedom bestowed by us, for mysterious reasons of our own, on worthless young men to launch open attacks on all authority, blackguard their opponents, intimidate the public, distort the truth, and, at the least pretext, have recourse to hooliganism and violence. To almost all old and middle-aged men, and to the best of the young men as well, this is not liberty but a pernicious form of licence. In case I should be thought to exaggerate let me repeat the verdict of the independent arbitrators in the Kano Reconciliation Committee. After hearing extracts from recent political speeches, they were asked how people who said such things should be dealt with. Their reply was: 'three warnings and then death or banishment'. At present, however, for a variety of reasons, it is difficult to get convictions. Speakers therefore say pretty well what they like and play openly upon the rebellious and lawless streak in their audiences.

The consequence of this licence is that, among the respectable, not only the principle of liberty but the whole art of politics is falling into disrepute. This is a trend which suits NEPU admirably because the fewer people who vote the more likely they are to win. Their tactics have therefore consisted largely in abuse and intimidation with the object of making politics so rough that it remains a young man's game. If they had a monopoly of integrity and brains and represented a good cross-section of the community this might be tolerated. In fact, however, their standards of honesty and learning are low and their strength is drawn from a narrow segment of society. Furthermore they have brought into being, in the hooligan wing of NPC, an opposition as disreputable as themselves. If these young men are now given their head, and if Kano's past experience of riots, affrays and constant vilification became general throughout the Region, then personal liberty and parliamentary democracy are probably doomed. And if these two principles fall, then the rest of our structure will also come down in ruins.

The only remedy that I see for these calamitous prospects is to place, without delay, some restriction on our very wide conception of political liberty. I know what a dangerous exercise this is but suggest that if the restriction were based upon an insistence on truth in public utterances then no essential freedom would be lost.[19]

Tim then attached a draft showing how he thought the legislation for the control of political meetings and processions could be amended to curb licence without encroaching upon any fundamental liberties.

At the end of the year in his annual report on the Province, Tim warned:

Without doubt the people of the Province are on the move towards better things and, though there is far to go, they now have on their side more money, sounder health and greater knowledge and enlightenment than they have ever possessed in the past. If they are to continue to advance, however, they must preserve their ancient virtues of loyalty, tolerance, and good sense and disregard the false prophets whose stock in trade is destructive criticism, barren controversy, and defiance of constituted authority. The future depends upon the ability of average men during the next two decades to distinguish between the true and the false, to keep their eyes upon their ultimate objectives, and to put their faith in leaders who will take them there. If they fail in this, however, there is a danger of their drifting out of the broad stream of progress, on which they have hitherto made such notable advances, and losing themselves in the turbid backwaters of schism and anarchy.

Kano and Kaduna 1957–59

In May another London Conference was convened at Lancaster House to revise and update the 1954 Constitution. The Conference agreed that the Eastern and Western Regions would become fully self-governing within a matter of weeks and that the Northern Region, which was not yet ready for self-determination, would take over from the Governor control of the Civil Service, Finance and Information Services. This meant that the posts of Civil Secretary and Financial Secretary, held by KP Maddocks and Peter Scott, would be abolished and they would lose their executive functions. Hedley Marshall would have to remain as Attorney General as there was no Northerner qualified to take over from him. The Conference also decided that the post of Prime Minister of the Federation should be created and that there should be more ministers.

The Premiers of the three regions then asked for independence in 1959 and were promised that if, after the 1959 federal elections, the new House of Representatives should make a request for independence within the Commonwealth, the British Government would then do its best to accede by the date designated.

Tim returned to Kano at the end of June.

> Here we are, safely arrived after a good and uneventful journey. The plane was a Stratocruiser and we stopped at Rome but not Tripoli. There were not many people and I had no neighbour and plenty of elbow-room.

On arrival here I found the Sardauna and Co about to set off on the pilgrimage so within a few hours of landing I found myself going back to the airport to see them off.

The new room downstairs has been built and looks quite nice. For the Queen Mother's visit, in case of long delay, I shall have to set a camp bed up there and leave one wing for the QM and the other for the Lady-in-Waiting. North Carter, when drafting the programme, forgot that you weren't here and proposed to outrage decorum by leaving me alone in the house with the QM!

Next Monday and Tuesday are public holidays for Salla and the break will help me get things sorted out. I miss you very much and have no joy in life now. I hope you are all well.

Although getting used to another separation was always difficult, Berrice was perhaps quite glad of the excuse of the children to escape the social whirl of Kano.

After the royal visit and the Sardauna's return from his pilgrimage Tim wrote:

Well the Queen Mother's visit is safely over, thank goodness. We made the usual arrangements and, with two exceptions, everything went off as planned. The first slip was made by the Judge who failed to keep in touch with the Airport, consequently did not hear that the aircraft was arriving twenty minutes early, and missed his cue. I am sure that no one in the royal party noticed his absence but of course it was embarrassing for him and I think he feels it was our fault. The second slip was made by the Emir's wives: they were supposed to be waiting in their private 'saro' leading off the garden but when Lady Sharwood-Smith took HM in there the place was empty. Pam McClintock then scurried about and rounded up a couple of them for presentation. I thought Sharwood would explode when this news came through but he took it very calmly. The QM of course said and did all the right things but our private opinion was that it was duty rather than interest that impelled her. HE, however, seemed to think it was another great success and went away happy.

We should hear soon who his successor is to be: he said he thought he was not the best but the second best of the possible candidates. KP and Peter will soon cease to be members of Exco, KP becoming Deputy Governor and Peter Economic Adviser. Residents at the Conference asked for more pay but no promises were made. Meanwhile the Permanent Secretaries in Lagos get more than we do!

Great excitement in Kano over the arrest of Mahmuda dan Tata, the ne'er do well son of old Alassan. He got his pilgrims into an awful mess this year by failing to produce the money which they had deposited with him at the right place and time. Many of them are still stranded in Arabia or the Sudan and according to the Sardauna feeling against him was running so high in Jedda that if he had appeared he would have been lynched. This was after his agent there had been arrested trying to cash forged Bank drafts which had been stolen in Kano earlier in the year. Mahmuda was of course suspected of being implicated in this but there was no proof to connect him with it. Well last week the police got a search warrant and had a look in his safe and what do you think they found – not the evidence they were looking for but a forger's kit and £4990 in forged five pound notes. There is a rumour that his operator was one of the Indians.

I had a well-written letter from Carolyn today, except that she put Mr. H.A.S. Johnston Esq. on the address. I'm sorry Robin has been bored but soon he will have her to go out with. His wheel-marks still show in some of the garden paths: I had quite a pang when I came across them the other evening. Are you missing 'pole old Dad'!

Mallam Isa Wali came to drinks the other night. If I gave you fifty guesses you would never come up with what he proudly announced: that he can rock 'n' roll!

On the question of Sir Bryan Sharwood-Smith's successor, the Governor-General, Sir James Robertson had written to Sir John Macpherson at the Colonial Office in the following terms: 'The North will be the key Regional Governorship in the next five years. I believe that the North is far more potentially difficult than the south, and that while the Western and Eastern Regions can give us trouble and unrest, the Northern peoples are more warlike, far less assimilated to the Western way of looking at things and much more dangerous. During the next five years, the first results of the recent educational drive will begin to appear; and there will be a big output of new young semi-educated 'Mallam' class who, on all past experience, will question the basis of the existing authoritarian rule of Emirs and Native Authorities, and will wish no doubt to get rid of the British administration who at the moment keep the Region together. It is therefore essential that the new Governor should be the best man that can be found.'

Sir James had gone on to suggest three possible successors. His first choice was Sir Gordon Hadow of the Gold Coast, although he was not sure if he had enough experience with Muslims. His second choice was Ralph Grey but he was known to be unsympathetic to the North. Lastly he suggested Gawain Bell who had served in the Sudan for many years and since 1955 had been HM Political Agent in Kuwait.[1]

Not long afterwards it was announced that Sir Gawain Bell had been appointed Governor of Northern Nigeria and Berrice was keen to know more.

What do you know about Bell who is to be our new Governor? Kuwait to Kano seems rather a violent change, one so rich and the other so poor, but I suppose a knowledge of Arabic will help him a little in the north.

I decided to go to Poole to collect Carolyn. This as the result of a programme – actually in Panorama – drawing to the attention of parents the dangers of children, male and female, going about alone. It was horrifying, and over 8000 children under the age of ten are sexually assaulted a year, plus thousands more over the age of ten.

15. The Residency, Kano

C's report is very good and I'm sure she has worked hard. She is fourth in her form which has fifteen children in it. Her class work average was 84% and her exam average was 78%. I think she has done extremely well, perhaps you would write and congratulate her.

Robin had a most successful birthday but he misses you and keeps saying he wants to go home to Kano. I told him what you said about the wheel marks and the pang. He was pathetically pleased to know that you had thought of him and kept asking 'Does Daddy want me?' and 'Does Daddy love me?'.

As a result of the Lancaster House Conference a number of new ministries were being formed and much of the work of the Governor's office was going to be taken over by the Premier's Office. The new ministers would need expert advice from their civil servants and Sir Bryan was busy working out the redeployment of the entire Service. Naturally there were rumours going round that changes were afoot.

A lot of rumours are flying about concerning the impending changes. With Self-Government approaching so fast the theory is that we can no longer have the 2nd XI of the Administration at Kaduna and the 1st XI in the Provinces and that it is time to start swapping round. According to David Muffett, we are among those tipped for Kaduna. Does the thought appal you very much? Whatever job I got, there would be plenty of people senior to me and so life would be much less public than it is here. For you it would not be such fun as Sokoto or Bornu but once settled I think you would be happier than you have been here. Well, we must see what the future brings forth.

Berrice was not certain how she felt about Kaduna, but on the whole thought she would like it better than Kano because they would no longer be responsible for entertaining the most important VIPs. She was already dreading the thought of the new Governor's tour of inspection of the North scheduled to take place soon after her arrival.

Meanwhile, the Asian flu that had first been identified in China in February had reached Nigeria.

No letter from you for a whole week: I hope you are all right. Here the Asiatic flu has arrived and quite a lot of people have succumbed.

Well, our worst fears about Dan Amar were realised last week: little Alhaji suddenly got cerebral malaria[2] and died a few hours after being admitted to hospital. I wrote to Dan Amar the same evening and a couple of days later he came here and told me all about it. It was most harrowing: he broke down several times (the first time I have ever seen any of these people really over-mastered by emotion) and I felt like bursting into tears myself. This is the third son that he has lost and I am sure that Alhaji meant more to him than the rest of his family put together.

By the way, you were right all along about DG. Apparently he has made himself very cordially disliked in Kaduna first for his sycophancy towards the Sardauna and second for his rather unscrupulous use of the Premier's authority for furthering his own ends. Things have gone so far that people like Bruce Greatbatch and Hector Wrench are refusing to serve with him.

In Kaduna, Sir Bryan was finalising the restructuring programme. It was a delicate task because he had to be sensitive to the ministers' wishes but he was also determined that they should have the best top civil servants. Having served in Northern Nigeria since the 1920s he had become very close to the people and was afraid that unchecked power might lead to abuse, and that nepotism or personal prejudice might influence postings and promotions. The Premier was a very flamboyant character who could be warm-hearted, charming and generous, but he had always reacted badly to criticism or opposition. Lately he had become uncommunicative and remote, even shutting himself away in his home for days at a time and refusing to deal with the matters of state. Sir Bryan therefore considered it vitally important to choose a man with the right personality to be his Permanent Secretary. Although Tim was the youngest, by far, of the Senior Residents he was already outstanding. Both able and forceful he always said and did what he thought was right and Sir Bryan was confident that everyone would trust him, especially in times of doubt and difficulty.[3]

Tim's appointment as Secretary to the Premier contrasted very much with the fate of his great friend Peter Scott.

Well, we are definitely posted to Kaduna and I have to go there before the end of the month. I am to be Permanent Secretary to the Premier and Bruce Greatbatch is taking over Kano. My job was first offered to Waddle but he declined it on the ground that he did not want a change when he was so near the end of his service. At that time the post was to carry a salary of £2880 and an entertainment allowance. Now that I am to fill it Sharwood in his odd way decided that (I think) £2750 was enough and that no entertainment allowance was required. I don't mind about the entertainment allowance, though I think we should have had a small one, but I am rather annoyed about the reduction in salary. Its object was to avoid rousing the wrath and envy of the Directors though I don't think any of them would have grudged us the extra bit. Well, we mustn't grumble: I think that we shall be a good deal better off in Kaduna than in Kano.

My job will be (a) to run the Premier's Office and (b) co-ordinate the other Ministries. In the Administrative hierarchy I shall rank No 3 after HE and KP Maddocks, who is to be Deputy Governor, but when someone has to act as DG it will probably be Waddle and not I. In other words I shall be something of a back-room boy and I think that will suit us very well. Apart from HE and KP there are the Chief Justice, Brigadier, Attorney General and all the Ministers to take precedence over us and therefore to bear the burden of entertainment and visitors.

Now here is some news about pensions and lump-sum gratuities. In 1959, when the Region will be fully self-governing, civil servants will be entitled to retire and draw gratuities designed to compensate them for the premature termination of their careers. These will be calculated in accordance with their salaries and ages. Alternatively, if the Region wants them to stay on, they will be entitled to freeze their gratuities (which otherwise taper off to nothing) at the point most advantageous to themselves and continue in service. What is more, they will be allowed to cash in a part of those gratuities in the period between freezing and final retirement. Personally I think these terms are pretty generous and I hope that they will put an end to our financial worries. The prospect of having some capital to draw on by 1959 I find very cheering. Perhaps at last we can let ourselves go a bit and have a really good holiday.

Finally a word about Peter. I told you I think that the idea was to make him Economic Adviser. That of course meant the creation of a new post which only the Ministers could approve. At first they agreed to do so but suddenly the resentment that some of them feel against him flared up and they said that not only would they create no post but that they wanted him out of the country by September 1st. As KP is on leave and Peter was not only counting on his new job but on being Acting Deputy Governor as well, this fell on him as a terrible blow. It is pretty definite that Peter will have to go and his friends are now mainly concerned to secure a decent exit for him.

Unfortunately Peter had become involved with a Nigerian woman who was said to be the mistress of a high ranking African. Although he was highly respected by everyone for his intellect and wit, it was his excessive love of knowing what was going on behind the scenes in African ministerial as well as other circles that eventually caused his downfall.[4] It was sad because over the years he had probably done more than anybody to help young intellectual Africans adjust to the changing environment.

Berrice was naturally distressed to learn about Peter's misfortune but delighted at the prospect of leaving Kano and going to Kaduna.

Your long letter about Kaduna came this morning and I feel about twenty years younger. I'm so delighted that we are not returning to Kano: the thought of going back there has been hanging over me like a blanket and I have had awful waves of panic at the very idea of Kano again. I'm not saying that I shall never get het-up in Kaduna, but I know I shall be happier there – at the moment I'm simply bubbling over with relief. You'll never know how near I was to breaking point in Kano. What about you? Will you enjoy the work or not? I do hope you are pleased about it. I think we must make it quite clear at the beginning that we don't want too much social life. I think it would be quite a good idea if we followed Andrew Armstrong's example and only entertain at the weekends.

The pension and gratuity are very generous and it is marvellous to know that we shan't have such an uphill financial struggle. Oh, I feel so excited and happy about the change.

Poor Peter, what an end to his career in Nigeria and I feel very sorry for him. I'm sorry too that he won't be in Kaduna with us. I'm sure all this trouble could have been avoided if only he had found the right woman to marry.

Tim was relieved at Berrice's reaction to his new appointment and their future in Kaduna.

I can't tell you how relieved I was to get your letter and learn that you were pleased at the prospect of going to Kaduna. I was afraid that you might feel that you were exchanging the frying pan for the fire. In fact I am sure that we shall have a much more normal life there than we have ever had here. I do hope, however, that you will get out of the way of undervaluing yourself as you do: everyone here has enquired most kindly about you and people are ready enough to like you if only you would let them do so. In Kaduna we will make it plain that we need a rest from entertaining and I shall probably have to do a good deal of work in the evenings until I get on top of my new job. Anyway, whatever it is like, let's make the best of it. Yes, it is quite true that I didn't realise last tour how stretched you were. Not, at any rate, until the time of the Governor-General's visit and then I reproached myself for selfishness in not having let you go home. It was selfish I suppose but you know I do miss you badly when you aren't here. I also had the feeling that if you went then you would always want to go whenever anything of the sort appeared on the horizon. Perhaps I was wrong but I think I may have been right because I went through the same sort of crisis myself in the war when I returned to operations after being shot down. If you hang on you come through.

Wish you were here now because I feel the need to give you a very big hug. Anyway, I am delighted that you are so pleased at the change.

Tim left Kano and moved to Kaduna at the end of August.

Well, here I am, already installed in 7 Race Course Road, next door to Peter. We drove down from Kano yesterday and arrived about dusk in pouring rain. This didn't matter because Peter put me up for the night and I have spent today, Sunday, moving in here. I left most of the packing to the boys and I must say, on the whole, they did it very well. So far only two breakages have come to light, a white plate and an autumn spray. This house used to be Bruce Greatbatch's and it is just as well that you were not here to peer into corners because it was left very dirty. Still, by and large, it has been less of a struggle moving than I expected. I'm glad it is over though.

Controversy is still raging round poor Peter. He has been made Acting Deputy Governor but probably for only a month. Waddle is being recalled from leave to take over from him and he now suspects that he is being made to go not because of the hostility of the Ministers but because Sharwood wants to make good some of his promises to Waddle. I don't think this is true but he has come to believe it and is consequently very bitter against Sharwood. The result of it all is that Peter will probably be leaving for good at the end of September. For good, that is, so far as the north is concerned but he has been offered a Permanent Secretaryship in Lagos and is thinking of returning there. In his place, with a pension of £1900 p.a., I should go for good but of course it is rather different for him with few ties at home.

He says his house is better than this one and wants us to take it when he goes. You will be able to decide this when you have seen them both. As they are next door a change would be easy.

Inevitably, Tim's first week in the new job was hard work.

I have had an awful week, working twelve or more hours a day every day and no exercise or amusement of any kind. When I shake down I am sure that I shall enjoy my job but at the moment there is too much chaos and intrigue for my taste. The Sardauna, however, is being very easy and affable and I hope we shall get along well together.

Sharwood's time is nearly up now and next week will be full of functions including a dinner for 200 and a cocktail party for 500. KP arrives just before he goes in order to act as Governor until the new Governor arrives. On top of all this the House of Assembly and House of Chiefs are meeting and the new Prime Minister, Abubakar Tafawa Balewa, is paying his first formal visit to the North. By the time you arrive everyone (not least poor old dad) will be exhausted.

Berrice was pretty busy herself getting Carolyn ready for the new term and preparing for the journey to Kaduna.

I'm sorry you are having to work so hard and I hope you'll soon be able to ease up a bit.

We are in the midst of packing up and, as usual, I feel we shall never be ready in time. Carolyn has been frightful most of the time, she sulks and shouts at Robin and she never says please or thank you for anything. In fact, I shall be thankful when she goes back to school.

Simply longing to see you and don't forget you have to give Robin a big bear hug when you see him!

* * * * *

Kaduna 1958

In May KP Maddocks accepted a new appointment as Governor of Fiji and the Governor then offered the post of Deputy Governor to Tim. At great financial sacrifice, he turned it down because he felt he should continue to give the Premier his help and support in the difficult days leading up to self-government. Sir Gawain replied that he much admired the way in which Tim had put the interests of the Service and the Region before his own immediate personal prospects. He went on to say that although he would have preferred to have had Tim rather than anyone else helping him, he felt sure that he had in fact made the right decision.[5]

Berrice and Robin returned to England in June and Tim followed shortly afterwards, his leave for once coinciding with Carolyn's school holidays. In the three years since she had been a boarder they had spent barely six months together.

At the end of September delegates assembled in London for the resumed Constitutional Conference and a special reception was held at the Tate Gallery to welcome them.

The reception in the Tate was not as bad as I had feared. Ben Enwonwu's statue of the Queen was on display, a seated figure, and surprisingly good it is. Very dignified and very like. The nudes were discreetly screened but unfortunately one of the Ministers, probably quite innocently, was detected by a journalist peeping behind a screen. Or so we assume because the columnist William Hicky of the 'Express' has been ribald about this alleged curiosity and has thereby deeply offended the Ministers.

As I was saying goodbye to Lennox-Boyd he asked me if I was happy about everything and when I replied no, not altogether, he told me to go and see him next day. This I did. He was very affable but did not say at first what he wanted so I asked bluntly whether it was because he had heard of my throwing my weight about in the Colonial Office.[6] He grinned and said it was, so I apologised for having outraged the feelings of the officials but added that they on their side had made me cross by not keeping open minds. 'O never mind about that' he said 'all to the good'.

He then gave me five minutes to develop my argument and, as there was no more time, told me to write a brief paper for him personally to study and discuss with the Premier at Chequers next weekend. All this, as you can imagine, encouraged me a great deal after my frigid reception in the Colonial Office.

At Lancaster House the previous year, the question of Minority Groups had been raised and the Conference had referred the matter to a special Commission headed by Sir Henry Willink. Its remit was to advise what safeguards should be included in the Constitution to protect minorities, and, as a last resort, to recommend the creation of one or more new States.

The Commission toured round the country for several months listening to the problems, fears and aspirations of the different minority groups in each of the regions. In the Northern Region they found that the minorities were afraid of a swing back towards Islamic conservatism and the autocratic rule of the Emirs. Most of the greater chiefs were Muslims and it seemed likely that after independence they would become more powerful. Politically they feared that the Alkalai would use their position to act as agents for a political candidate and that the Emirs would use their bodyguard as a means of intimidation to prevent criticism. Socially, they objected to the fact that strict Muslims would not eat with non-Muslims and called them by contemptuous names, and that women were not allowed to vote in Muslim communities.

As far as the law was concerned, there were three kinds: Nigerian law based on the Common Law of England, Koranic Shari'a law, and Native law other than Muslim law. Shari'a law distinguished between Muslims and non-Muslims and the judiciary was closely associated with the executive. The evidence of a male Muslim was considered of greater value than that of a woman, a Christian or a pagan. In a homicide case, if the deceased was a Christian, Maliki law prescribed that the compensation should be half as much as for a Muslim while if the deceased was a pagan then the amount should be one fifth. There was therefore a real fear that Shari'a law would be interpreted more strictly in the future to the detriment of non-Muslims.

There was also the question of religious intolerance. In the North, there had long been hostility towards Christian missions, which had difficulty obtaining permission to build churches whereas Muslims could set up a mosque wherever they liked. The Minority Groups, both Christian and pagan, wanted the new Constitution to embody a statement on human rights that would give them freedom to practise their own religion.

Lastly, some of the non-Muslim, non-Hausa people who lived in the Middle Belt wanted to create a new State so that they would not be dominated by the Fulani and Hausas. The Prime Minister, Abubakar Tafawa Balewa, objected to this suggestion and told Sir Henry it was wrong that, having done so much to create a unified Nigeria, Britain should now divide it just before independence.

After due consideration, the Commission came out strongly against the creation of any new States. It argued that separation might cause more problems than it solved and that the human rights of the minorities could be better safeguarded within the existing political framework and by making it impossible to amend the constitution without the consent of the whole country. Finally, it insisted that the police should remain a national force and not be regionalised.[7]

At the start of the Conference *The Times* published two letters from eminent Nigerians expressing their views on how to resolve the major problems. Mr S.G. Okoku, Leader of the Opposition in the Eastern House of Assembly, wrote: 'The three major problems awaiting solution are the creation of more states, the adjustment of boundaries, and the entrenchment of fundamental rights in our constitution. ...If the conference cannot reach agreement on them they should be settled in the only way acceptable to citizens of democratic countries – that is through the ballot box. All issues on which the conference cannot agree should be referred to the people to decide... In the view of the Action Group the British Government has a primary responsibility not only to grant independence to Nigeria on April 2, 1960, without fail, but also to ensure that all the major outstanding problems are settled by democratic processes, if need be, before that date.'[8]

Mr M.E. Ogon, Chief Whip of the NCNC contested this view by saying: 'It has again and again been emphasised by the Action Group that Nigeria is a British creation and the solution of these major problems can best be handled by Whitehall. This unfortunate argument foreshadows a fallacious conclusion that the problems confronting Nigeria cannot be solved by Nigerians themselves. No one argues that an attempt should not be made to solve these problems, but it is the opinion of the majority of Nigerians that independence is an over-riding issue and that major problems left unsolved at the present constitutional conference should be solved by Nigerians themselves after independence.'[9]

The first week of the Conference passed off fairly well and Tim wrote:

> We have had a successful first week and have got through a lot of our agenda. If we could keep up the present pace we should finish before the 18th but I'm afraid we shall run into trouble over Minorities and possibly over Finance. Among our lot the federal tail is wagging the regional dog in a way I find rather disturbing and the Premier has more or less abdicated in favour of Abubakar Tafawa Balewa. The Emirs, moreover, are kept on the sidelines and, as far as I can see, seldom consulted.
>
> I ran into Hudson [CO] at the Colonial Office and he promptly asked me to lunch. The Secretary of State has also bidden us to a buffet supper at his house on Monday: I shall be interested to see what it is like. Otherwise no boats being pushed out by our friends from the Colonial Office.

The second week of the Conference was much more difficult. After consideration of the recommendations of a special finance commission, which concluded that the Western Region was receiving too much and the Northern Region too little, agreement was reached on the redistribution of revenue among the governments of the Federation, and the North was allocated £500,000 for the year 1958–59. On the minorities issue, some of their fears were allayed by granting their request for basic fundamental human rights to be written into the new constitution but the question of new states remained unresolved. At the end of the week, the Secretary of State for the Colonies proposed three possible solutions: '1. The plan to grant independence should go forward without any further consideration of the problem of new states. 2. Attention should be given to the creation of new states now, but that the British Government would have to be satisfied of the economic and administrative stability of any new states before granting independence to the Federation as a whole. 3. Entrenchment should be made by the conference in the constitution providing for the consideration of the problem after independence had been attained.'[10]

Tim was unable to go home for the weekend and Berrice was sympathetic:

> It is disappointing that you are not here for the weekend. You did sound depressed and I'm very sorry things are going badly, especially after all the effort and trouble you have taken. I was shattered to hear that they hadn't pressed for more money for the North – is it sheer laziness or are they really not interested.

After nearly sixty years of British rule, Nigeria was still one of the most socially backward and economically underdeveloped countries in the Commonwealth. In the North, this was partly due to Islamic self-sufficiency and reluctance to adapt to Western ways which could be construed as the fault of the people, but, in Tim's opinion, the UK had not fully discharged its material and moral obligations and should share responsibility for the Region's plight. No other territory in the British Commonwealth had received so little grant-aid or reached the brink of independence so poor as Northern Nigeria.

During the four decades from when the North became part of the Protectorate and Colony of Nigeria (1914), it had received much less than its fair share of Nigerian funds and had been left to manage as best it could. Nor had it received its fair share of grants from the CD&WF. In this case, if distribution had been proportionate to population it would have got double the amount and if it had been based predominantly on need (the principle which the British White Paper of 1955 laid down) it would have been entitled to even more.

Successive British and Nigerian Governments had done nothing to prevent a gulf opening between the two halves of what was then a unitary country, and this neglect constituted the first of a series of financial deprivations that the North had experienced.

The second occurred when the Federal Constitution was introduced in 1954. Because of a faulty formula for the division of revenue between the regions, the North during the ensuing years received at least £2m and perhaps as much as £4m less than it should have done. And now the Fiscal Commission had just succeeded in imposing further deprivations. After pointing out the previous Commission's error, it not only omitted to recommend any reimbursement but did the North a further disservice by awarding it only 40% of the distributable pool of revenue instead of the 54% to which, by virtue of its population and need, it was entitled.[11]

During the third week, all the delegates accepted the Secretary of State's third solution to the question of new States. They also agreed that any subsequent resolutions to alter the boundaries and status of the Regions after independence must first be approved by both Houses of the Regional Assemblies concerned, then by both Houses of the Federal Government, and finally by a two-thirds majority in a plebiscite held in the area to be altered.

Finally, the conference agreed that the granting of independence in April 1960 would necessitate a rush in handing over the administration and that October would be a more acceptable date.

Tim left feeling gloomy. The policy of HMG to deny grant-aid to colonies after independence did not augur well for Nigeria's future prospects. To attract private investment, first there needed to be an adequate infrastructure and second political stability. Unless they received further substantial aid they would be unable to develop the one and in danger of losing the other. Their reserves were very low and if they were cut from grant-aid they would have to rely for future development on what they could raise in the way of loans. What infuriated Tim was the inconsistency with which HMG applied its policy since some of the other African countries were being offered far more generous grants.

Although he had found one or two people who were sympathetic to the North's predicament, the reception given to their arguments in the Colonial Office had been cold and hostile. In an unguarded moment one official had told Tim: 'You know if the North opted out of the Commonwealth I don't think that anyone in this country would lose much sleep'. Another, more eminent, had said 'We have a lot of commitments in East and Central Africa and I don't know that we shall be able to do much more for your people in West Africa'.

Tim was convinced that it was not simply an economic problem. Although the North currently had some economic momentum, if this were lost through lack of development funds they would soon stall and spin. The sequence of events that he could foresee was that failure to progress in the economic field would strengthen the opposition, most of which was in any case irresponsible, to a point where the Regional Government would take fright and have recourse to repressive measures. Then, when the lid had been firmly screwed down for a few years, the pressure would gradually build up until the inevitable explosion took place. Finally, when stability had been lost and a revolutionary government was in power, there would be a demand at home for aid, probably on a much more massive scale, to be given to the North so that it did not fall into the clutches of the UAR or the USSR.

At the beginning of November he returned to Nigeria and Berrice was disconsolate.

> You've been gone just a day and I feel completely lost and sick without you. To me, these awful partings get more and more dreadful and I long for the day when they will be over. What a wonderful day it will be.
>
> I pray that you'll have a safe journey. Do take care of yourself and don't work quite so hard this tour. I must get busy with some sewing and house cleaning to try and make the next twelve weeks go quickly, but I'm afraid they'll seem more like twelve years. It is wonderful to love you even more now than I did when we were married.
>
> Robin is feeling your departure very much. He was aggressive and troublesome yesterday and wouldn't go to sleep at night. At 10 p.m. he burst into tears and said he wanted to be with you. The first thing he said this morning was that he hated this house and wanted to go to Kaduna. I'm afraid he feels things very deeply and it is distressing to see him trying to bottle things up.

When Tim arrived back in Kaduna there were rumours circulating about the Conference.

> There has been a bit of unpleasantness here this last week. The cause this time was an allegation that officials were going round Kaduna criticising the results of the London Conference and saying that the North could have done much better than it did.

This, as you can imagine, caused great umbrage. It looks as if it all arose out of an indiscreet remark of Richard Adams's [DO] which the Emir of Kano passed on to the Premier. Having been very careful myself in what I said, I was particularly annoyed at getting involved in this way. I think the misunderstanding has now been cleared up.

These events, as you may imagine, have made me think more about the future. I told Bruce when I returned that I was thinking of applying to freeze for three to five years but hadn't made up my mind. He advised at least five to give other people confidence but this last episode, coming on top of the others, has made me feel that my welcome will not last nearly so long. I think I shall put in for three but make it clear to Himself that I am ready to go sooner if we don't get along. This would mean a smaller pension, of course, but I know you wouldn't mind that. I was looking at a UTC calendar the other day with coloured photographs of Switzerland and thinking how lovely it would be, when both children are at school, to have enough money to wander quietly about the Continent. My sense of duty makes me feel that I must hang on here as long as I am needed but if, through no fault of mine, I become a political casualty, then I shall be quite ready to go and shall not eat my heart out like Peter.

Tim then went off to visit Kano and Wudil where the Premier had just opened the Teacher Training College. It was a nice break and he enjoyed escaping from Kaduna.

Sorry not to have written sooner but I have had a frightfully busy week after being away in Kano. I came back by the new road. About twenty miles is not made up and there is a bridge to be finished but even so it is much quicker and I took only four hours instead of the usual five. The country is more interesting too.

Do you remember Mrs Akilu, the African wife whom you rather took to? I'm afraid she has just died in hospital of strangulated hernia. The doctors operated but the thing had gone too far. On top of that, the day before Akilu returned from Arabia, his younger child also died. I feel terribly sorry for him.

The Premier is going to Sokoto for twelve days over Christmas and the New Year. Much as I should have liked to go too, I feel that I must go and see the Provinces I don't know while I have the chance. I am therefore planning a visit to Kabba and Ilorin. It is a pity that you will not be here because I hope to have a nice quiet Christmas on the barge.

HE took me aside the other day and said that they proposed to give me a CMG in the New Year's honours and was it acceptable? I had long suspected that in honours, as in most other things, the North got less than its fair share so I said I would think about it and let him know. I then searched the Colonial Office list and found that although we got more than the E & W we came off worse than the Federation and the East African colonies. I therefore told him that I didn't want the thing. He seemed faintly horrified and told me (a) that he thought by refusing it I should do the North more harm than good and (b) that in this list the CO had treated us very handsomely with a KBE for the Sardauna, a CBE for the Makama and CMGs for Tom Letchworth and myself. Anyway he talked me round and I have accepted but I don't know whether I have done right or not. It elates me far less than getting my colours at school.

Now here is a tit-bit of scandal. T-L and Miss L went away together and registered in the Kano Central Hotel as Mr and Mrs T-L. This was a bit risky in itself but what they had overlooked was that their illicit weekend coincided with the end of the school holidays with the result that the KCH was full of Kaduna parents seeing off their children so the guilty couple were almost constantly on the run!

Berrice was pleased about the CMG but exasperated with her daughter.

I'm very glad that all your hard work is being recognised in the New Year – congratulations. I understand how you feel about it, but I can also understand how HE felt. Anyway, I'm glad you have accepted it, but you'll be more difficult to live up to than ever!

Carolyn's report was quite good – average term marks 71% – and fourth in her form, but she had five order marks and Miss Jeanes and her form mistress are not at all pleased with her conduct.

Since she has been home she just wanders about the house all day and never wants to do anything. It has been a glorious warm sunny day, but she said it was too cold to go out in the garden. I forced her into a walk this afternoon, but she baited Robin all the time and we were all thankful to get home again. I know it is boring for her here, but she doesn't make any effort at all to amuse herself. She couldn't even suggest one thing she wanted for Christmas.

I really am very worried about her and I wonder if we should write to Miss Jeanes about her. She couldn't even be bothered to get on with the Christmas decorations. She is very well and eats well but complains about the food and says we never have anything nice, although I always ask her what she wants. Robin gets very upset and I'll be glad when the holidays are over.

After Christmas Tim described his trip down the river.

I set off from Kaduna after lunch and got to Bida about 7 p.m. It is 210 miles and the road is not good. At Bida I stayed in the CRH but was bidden to dinner by the SDO. Next day I went on to Baro which is 55 miles beyond Bida. I had never been there before and was interested to see it. There are some low hills coming right down to the Niger and the port is perched on a rather narrow ledge between them. We found our launch all right but, as the river was rather low, had some difficulty in getting the car onto the barge. In fact it got stuck twice and finally had to be man-handled on board with much heave-hoing.

The Nedeco launches, which have now been taken over by the new Inland Waterways Department, are very superior to anything we have ever met before. The forward cabin has two big berths with Dunlopillo mattresses and doors on to the fore-deck so that there is a through breeze. Then comes the saloon with dining table and chairs and finally galley to starboard and BG and small bath to port. The run from Baro to Lokoja took us eight hours and we got there just at dusk. At first the country was pretty flat but for the last thirty or forty miles the river runs between flat-topped hills. John Baker is Resident now and he put me up for the first night. After a night in Lokoja John and I went on together by launch to Idah. The first half of the journey is through the most picturesque stretch of the whole river with quite big hills on both sides. I took quite a lot of snaps which I hope will give you a good idea of it: I had no idea it was so pretty.

At Idah we were met by St. Elmo [Nelson] who put me up and fed both of us. The little princess has gone her way and there is now a new wife, a young Australian. St. Elmo has plenty of money of his own and by spending it on the house and garden he has made them most attractive. The new Government Reservation Area is on a ridge with a very fine view of the river. There are about a dozen people in the station, all told, and they all came in for drinks. Afterwards he gave us a very good dinner for which, at his special request, we dressed. I had been told by John that he was particularly keen on this so I agreed gracefully when it was suggested. The new doctor there is Imam and I got the impression that, though slightly appalled at the remoteness of Idah, they were both pleased with the way the Europeans had accepted them. They now have two children.

Next day we crossed by ferry to Agenebode in the Western Region, and drove 95 miles to Okene which stands at 1500 feet and is set among hills that look very like the hills of the Plateau. The town is quite large but, as nearly all the roofs are pan, far from picturesque. In the station there is a reservoir for the water supply which constitutes a very pretty lake where people can fish and even sail. Just below this there is a small swimming pool where, after we had done our work, we had a bathe and a picnic lunch. Very nice except for troublesome sand-flies. Trevor Clark is the SDO there and has his old mother with him. In the next dispositions list they are thinking in Lokoja of showing: i/c Division – Mrs Clark and 1 child.

The West is very different from the North: few people and obviously much richer. In the villages and towns, instead of there being a few big houses, it seemed that practically everyone could afford a two storey house with a pan roof. The other thing that struck me was the lack of cultivation: the people there must import nearly all their food.

From Okene we drove back to Lokoja the same day, Christmas Eve. I then took up residence in my house boat. It had only a shower instead of a bath and the BG was rather cramped but otherwise it was nearly as good as the launch in its accommodation and fittings which included electric light and fans. It got rather hot in the evenings but when I was there always cooled off at night so I was very comfortable and had three days relaxation.

On Sunday we set out for Kabba from Lokoja and drove through the hills where David got his lion. I gather that he shot it out of the window of his car. Needless to say, I saw nothing. Kabba is a much more attractive place than I had ever imagined, in fact I preferred it to Okene. It is about the same altitude and has black granite hills round about and excellent views. You would like it very much. The DO there is a young man called Davies who had his fiancée staying with him, a girl who works in the Ministry of Land. She struck me as rather prim and tight-lipped and I decided that she stood in no great moral jeopardy. After lunch I said goodbye to John Baker and set off for Ilorin, 150 miles away. One of my tyres had already developed a blister and been changed for the spare and I had not covered 20 miles before another one went. I reduced speed to 35 mph and drove very gingerly with the blistered tyre making a slapping noise at every revolution. Darkness descended when I was still thirty or forty miles out and I was most thankful to arrive safely.

I enjoyed my five days in Ilorin very much and Chris was a very good host. The Residency is like the Bauchi one, very nice but slightly marred by poor timber. My programme was not too arduous and so, besides seeing a good deal and meeting everyone, I got two games of tennis and one of squash. On New Year's day I drove out with the two African ADOs to Lafiagi. It is one of the few remaining one-man stations and, after hearing Bob Longmore on the subject, I expected it to be pretty grim. Actually it is not a bad little place at all though the NAs are minute and penniless. We saw the grave of the DO who was shot by his cook. The story about their playing dice to decide who slept with the cook's wife is a myth!

On the way back I stopped at Jebba and climbed the hill to look at the old station where Maiholi started as a small-boy in 1896. The stilts on which the houses were built show exactly where each one was and there is a well-kept little cemetery.

On arrival back here I got your rather gloomy letter. I am sorry and worried to hear that Carolyn is behaving badly again but I can't help feeling that the cause is boredom and the fault partly ours.

Just before flying out to join him, Berrice was in her usual state of panic.

Carolyn and Mummy were very pleased to see your CMG in the paper this morning and send their congratulations.

I have at last got Carolyn interested in a book by Gerald Durrell and it is being a great success. His books are about animals and I love them. I must try and get her some of his other books.

She has been a great help in the house recently and seems to be much easier to live with. She still has her off moods, but things have improved enormously.

I'm afraid this is going to be another gloomy letter, but I'm worried to death about money. We owe £154–0–8 for bills plus school fees £79–4–4. Can you do anything to help please? I'm absolutely desperate and if we are in this state now before Robin has even started school we must try to sell the house.

I dread all the packing up and cleaning, but I shall be thankful to have a change. Things have got on top of me and I worry about all the things that need to be done to the house. I think the thing that gets me down more than anything is not having a soul to talk to except the family. Next leave we must try to have a real holiday for a short time – I feel it's too much to come straight home from Nigeria and plunge into housework at once. I'm always in a 'state' by the time we come home and I never seem to have time to recover. It will be easier when Robin and Carolyn are both at school. At the moment the housework is like a treadmill – I just go on and on and there is nothing to show for all the effort. In other words I'm completely down in the dumps. Still I shall feel better when I'm with you again. I simply hate being away from you.

* * * * *

Kaduna 1959

Northern Nigeria was set to achieve self-government in March and the date chosen was the 15th because it was the anniversary of the overthrow of the Fulani Empire by the British.

Tim thought it would be fitting to make a symbolic gesture to the Northern Regional Government to commemorate the occasion. His idea was that the Queen's Own Nigeria Regiment should return the flag kept in their museum, which was believed to be the original Holy Standard raised by Usuman Dan Fodiyo. However, when he approached Major General Exham, GOC Nigerian Military Forces, there seemed to be some doubt as to its authenticity. Research had revealed that the standard captured at Sokoto in 1903 had subsequently been lost and that the flag in QONR's possession, which was taken at the Battle of Burmi, was unlikely to be the same one. Even so, as Burmi was the last stand of the diehards,

Tim was sure that this flag would have great sentimental value for the Northern Muslims generally and the Sultan's family in particular.

He had recently read *Maimaina*, the reminiscences of an old gentleman in Bornu called Sarkin Askira who had been present at Burmi and who, in company with Captain Mundy, had found the body of Sarkin Musulmi Atahiru and identified it with the help of some of the wounded in the vicinity. Although he made no mention of it in his book, Tim had little doubt that he would remember the flag being found if it was retrieved at the same time. He therefore wrote to the Resident of Bornu, Robert Eustace, requesting him to find out whether there had been any weapons or standards near the body of Sultan Atahiru. Sarkin Askira told the Resident that there were plenty of dead bodies around and weapons, and he could remember two very soiled white flags which were partly furled and tied to two short bamboo sticks. He said two white cloth flags were always carried on either side of the Sarkin Musulmi in battle and they must have fallen from the hands of the flag bearers when they were killed. He added that he had not mentioned them in his book because they were of no value to anyone and once Atahiru was killed they were of no use.

Having satisfied himself that the flag was indeed one of the two carried by Sultan Atahiru at Burmi,[12] and having therefore confirmed its historic value, Tim wrote again to the GOC asking him to approach the 1st Battalion on the subject of giving it up. He argued that it would be inappropriate for the Battalion to retain the flag as a trophy and that if it were not restored voluntarily there would almost certainly be a demand in the future that it should be given back. He thought it would be much better to anticipate events and make a gesture that was appreciated rather than to delay until they found themselves in a position of having to bow to popular demand or enter into a damaging controversy.[13] And so, at the self-government celebrations that were held after the end of Ramadan, Tim presided at a short ceremony during which the Queen's Own Nigeria Regiment handed back the flag to the Sultan of Sokoto. To commemorate its surrender, Tim presented their Commanding Officer with a silver statuette of a Nigerian soldier of the 1903 period, subscribed to by the Northern British administrators. The Premier expressed his appreciation of the gesture by saying, 'The exchange of this standard and this statuette symbolises all that has been achieved in a half century that began as war, and now ends in co-operation and friendship between us and the United Kingdom. May I say too, it is also a symbol of that characteristic British trait of turning enemy into friend.'[14]

At the end of the summer term, Carolyn joined the family in Kaduna for a happy holiday. Robin, who was now six years old, had a passion for cars and liked nothing better than to 'work' on Tim's Chevrolet during the breakfast hour. Much to everyone's amusement, Tim often went out to find that Robin had jacked it up and taken off a wheel! His reaction was a mixture of irritation at being held up and admiration that Robin was so mechanically minded. The Sardauna, who was very fond of children, nicknamed him Makaniki, which is Hausa for mechanic.

In August there was a small ceremony at which HE the Governor presented Tim with his CMG in the presence of the Sardauna and the Emir of Kano. Shortly afterwards Berrice and the children had to return to London to buy Carolyn a new uniform for her secondary school. Meanwhile, Tim's future had become rather uncertain.

> Many thanks for your cable. Having had all my eggs in one basket, I was very relieved to hear that you had all arrived safely.
>
> On Friday the question of my future was brought to a head in an unexpected way. A deputation of ministers, led by you can guess who, went to the Premier and said that Mr. J. must go because he was thwarting the Regional Government. The particular instance they gave proved on investigation to be groundless and was easily explained away. The Premier has been very good in supporting me but of course cannot ignore a concerted move of this sort. His solution is that I should succeed Waddle but he and HE naturally have to be sure that as Deputy Governor I should be acceptable to the others and that is where we now stand. After this I clearly cannot go on where I am nor do I want to. As for becoming DG, I am so sickened by this treatment that I am by no means certain that I want even that and I have told HE that unless I am accepted wholeheartedly and without any reservations whatever I shall go. This move explains all the odd things that have happened in the last couple of years and personally I am glad that things have come to a head. I feel

that all the right is on my side so I have not worried and have let things take their course without losing any sleep.

Whichever way things turn out I expect to take leave fairly soon. Bruce, who will probably succeed me, returns from leave on Sept. 21 but, as Nicky will already have gone, a new Resident Kano will have to be found before he can come here and take over. It is too early to predict the date but I think late October or early November are probable. If I am to go for good I think that I shall try and get a job in the Commonwealth Relations Office: it was revealed the other day that they are short of staff and they were advised to recruit more from HMOCS. Furthermore I noticed in the paper that Cumming-Bruce had been made High Commissioner for NZ (= Ambassador) and I thought that that was pretty revealing. He struck me as just the type that NZ'ers would not take to. If I was successful in getting a job with the CRO – and I think that in these circumstances even the Colonial Office would give me a helping hand – I should no doubt start at HQ in London and then go abroad later. Still, it may not come to that and we must wait and see.

Tim was considered to be very tough and had been described as 'the man of steel' by at least one expatriate Permanent Secretary. He was an ideal administrator but he perhaps lacked the flexibility and social ease required of a politician and in those years of transition of power all the officers had to be politicians to some degree.

Having attained internal self-government, the countdown had started towards independence and the Sardauna and ministers generally were taking stronger lines. Appointments to senior jobs were a significant issue. They were not keen on many of the older generation expatriates who had known them a long time. A good number had upset NPC members in the past, often quite innocently and usually fairly, but it could be held against them and several either retired or were posted 'out of the way'. As head of the Civil Service, Tim had to arbitrate on every case and it was a wretched burden for him[15], but he was always at pains to maintain his impartiality and be fair when everyone seemed to be at cross-purposes with one another.

One theory suggests that it was the Sardauna himself who wanted a new Permanent Secretary – one who would acquiesce to his wishes – but because he liked Tim personally he asked the ministers to push for his removal. On the other hand, the Federal Minister of Defence, Muhammadu Ribadu, who was a prominent member of NPC, had it in for the Northern Administration generally and might well have led the deputation. Equally there may have been a Sokoto or Kano minister who had crossed swords with him when he was Resident and saw the opportunity for revenge.

Because of his accelerated promotion, Tim had been a victim of back-biting and another theory suggests that it was an expatriate – old rival of Sharwood-Smith – who led the deputation of ministers against him, although it might have been the ministers themselves who were anxious to get the top administrative jobs.

A further factor was the alarming degree of corruption that existed at almost all levels in both the Public Service and the NA Service. Some of those who were specially trained to protect Public funds were themselves perverting their skills in the direction of deliberate fraud.[16] Tim would have found this dishonesty totally unacceptable. Some people said that he was too straight and should have bent a little but he knew that the Westminster-style of government would never survive in Nigeria unless there was a drastic diminution in corrupt practices.[17]

In his next letter Tim had more definite news about his future.

I thought of you and Carolyn yesterday and hoped that you got on all right. Tell me all about it when you write. You must try to get someone for her to play with in the Christmas holidays because she seems hopelessly lost on her own.

I learnt today that the Premier told HE that his colleagues would have no objection to my translation into Waddle's shoes. I had made it clear that I could accept no reservations but they apparently expressed themselves as 'perfectly happy' at the arrangement. So that, unless they suddenly change their minds, is what it is to be. In a way I feel relieved that this time the choice was made for me and that I really had no option. After the hurly-burly of the last two years I am looking forward to a quieter life. Waddle always complains that there is nothing to do but I think I shall occupy my spare time by digging among the old files for literary material that I can perhaps use after I retire.

We don't yet know who is to succeed me but I think that it will be Bruce Greatbatch. Dougie Pott has at least as good a claim but I doubt whether another of our generation will be wanted in that job. If Bruce comes here we shall have to look round for a new Resident Kano and until we find one I shall not be able to hand over and come on leave. I shall try to get away by October 20th at the latest so that I can have three clear months at home.

The Premier and party are off to Ghana tomorrow for five days. He has been extremely affable to me recently, touch wood, and the trouble with the others also seems to have blown over.

Berrice was very relieved at the prospect of Tim becoming Deputy Governor.

I have just read your letter and I feel I must write to you at once to tell you how delighted and relieved I am that you will – barring accidents – take over from Waddle. The thought of your getting a job with the CRO and probably vanishing to the wilds of Australia or somewhere, has depressed me most dreadfully this week and now I feel quite light-headed with relief. Does this mean that if you do – or are able to do – two or three years as DG you will be able to retire for good? I do so hope it does for many reasons – mainly because of the children and because it is high time you and I had some time together without having Robin or Carolyn hampering us. Anyway, we can talk about this when you come home. It really is heavenly to think that you will be home next month and I'm longing to see you. I'm more than thankful that you won't have much work to do in Waddle's job: I've been very worried about you for some time because you work too hard and you have had such a very difficult time recently and I do so hate to see you looking so tired.

Mummy saw Reggie yesterday and found out a bit more about the caravans in the field next door. They are owned by a London man who has bought the two bits of land and he intends to develop the sites. This sounds rather alarming.

Meanwhile Tim was still awaiting confirmation of his appointment.

I had hoped before now to have had news about my future but there is still none. I saw HE tonight for a talk and he said that he had followed up his letter with a cable. If I became DG there is always the possibility that the job may be abolished next year and that I may have to look for another. This is a risk that has to be accepted and if I had once acted as OAG I imagine that I should be able to pick up something else without too much difficulty. It might even be UK Commissionship in Kaduna which would probably mean half the work and twice the money.

The Emir of Argungu[18] has retired in order to avoid dismissal. I must say I feel sorry for him. I had to go and see him the other day to find out where he wanted to live and it was clear that the bottom had fallen out of his world. When he is settled I must send him something in place of the things he gave us.

I'm afraid there is little or no hope of getting back in time for Carolyn's half-term, but I don't think it will be much longer.

Berrice was naturally sorry about the delay but had some interesting news for Tim.

A most odd thing happened this afternoon. A very nice woman called and when I opened the door she said 'I hope you don't mind but I've come to ask a personal question – is your house for sale?' I replied no and then she said she had always had her eye on Four Winds and that it was just the sort of house she wanted. By this time I had asked her to come in because there was a terrific gale blowing. She was so interested that I took her over the house and she said it was just what she wanted and would we let her know if we thought of selling.

Tim at last received the confirmation he had been waiting for but there were several things he had to do before going on leave.

I was hoping to get away early next week but I'm afraid it will not be until the 5th of November because the Premier is giving a cocktail party for me on the 4th – the only day he can manage.

So far as I am concerned the time can't come too soon. In the last week we have been overwhelmingly busy with about three major problems to deal with simultaneously. On top of all this Charles M. has got involved in a bitter controversy with a Committee of Enquiry – mostly African – appointed to investigate the alleged waste and muddle at Samaru. I have been roped in to try to settle the dispute and waste a lot of my time listening to each side thundering against the other. Charles I think is right but his manner has antagonised the Committee and the result is that both sides are as stubborn and b-minded as they can be.

The news of the enquiries about Four Winds is particularly cheering because I have been worrying about it ever since we first heard about the caravans. We must not appear to be too eager to do so, but if she is prepared to pay a decent price I feel sure we should sell.

I think I ought to have a night in London to see the Aunts so I shall catch the 11 o'clock train, d.v., on Saturday 7th. It is a wonderful thought and I feel happier than I have for weeks. This leave I intend to put Nigeria out of my head.

Longing to see you again.

Kaduna 1960

Tim was due to return to Nigeria as Deputy Governor at the end of January and Berrice would remain in England so that Robin could start school. Although there was a good little school in Kaduna that he could have attended, it seems she had not been able to conquer her demons and preferred the lonely life of Devon.

Before leaving England, Tim visited the Colonial Office and wrote a quick farewell letter.

> I got all my chores done yesterday and so have time today to sit down and write you a letter before I go off.
>
> At the Colonial Office I was taken in to Hilton Poynton and had about twenty minutes talk with him. He seemed very affable and had not forgotten, as I thought possible, that he stayed with us in Kano. Afterwards Eastwood took me to his club for lunch. He too made himself pleasant and gave me a good meal. I think HE must have dropped them a hint that I rather resented their past neglect. Nothing was said about my future except by Hilton P who enquired if I intended to stay on and then seemed surprised to learn that there was a probability of my job being abolished. That just showed, I thought, how ineptly the CO runs our service.
>
> After lunch I went to Nigeria House to see Gilbert Stephenson. He hasn't got a job yet and has no idea what he will do when he retires in July. He told some alarming stories about the new northern Commissioner – orgies in the small and not so small hours bringing complaints from the neighbours, staff

always giving notice, Selfridges pressing for the payment of £500 in unsettled bills, whisky ordered and consumed by the dozen, in short fine goings-on for a Muslim diplomat.

I hope Robin is settling down well at school and that all is well for both of you.

The new job meant moving to the Deputy Governor's House, which was on the other side of the racecourse and only a few minutes away from their old house.

Here I am, safely installed in the new house. We had a good flight and arrived at Kano just after dawn on a brisk morning with fairly thick Harmattan.

I had breakfast with Dick Greswell and then drove out to Dambatta to have a look round. Unfortunately young Sarkin Bai was away in Lagos but I was able to turn aside and look at my Fogolawa road, which I was glad to find in good condition even though it had just come through the groundnut season. The faithful Maiholi[1] showed up of course and drove out to Dambatta with us. This trip occupied the morning very satisfactorily and at 12.30 we flew on to Kaduna in a Dakota.

Yesterday evening the Premier gave a big farewell party for Waddle and Sylvia. It was very like mine in November with speeches and Waddle having to wear his presentation riga. The Premier seemed very affable and enquired after you all with his usual special mention of Makaniki.

The party gave me a good opportunity of getting round and meeting people again and there were of course dozens of enquiries after you and the children. Today, Sunday, I have been able to do very little because all our loads are still in store. I suppose I should have mentioned them in a letter but I thought that someone would have the sense to take them out before the weekend. This house is rather ramshackle but I think I shall be comfortable when I have settled in. In the dining room we have Lugard's table which still has the stains of his medicine bottles. If you remember, he suffered regular bouts of malaria and dysentery. The noise of the traffic has not worried me and at the back there is a very nice shady veranda, with cane chairs, which overlooks the lawn and flower-bed. Waddle has left the garden in very good shape, lots of phlox in flower and plenty of vegetables.

Tim soon settled down in the new job. One of his first tasks was to submit the Regional Intelligence Committee's report, which presented a fair picture of the Federal Elections in the Northern Region. He added his own comments in a covering letter to the Secretary of State for the Colonies, Iain Macleod.

The NPC had originally hoped to win at least 150 seats but the reverse that they suffered in the Northern Cameroons plebiscite filled them with apprehension lest there should be a similar landslide in the Federal Elections. Consequently the results came as a relief to them. Since the elections they have had some success in persuading other members to cross the floor and they hope that with further accessions of this kind they may still reach their target. Where the party failed their failure for once was not ascribed to the Administration. I gather, however, that some of the Ministers are inclined to blame the influence of the Christian Missions for their losses in the non-Muslim areas and if this idea takes a firm hold it will, I fear, lead the Regional Government to adopt a less liberal attitude in the future than in the past.[2]

In his next letter to Berrice he had some news about salaries.

I was delighted to get your letter and learn that you were not feeling too depressed or downcast. I hope things continue to go well and that Robin is happy at school.

The salary revision committee have recommended increases of 15% on the lower salaries and 12.5% on the medium with a maximum increase of £300. We of course shall bump against this ceiling but all the same we shall go up from £3240 to £3540. What is more, if Exco accept the recommendations as is expected, there will be arrears from Sept. 1st.

The Premier is said to be contemplating a sweeping re-shuffle of his Ministers and this may include some dismissals. The Ministers whose heads are said to be in danger of rolling are Mallam Audu Buba, the Minister of Social Welfare and Co-operatives, Dan Buram Jada, Minister of Northern Cameroons Affairs, and Mallam Mu'azu Lamido, a Minister of State. It is possible that as a corollary to changes among the Ministers the Premier will advise me that parallel changes among the Permanent Secretaries are desirable. Relations between Ministers and Permanent Secretaries have been better in recent months however and I am in no way alarmed at this prospect.

I am sure that I shall be happy in this job but I am missing you very badly.

As expected, Tim found the workload very much reduced compared with his last job and a lot less stressful.

> Life in the office is very placid and I am enjoying the change. It is ironical that I should be paid a third as much again for doing a third of the work. Bruce is not finding things easy although he has Harry Seaford and Pat Grier and Ali Akilu as Nos 2, 2a and 3.
>
> Margery Perham was here not long ago and I had her to dinner and then next day took her along to a meeting of the historical society. I had about twenty minutes alone with her but it wasn't enough and I got no chance of saying a lot of the things that I wanted to. She is bringing out the second volume of Lugard in July. I liked her better this time.
>
> I have just had a nice man called Owen staying with me. He is Chairman of the UN Technical Assistance Board and is based in New York. He told me that although he has to entertain a good deal it is all done in restaurants so that at home his family life is not disturbed. Even so, he gets an allowance of $2000 a year.
>
> Yesterday I had lunch at Government House to meet Billy Graham. He was young and good-looking but HE and I agreed afterwards that we had detected no magnetism and that if we hadn't known we should have taken him for a perfectly ordinary young American. In other words amiable but undistinguished.

Other foreign visitors included Douglas Bader from whom Tim learned news of some of his wartime friends. With more time on his hands, he started playing polo again.

> You will be surprised to hear that I have taken up polo again, for the moment anyway. Hector Wrench has a bad knee and can't ride at all and with the Army out on exercises the polo club is short of players so at the moment I am playing two chukkas on one of Hector's horses. I have even scored a goal and am enjoying myself very much. Don't worry: I am wearing a hard helmet also borrowed from Hector, and I am not being too intrepid.
>
> Andrew Armstrong was here the other day and came to lunch. He is just the same. Among other things he said that no-one in Lagos thinks much of Gardner-Brown and that they were all surprised when he and not Newns was made Deputy Governor-General. He attributed this to the preference of Sir James. Incidentally when G-B was here about a month ago he put his foot in it by talking rather disparagingly about the North

to Ian Lewis at the dinner table. This would not have mattered if Isa Kaita had not been sitting opposite listening. Afterwards Isa Kaita thanked Ian for standing up for the Region. The story got back to HE who told the Governor-General who rebuked G-Brown.

HE is going on leave a month today and is taking three months. That all fits in nicely with our plans. The question of the retention or abolition of Deputy Governors is under discussion right now. Rankine and Stapledon are both due to retire this year and may be succeeded by African Governors. This being so, the East and West may change their minds about abolition and retain their European Deputy-Governors, at any rate for a time, to help the new Governors. Here in the North I think that they will want HE to finish his term but what they will decide about the Deputy Governor no-one knows. From the standpoint of pension a reprieve would be very useful because an extra eighteen months in the job would make a difference of £250. If you were with me I should be very happy to carry on. As it is, I don't know what to think. When Robin goes to St. M. do you think that you could face two spells of two to three months each tour, that is spending the holidays with the children and part of the terms with me? That would reduce the separations and make them more bearable while the coming and going would effectively safeguard you from Red Crosses and Girl Guides. You always pretend that I can get along very well without you but I can't, you know, I miss you very badly.

Berrice replied that she thought she would be able to brace herself enough to go out for two to three months. Although she hated the separations, in Nigeria she always felt so nervous and dreaded the phone ringing in case it was someone asking her to do some charitable work or inviting them out to dinner.

Shortly afterwards the ministers made up their minds and decided that the post of Deputy Governor should disappear.

The Premier has agreed that the date of its abolition should be postponed a little so that I can be here to help at Independence and so I am likely to finish at the end of October. By then I shall have over six months leave in hand and this will carry me through until the end of April 1961, just three months short of twenty-five years service. My pension should work out at about £1500.

I don't know whether to be glad or sorry. If you were happy here I should definitely feel disappointed at going but as it is I think I'm rather relieved. There will, however, be the business of looking for another job but we can worry about that later.

The return air fares by tourist class are now £124 for Carolyn (student) and £82 for Robin (child), making a total of £206. As the allowance is £230 it won't cost us anything if you all come out for the summer. In fact it will be cheaper to be together than in two households. The tourist seats are already heavily booked so let me know the date when you would like to come out. There is no need to wait for Carolyn and in any case I should prefer you to fly in separate planes. For you and Robin the nearer mid-July the better, I want a big bear hug.

How is Robin getting on at school? I mean is he making any progress with his 3Rs? I hear from Carolyn about once a fortnight and she seems cheerful enough.

Tim then travelled down to Lagos and his next letter was from Government House Lodge.

Just before I came down here, the Rothschilds passed through. They were a pleasant couple, and he was lively and interested. There was nothing to indicate great wealth except that at one point they let slip the fact that they had a town chauffeur as well as a country chauffeur. She, poor woman, had lost a suitcase and had only one dress so I took her to Kingsway to buy another. It was odd to reflect that, had she wanted to, she could have bought the whole shop.

For almost the first time in my life I am enjoying a visit to Lagos. I flew down here on Wednesday and spent the first two nights with Peter Stallard. On the first evening we were bidden to dinner at Government House but on the second we had a quiet supper at home.

Each day I have had a full programme of visits to Ministries, Corporations etc. but as this has involved nothing more than general talk it has not been at all exhausting. On the contrary, rather stimulating. Almost all the big shots are air-conditioned now, in their offices as well as their homes. Peter S. lives very unpretentiously in a house which, if I had been he, I should long ago have exchanged for a better one. It is rather small and scruffy and does not even enjoy a decent site.

I had forgotten how big this house was: it is almost a small hotel. There are three floors and on the top one are six self-contained suites. The one I am in has a bedroom the size of the Queen's room in Kano with a sitting room and dining annex adjoining it on one side and bathroom and BG on the other. There is a fine view over the harbour and as it is air-conditioned I have been most comfortable. The quality of the furniture and furnishings is very good and clearly expense has not been spared. Similarly the service is excellent. There is a boy who goes with the room and acts as valet, waiter etc. In fact it is what Carolyn would call ever so posh.

On Sunday we all went over to Lighthouse Beach where HE has three chalets in a group among casuarina trees. That is where Governor Bourdillon used to conduct his amours and a very pleasant spot it is. We bathed and there was enough sea for surfing, in fact the waves were bigger than they are on all except the best days at Westward Ho!

The Robertsons made themselves very pleasant and I got on better with them than I have before. I think that the old malice towards the North and northern officers has now evaporated. On the last evening I had supper with G-Brown. His house is next door to Government House and is well designed and expensively furnished, a startling contrast to the Deputy Governor's house in Kaduna. I gather that he is unpopular with the Colonial Office and he does not expect them to offer him anything in October when his job, like mine, comes to an end. Did I tell you that Stapledon was going to the Bahamas as Governor? The population of the place is about 130,000 (less than Argungu's) but the Governor gets £8,700 in pay and allowances, far more than HE here.

In April, shortly after returning to Kaduna from Lagos, Tim moved into Government House to act for the Governor while he was on leave.

Well, here I am in the big house and I am writing to say how much I wish you were with me. HE went off by air at 4 p.m. today and I spent the evening moving my things. At 7.30 we assembled for the swearing-in but had to wait about half an hour because the Makama, who was representing the Premier, did not turn up. The oaths only took five minutes and afterwards Hedley and John Smith stayed for a drink which we had on the lawn.

There is more room and more privacy here than I had imagined. HE's suite, in which I am living, is at the rear of the house (as you approach it) and consists of a private sitting room, a double bedroom, a child's bedroom, bathroom, BG and plenty of cupboards. I like the idea of the private sitting room very much indeed: it means that even with people in the house you can escape and live a bit of private life.

Of the boys, Ali is going to stay behind as caretaker of the other house and his salary will be paid from the vote. M. Lawan has come here (a) to look after me upstairs and (b) to pick up tips in the kitchen and improve his cookery. Him I shall still pay. Buba has also come here but he has been fitted into a vacancy on the staff so that I shall not have to find his wages. This arrangement is cheap and yet satisfactory and I am well satisfied with it.

There has been some quite serious trouble in Benue, first in Wukari, then in Lafia and finally in Tiv. The crises followed one another in quick succession and Mike Counsell had to dash from place to place to keep up with them. I think that he has done very well. In Wukari a village of Tiv killed an NA policeman and put themselves in a state of defence but they were taken by surprise before dawn and disarmed. In Lafia an Arago village refused to give up ten men wanted by the courts and when Mike went there with 150 Nigeria Police they were met by a hostile crowd who, after some abortive parleying, finally started shooting poisoned arrows at them. To extricate themselves the police had to open fire and in doing so they killed five (not eight as some of the papers said) and wounded five. No sooner had this trouble been cleared up than word came from Gboko that the Tiv were refusing to be counted for tax and defying their clan-heads and courts. The first cause of all this turmoil was the election campaign in which the Action Group and UMBC not only did their best to discredit the NAs but made wild promises about remitting tax and so on. Tiv is still highly explosive and might go up any day.

Tim was enjoying life at Government House and was feeling very pampered.

A PS, ADC and private sitting room make life here much simpler and pleasanter than it was in Kano. Everything is done for me and I have no worries in the house. The ADC is a young man called Egremont-Lee. He is rather like Hanson-Smith and seems very pleasant. The PS is John Smith who is first class. In addition we have taken on a housekeeper and I don't have to worry about the house at all. If there are no guests I have lunch with the ADC but I breakfast alone downstairs and have supper alone in my sitting room upstairs. The work in the office just keeps me occupied but no more and there is no rush or urgency about it. It is a constant surprise that for doing far less than half what I did as Sec. Prem. I am at present paid more than twice as much. If you were here, everything would be perfect. I jog along happily enough but I miss you all the time.

At the end of the month the Queen's Birthday Parade was held on the Racecourse.

On Thursday I had to officiate at the Queen's Birthday Parade. It was rather a dull parade, consisting of a whole series of royal salutes, one when I arrived, three for the Royal Standard, and one before I left, but my part was quite easy and it all went off well. I borrowed Jackie Noble's horse and he behaved admirably until right at the end when he suddenly shied violently as I was skirting the Pavilion to depart. However, I remained on board all right and my hat did not fall off. The tunic which the A&N made for me, after having a new collar put in and being twice altered, at last fits me properly. I am glad, however, that I took the trouble to get it right because otherwise I should have felt very uncomfortable with 1000 pairs of eyes boring into my back as I took the salutes.

Last week we had a tea party for members of the House of Assembly but of the twenty invited only half came. Some like the Galadiman Kano were admittedly away but of the others none of the four Sokoto members and none of the three Parliamentary Secretaries either came or even bothered to answer the invitations. However, though small, the party was successful so this week we are going to try again. I have also taken to asking some of the younger people, Africans as well as Europeans, to a drink before lunch on Saturday. I think this is quite a good idea too because it throws them together and otherwise they hardly ever get asked to Government House.

Randall Ellison has been under fire in the House of Assembly as Chairman of the Public Service Commission and the fact that neither the Premier nor any other Minister spoke in his defence suggests that the criticism was not spontaneous but inspired. He was appointed on contract in 1958 with the Premier's blessing for a period of five years, but lately the Ministers appear to have changed their minds and to have decided that with independence approaching the time has come to appoint an African. The Premier recently told me that the pressure for the change is strong and that he and his colleagues feel that Ellison should not stand on his legal rights but should offer his resignation. One of his assailants was the Madaki of Kano and the Premier also told me that he was paying off an old score because years ago, when Ellison was PEO Kano and the Madaki a young schoolmaster, E refused to let him have a bicycle allowance. I wonder any of us survive.

Tim's next duty was to open the House of Chiefs.

On Wednesday I had to open the House of Chiefs. The ADC and I drove down in state in the old Humber – open for the occasion – and on arrival I inspected the guard of honour. Then I was escorted into the Chamber by the Emir of Gwandu, as President, and the Premier. Having bowed three times, I settled myself and read the speech first in English and then in Hausa. There were only five pages all told but it seemed to take a lot of getting through. However, I had of course prepared it beforehand and I got through without any stuttering, stumbling or unfortunate spoonerisms. I wasn't really nervous but was relieved when all was over.

The Premier flew off yesterday and, if all went well, is probably in the Abbey now watching Princess Margaret's wedding. He came to say goodbye and was very frank and affable. Within the party there has been a strong movement against the Makama who they accuse, along with Ribadu, of running the party machine in an arbitrary and high-handed manner. The Premier has had to intervene and settle the trouble. He is in complete command again and I think fitter and more relaxed than he was last year.

I wrote to Maiholi asking him if he would like to come and stay here and he came like a shot. He is just the same and seems in good form. He has to return tomorrow, and anyway we are off to Jos, but he has promised to return next month so that I can record notes about his life. Seeing me in this house has, I'm sure, fulfilled one of his ambitions. With the Chiefs here, he has been able to call on his old friends like the Sultan and Emir of Gwandu and has doubtless not come empty away. He told the ADC on arrival that he was 95!

Tim then went on tour to the Plateau and stayed at Tudun Wada, the Governor's hill-station retreat near Jos.

I was relieved to hear that Carolyn had promised to do better at school and hope that she will try to conquer her rebellious temperament. I am glad too that she behaved well in the last week of the holidays and helped about the house.

I was sorry to hear that you had been feeling lonely. When we buy or build another house I think we must go to a village where it is easier to get to know people.

I had a comfortable journey here in an air-conditioned coach. This is a nice house and the garden is looking lovely so it has been very pleasant staying here – perfect if you had been with me. As it is, I too feel lonely and often rather depressed.

We went first to Vom and saw the Veterinary Research Establishment. Then we spent two days in Pankshin. It is a delightful place with glorious views of the plain and an excellent climate. One day we spent visiting Wase whose rock you probably remember seeing when we went to Shendam. When you get there it is certainly a most impressive feature, sticking up 800 ft and practically sheer on all sides. Julian Wallace finally succeeded in climbing it last year but only by dint of preparing a route with pitons (steel hooks on rings that you hammer into the rock) on many previous visits. His companion on the rope, of all people, was his cook, a Fulani called Alhaji. Wase is a nice little place – a typical small NA HQ – and we had a picnic lunch there and drove back in the afternoon. St Elmo has accompanied us everywhere and is a most cheerful companion.

Meanwhile, the ministers had returned from constitutional talks in London well satisfied over everything except future aid. The Premier had for some time been apprehensive lest the conclusion of a defence agreement with the United Kingdom and the cession of land should cause Kano Airport to be regarded as a British military base. Consequently, HM Government's decision to forgo a formal agreement had given him particular satisfaction.

Soon afterwards he departed for the pilgrimage. Salla was expected to fall on 6 June and Tim decided to go to Katsina for the celebrations.

Here we are at Katsina, staying with Oliver [Hunt]. We were very lucky in the weather because it rained the night before and yet was cool and sunny on Salla day. I wish you could have been here to see the show which was full of colour and distinguished from Sokoto and Kano by having the *Ja'afi*, each District Head and his men coming up in turn.

Yesterday we went to Daura and saw the legendary sword with which Abuyazidu struck off the head of the gigantic snake that lived in the well. Here is the first part of the legend which you can read to Robin.

There was once a prince of Bagdad called Abuyazidu who quarrelled with his father and left his home in the east. After some time his wanderings brought him to Bornu. There he was given a daughter of the Sultan in marriage, Magira by name. He stayed in Bornu and his affairs prospered so much that in the course of time he became rich and powerful. His wealth and authority only excited hatred and envy, however, and the Sultan began to plot against his life. But Magira, being a daughter of the palace, heard what was afoot and warned her husband. Although she was with child, they decided that the only safety lay in flight. So with nothing but a mule to carry their possessions and a slave-girl to wait on them, they took the road to the west. When they reached a place called Garun Gabas Magira's days were fulfilled and she gave birth to a son. Abuyazidu left her there and, taking the concubine with him, continued his journey.

After a time Abuyazidu came to the town of Daura which was then ruled by a woman, the last of a line of nine Queens. He lodged in the house of an old woman called Waira and in the evening he asked her for water. 'Young man' said the old woman 'in this town there is no water to be had except on Fridays. Only when all the people are assembled can we draw water.'

'Nevertheless' he said 'I am going to get some now. Give me a bucket.'

He took the bucket which she gave him and went to the well. Now a gigantic snake called Sarki lived in the well and when it heard the bucket being lowered it lifted its head out of the well and tried to strike Abuyazidu. But he drew his sword and struck off its head which he then hid. After that he drew water for himself and his horse, gave what was left to the old woman, and went to bed.

Next day as soon as it was light the townspeople saw that the snake was dead. They marvelled at its size and the news was quickly taken to the Queen. Escorted by all her warriors, she rode down to the place and she too marvelled at the size of the snake which was still lying half in and half out of the well. 'I swear' she said 'that if I find the man who killed this snake I will divide the town into two and give half of it to him.'

'It was I' said one of the bystanders at once.

'Where is its head then?' said the Queen. 'If you cannot produce the head you are lying.' The man remained silent. Others also came forward and said that they had killed the snake but none of them could produce the head and their claims were all rejected.

At length the old woman Waira spoke up. 'Yesterday evening' she said 'a stranger came and lodged at my house with a strange animal as big as an ox. He took my bucket, went to the well, drew water, drank some himself, watered his animal, and gave the rest to me. Perhaps it was he who killed the snake.'

'Let him be found' said the Queen. When Abuyazidu appeared she asked him if he had killed the snake. He said that he had and when she demanded its head he produced it from where it was hidden. 'I made a promise' she said 'that I would divide my town in two and give half to him who did this deed.'

'Do not divide the town' he said 'because I for my part will be amply rewarded if you will deign to take me as your consort.' And so it came about that Abuyazidu, Prince of Bagdad, married the Queen of Daura.[3]

When Tim got back to Kaduna, Maiholi paid him another visit and they talked about his life in service to the British.

Maiholi was here again and I have been writing down his life story. It hasn't quite come up to my expectations because although he was present at so many of these events like the capture of Kano, the suppression of the Satiru rebels and the repulse (by the Germans) at Garua he was of course always in the background and consequently didn't see or hear much himself. Perhaps I expected too much. Do you remember the grave at Bauchi of an Hon. Oliver Howard who committed suicide in 1906? Maiholi was his boy in 1903–04 and says that he was the most brutal man in the country. His staff were constantly flogged and Maiholi finally ran away from him. The worst mistress he ever had was Winsome Cullen who would never give him more than one shilling market money. He says that he left them without notice when he could bear her no longer and that in 1945 Winsome recognised him and warned you against him.

President Tubman's visit went quite well. Here in the house we had Tubman himself, the British Ambassador in Liberia, and Tubman's ADC and Secretary. The President I rather took to: he was a very easy guest and proved to have a nice sense of humour without any pomposity or delusions of grandeur. In fact we got on very well together. He speaks English with an American twang and uses a lot of American expressions. In fact he seemed much more like an American businessman than an African politician and that I think is how he runs the country. All the time he was here he was receiving and sending a stream of radiograms and I gather his is very much a one-man band. The British Ambassador (6th Class) turned out to be a very affable chap and not in the least a stuffed shirt, in fact much less U than I expected from the Foreign Service. Between us we succeeded in creating an informal atmosphere which he said the President enjoyed much more than Lagos and Ibadan. In this we were helped by the ADC, a pure figure of fun. We had to give a lunch party and a big dinner but the house-keeper and ADC did it all and it was no worry for me. In fact compared with Kano – touch wood – this is money for jam.

I wrote to Waddle to congratulate him on his knighthood and had a nice letter from him in which he wrote 'Of course I owe it all to you ... this is real friendship and devotion'. I also had a letter from Charles Michie who, having failed to get any other job, has decided to become a schoolmaster. At first he thought of sinking his lumpers in a business. The result was that when he got his CMG the Duke asked him what he intended to do and he had to say he was thinking of selling bird seed and dog biscuits. This reply, said Charles, rather disconcerted the Duke who seemed to feel that the conversation was hardly maintaining the traditions of the Gold Room at the palace.

Well, a month today you should be on your way here. It has seemed such a long separation that I can hardly believe that it is at last drawing to a close.

I don't think that you need worry about entertaining. I shall try to clear off all the people who expect to be asked to drinks or dinner while I am here so that we should be more or less free of duty calls. In any case I hope there will be a lull before the independence celebrations.

Tim's next task was to draft a survey of the affairs of the Northern Region for the Secretary of State. In it, he first assessed the effect of President Tubman's visit.

[It] has provided an opportunity of gauging the attitude of Northerners towards their neighbours and towards the topical question of whether or not a United States of Africa should be brought into being. Beforehand there appeared to be little public interest in the visit but when the President arrived he was given a friendly reception and reasonably large crowds turned out to see him. In his interview with the Ministers he seems to have had no difficulty in convincing them that his proposals for future co-operation were not only more realistic but in every way better than Dr. Nkrumah's messianic delusions about federation. An argument of his that particularly impressed them was that a Federation would have but one voice in the United Nations whereas individual States could together form a solid African *bloc*. In social intercourse the atmosphere was friendly enough but the remarkable thing was how little the two sides had to say to one another. There was polite interest but little disposition to question, explore, discuss, or attempt to see into one another's minds. Quite apart from other considerations, this in itself suggests that Dr Tubman's approach to the problem of the future co-operation of African States is the realistic one. The President scouted the idea of the present national leaders being willing to subordinate themselves to one another. In this I am sure that he is right: few if any will voluntarily surrender the perquisites enjoyed by big fish in small ponds.

These attitudes of mind have a bearing on the problems facing Nigeria. In considering the future of the Federation we must bear in mind the fact that during the next few years the mere appearance on the world stage of little countries like Upper Volta and Niger is going to arouse jealousies and longings in the breasts of those who are dissatisfied with the limitations of regional status. Another possibility which might have dangerous repercussions is the breaking up of any of the neighbouring States of West Africa, especially if this happened to coincide with an internal crisis. Recent indications show that these risks, though they should not be exaggerated, cannot be altogether ruled out. The Congo is an obvious menace. Another is the Cameroun Republic where the French High Commissioner recently prophesied that the country would split in two and that the Muslim north would seek assimilation to Nigeria. If anything of the sort were to happen the NPC, tempted by visions of an overall majority in Lagos, might press for union, whereas the Action Group and the NCNC, appalled by the prospect of permanent Muslim domination, would undoubtedly oppose it to the bitter end. Clearly such developments could shake the Federation to its very foundations. They are unlikely to be initiated by the Northern leaders, whose attitude to empire-building is at present correct and responsible, but a conjunction of circumstances might bring them about. These latent dangers are mentioned here not because they appear to be imminent but in order to emphasise that even Nigeria, which appears on the face of it to be stable and tranquil, in fact enjoys only a precarious equilibrium which events elsewhere could easily upset.

He went on to comment on the decision taken at the Constitutional Conference, that the clause limiting the number of chiefs in Executive Council to a maximum of four should be deleted.

In seeking this amendment the Premier had two things in mind. First, he has always been very careful to ensure that all parts of the Region are adequately represented in the Government but in the past, with chiefs limited to four, it has been difficult to find room for representatives from both Bornu and the riverain areas. Secondly, he has come to realise that the talents of certain educated and progressive chiefs are wasted in administering small and remote chiefdoms and consequently he is thinking in the future of bringing one or two of this type into the Cabinet and giving them Portfolios. There is no question but that a man like the Emir of Yauri would make a far better Minister than all but one or two of the present commoners. These moves should help to reduce the danger of a collision after independence between Chiefs and Ministers.

Another matter concerned the legal and judicial reforms that had been passed by both Houses of the Legislature.

There now remains a great deal of preparatory work to be completed before the reforms are introduced on October 1st but this is being vigorously tackled and the auguries are good. A major problem, however, still remains to be decided and that is where the control of native courts will in future lie. At present control and general supervision is exercised by the Attorney General through the Commissioner for Native Courts who is responsible to him. So long as a British officer remains Attorney General this power will not be abused but for the future, when an active African politician succeeds, there is an obvious and very real danger that the native courts, which transact well over 90 per cent. of the judicial business in the Region, will be exposed to political influences and pressures. Logically control over them should now be transferred from the Attorney General to the Chief Justice and, in so far as they administer Muslim personal law, to the Grand Kadi. Unfortunately, however, the rift between the present Chief Justice and the Regional Ministers precludes this change at the present time but if Sir Algernon Browne were succeeded next year by a man who commanded the confidence of the Government it might then become feasible. For psychological reasons it would probably be more readily accepted by the Premier and the majority of his Ministers if the new Chief Justice were an Indian or Pakistani and no doubt it would help if he were also Muslim. The chances of introducing this change, which I regard as extremely important, and indeed the success of the reforms as a whole, therefore depend to a large extent upon the choice of the next Chief Justice.

In the economic field Tim reported that the Regional Government had at last woken up to the importance of agriculture. Arrangements had been made for a team of eleven international experts to survey all aspects of the agricultural economy of the Region later in the year and the government's plans for future development would be largely determined by their recommendations.

This is all to the good but the problem of finding finance to implement the recommendations will still remain. The Regional Government has followed the lead of the Federal Government in extending the Five-year Plan for 1955–60 by two years. Nevertheless the Ministers' thoughts are beginning to turn to the next Five-year Plan which will run from 1962–67 and they have at last realised that they will have to embark upon it with a kitty which will be almost completely empty. As financiers they have more in common with Mr. Micawber than with Mr. Gladstone and until now they have been sustained by a vague hope that something would turn up. At the same time they are shrewd and realistic politicians and they realise that they will be committing political suicide if they fail to preserve the present economic momentum after independence. No Government, said a recent memorandum of Executive Council, could contemplate this. Before long, therefore, they will set off on a search for funds. If their requests for help are not met in London they will turn to other Western capitals. At best they will be fortunate and will obtain enough in loans and credits to keep them going. As these loans and credits will mostly be tied to the goods of the creditor nation, however, the United Kingdom will suffer from this arrangement because its exports to Nigeria will be supplanted. At worst the Ministers will be rebuffed in the Western capitals and then they will reluctantly turn to the Soviet Union and the Russian Satellites. In doing so they will doubtless make the usual mistake of under-estimating the dangers and overrating their ability to accept Russian help without falling under Russian control.

While the Northern Ministers are slow to worry about finance for future development, they are all fully alive to the backwardness of the Region and united in their determination to advance with the utmost speed. They feel that in every other respect but western education they are better men than Easterners and Westerners and they are resolved never again to let the North be dominated by them. Even in education and modern techniques they contend that, given equal chances, the young Northerner is second to none and the fact that Northern students in British universities recently obtained first class honours in three subjects proves that they are justified in believing that the North has a rich potentiality in brains and ability. Their new determination to advance after years of stagnation is one of the most encouraging things that has happened here during the last two decades and surely deserves every possible assistance. The evolutionary gap between the North and the other Regions is already a cause of instability (which the geographical distribution of oil and the revenue from it will aggravate) and so it is not merely the future progress of the Northern Region which is at stake but perhaps the integrity of the Federation itself. In October the Nigerian ship of state will leave harbour and face the open sea. As she passes between the pier heads with bands playing let us not overlook the fact that she will have a heavy and indeed dangerous list which has been built into her during half a century of British rule.

In local government, the Region was facing a difficult problem in that past attempts to liberalise Native Authorities by teaming up chiefs and predominantly elected councils had tended to lead to deadlock and failure.

> In retrospect we can see that these experiments were premature. To borrow a parallel from English history, it was as if county councils had been brought into existence 60 years before their time and imposed willy-nilly on Lord Lieutenants who still enjoyed the power and prestige that was theirs when Wellington was Prime Minister. The result here was that some of the chiefs felt no more at home with their elected members than would a true-blue peer who found himself chairman of a county council dominated by radicals and chartists. In Ilorin, where the main issue in local politics was whether or not the Province should secede from the North and join the West, the Emir and his conservative councillors had to run the Emirate with elected members whom they regarded not merely as radicals or chartists but practically as Fenians. It was the failure of the experiment in Ilorin more than anything else that turned the Regional Government against the idea of liberalising native authority councils to the extent of giving them elected majorities. During the past few years this has prompted them to retreat but it would be wrong to suppose that this withdrawal indicates a triumph for reaction. Considering his antecedents, the Premier is in fact surprisingly liberal in his approach and has forced the hand of some of the conservative Northern Native Authorities like Sokoto and Katsina in adding elected members to their councils. Nor does the retreat seem unreasonable when it is remembered that the elected members in Ilorin and other riverain native authorities displayed, while they were in power, a deplorable irresponsibility in the conduct of public affairs. During the past year the Ministry of Local Government has been thinking the problem out afresh and the Minister has recently suggested to Executive Council that a new policy should be adopted based on native authority councils having a minority but not a majority of elected members, on portfolios being entrusted to committees instead of individuals, and on the control of staff being made impartial and impersonal. These proposals are realistic and as liberal as the present temper of Northern society permits and it is to be hoped that the Regional Government will adopt them.

In the Public Service, day-to-day relations with ministers had been easier than the previous year and morale had consequently improved. However, expatriates were still worried about the future. In the Administration, the Northern ADOs were doing well and twelve of them were in charge of Divisions. The majority were content with their lot but a few had discovered that the work was arduous, exacting, and often thankless and some of them were consequently looking round for easier billets.

Among African officials the group described as the 'Young Colonels' had not been very active of late but still constituted a force to be reckoned with.

> Most of them have already enjoyed rapid promotion but this excites their appetite instead of satisfying it. Being ambitious and well-informed they realise that the times have brought exceptional opportunities and they are therefore as impatient as bulls trying to make their fortune on a rising market. A typical example is Mallam Baba Gana who, after five years in the Senior Service, is acting as a Senior Assistant Secretary but is already dissatisfied with this status and aspiring to the post of Secretary to the Public Service Commission which carries a rank equivalent to that of a Permanent Secretary. The insidious lure of rank and power makes these officers restive and dissatisfied.

Among personalities, the Premier continued to dominate the stage.

> In spite of the extraordinarily exacting life that he leads he has kept fairly fit and seems to be more relaxed and confident than he was last year. This is probably because he is once again in complete command and has divided and subdued those of his colleagues who combined last year in an effort to impose their will upon him. As a politician and personality, he stands head and shoulders above the rest and, except occasionally when his pride is touched, he continues to comport himself in a responsible and statesmanlike way. His pride, however, is one of his two main weaknesses and it sometimes warps his judgment. For example, because the people of the Northern Cameroons spurned the Northern Region in the plebiscite last year, he refused afterwards to make any attempt to woo them back. Similarly, though he realises better than any of the other Ministers how badly the North needs external aid, his pride prevents him from appearing in the role of a suppliant and he therefore leaves negotiation in other less able hands. If pride is his weakness, his Achilles heel is undoubtedly extravagance

and this might one day bring about his downfall. He has a taste for princely generosity which he recklessly indulges. For the future, though addicted to power, he regards the hurly-burly of democratic politics with such aristocratic distaste that when Sir Gawain's term comes to an end he may well put himself forward as the next Governor of the Region. There are hardly more than three Northerners who would be acceptable in this office (the other two being the Emirs of Gwandu and Katsina) and of the three the Premier would probably be the most effective, though perhaps the least constitutional.

In recent weeks relations between the Premier and the Prime Minister have again come under strain. As politics in Nigeria turn on personalities much more than on principles, it is worth describing in some detail the nature and causes of their disagreements although doing so means going back a long way. When Usuman dan Fodiyo died he divided the empire between his son Bello and his brother Abdullahi who thenceforward ruled the two parts without interfering in one another's affairs. I believe that the Premier considers that he and the Prime Minister should adopt a similar arrangement and that he himself, though he may not always live up to his own standards, does try to manage things in this way. The Prime Minister, however, though in general he may be equally or even more forbearing, has on occasions intervened in regional affairs and as often as not it has been these interventions which have caused trouble.

The standing in the North of the Prime Minister himself is difficult to define. Some of the chiefs like to regard him merely as a useful instrument for the exercise of Northern control over the Federation. They do not forget his humble origins and will probably resent it if he is elevated so high that he begins to cast his shadow over them. Similarly among some of the influential commoners of the older generation there is a feeling that the deference paid to the Prime Minister in Lagos has made him proud and even arrogant. His reluctance in granting interviews has probably contributed to this impression and certainly the Waziri of Bornu was recently heard to say that the Prime Minister had become so pompous that he would see nobody. It is only among the younger men, and particularly those with radical or progressive ideas, that the Prime Minister commands a loyal and devoted following. Even here he has his critics but it is where his chief strength lies. In the nature of things the asset should be a growing and not a wasting one. Among the older men the opposition is largely based on snobbishness or jealousy and need not be taken too seriously but it would nevertheless pay the Prime Minister to cultivate these people with more care and tact.

The stock of the Makaman Bida, after the attacks upon him in April, appeared to have fallen very low. He is a consummate politician, however, and in three months he has re-established his position. This has now been consolidated by the appointment of the Minister of Health, who has long been the Makama's lieutenant, as General Secretary of the NPC. Politically, the Makama is as astute as ever but physically he is beginning to show signs of age and occasionally of premature senility. Unlike the Makama, Alhaji Muhammadu Ribadu has not yet succeeded in returning to favour but he too is a most astute politician and it will be surprising if he does not do so before the end of the year.

If the Premier were to retire from politics the Makama and Alhaji Muhammadu Ribadu are next in line of succession but it is unlikely that either of them would be accepted by the party or chiefs. After them comes Alhaji Isa Kaita, the Minister of Education, but he too probably lacks the personality and following that a leader must have. My belief is that if the post fell vacant during the next two or three years there would be a demand for Shettima Kashim, the Waziri of Bornu, to return to regional politics and lead the North.

By way of conclusion, let me touch on the subject of relations between Africans and Europeans in this Region. In the past there was a belief that Northerners were so gentlemanly that it required no particular tact or skill to get on well with them. During the last few years, however, they have shown that when thwarted or mishandled they can be as suspicious, touchy, prejudiced, deceitful, and downright offensive as African nationalists anywhere.[4]

A few days after submitting the review, Tim followed up with a letter to Christopher Eastwood.

[In my despatch] of the 11th July, which you will probably have seen by now, I dealt with the dangers besetting the Federation and you may have thought that I was being unnecessarily alarmist. There is, however, evidence to show that the thoughts of the Northern leaders are beginning to turn towards their neighbours in these latitudes.

An open manifestation of this interest was the invitation sent to the Prime Minister of the Republic of Niger to come to Kaduna during the Budget Session of the Legislature. He was unable to accept the invitation at the time but the Ministers still hope to see him later on. In the meantime they have sent one of the best of the Parliamentary Secretaries to Niamey to make contact with him.

What appears to be more significant, because they are still being kept secret, are the recent exchanges with the Republic of Tchad. I first heard about these from a private source about three months ago and mentioned the story to the Commissioner of Police who, I believe, instructed the Special Branch to keep their ears open. The rumour then was that a delegation from Tchad had visited Bornu in order to discuss the possibilities of a future union and that they had met with some success among the councillors but that the Waziri, Shettima Kashim, appeared to be unsympathetic. The Special Branch has now produced a report to say that another meeting took place in Maiduguri on June 20th which was attended on the Tchad side by the Deputy Premier and two members of the Assembly and on the Nigerian side by the Premier, the Waziri (Shettima Kashim), Alhaji Waziri Ibrahim (Federal Minister of Health), Abba Habib, a member of the Bornu Native Authority Council, and a Bornu member of the Regional House of Assembly. The report says that the visitors came at the invitation of the Waziri in order to meet the Premier and that the object of the meeting was to discuss the possibility of a merger between Tchad and the Northern Region after Federal independence. It is said that there was agreement on the possibility of such a merger and that future meetings were arranged but that these did not in fact take place.

The Commissioner of Police is away on tour and consequently I have had no opportunity of asking him how much reliance he places on this report. It is certain, however, that the Premier made a special journey to Maiduguri at this time and the explanation for it that he gave out at the time, namely that he felt it his duty to go and say goodbye to the Shehu in person, appears a much less likely one than this.

Provided that they continue to prosper in the Federation, I still do not think that the leaders of the NPC will take the initiative in mergers with either Tchad or Niger. The present moves are more likely to be a form of insurance in case things go badly wrong in Nigeria. If that were to happen, for example if the NPC lost control of the Federal Government, I feel sure that the contacts that are now being established would be taken up and that in certain circumstances, if the prospects within Nigeria appeared to be either hopeless or unendurable, the Premier and his friends would have little compunction in pursuing these aims regardless of the danger to the integrity of the Federation. If we were ever to come to such a pass the Premier might well find the Prime Minister against him but I believe that most of the other Northern Federal Ministers, if they had to choose, would side with him rather than with Abubakar. Similarly, given the sort of circumstances in which a situation like this might arise, I believe that the Premier would have a majority of the Chiefs and people, except in parts of the riverain provinces, behind him.

In describing these dire possibilities I am not trying to make your flesh creep nor am I suggesting that they are imminent. They do exist, however, and we must recognise that the potential danger is there.[5]

At the end of his stint as OAG, Tim went off on a tour of Niger Province, which he described in his next letter to Berrice.

I am writing this from the train at Minna. We have had an enjoyable tour so far. On Tuesday we came down the line attached to a goods train and arrived about tea-time. In the evening we drove out to the dam and that night I had to give a cocktail party at the Residency. Next day I had to attend the NA Council and reply to an address of welcome but that was no hardship. Afterwards a little *ja'ahi* was laid on in my honour. It was difficult to keep a straight face because the people here are Gwari with few horses and little skill so that among a turn-out of about a dozen there was one who had forgotten to tighten his girth and of course fell off. Still, they tried very hard. That afternoon we went on down the line to Zungeru.

As you probably know, Zungeru was Lugard's HQ from 1902 to 1906 and remained the northern capital until Kaduna was built. Government House in those days was a pre-fab which had been brought from Jebba and was taken on to Kaduna so there is nothing left on the site except the concrete pillars on which it was raised. In its heyday there was a European population of fifty but there is little left now except a cemetery with about fifty graves in it. One belonged to a man called Leith

Ross who died in 1908 and whose widow in 1959 came all the way from Australia to visit it.[6] The little suspension bridge in the Kaduna gardens used to span a river that runs through Zungeru and its piers are still there. Another relic is the platform of the tramway that used to run from Wushishi (which was the highest point navigable on the river, about fifteen miles downstream).

From Zungeru we drove over to Kagara which is the HQ of Kamuku NA. They had never before been visited by an Acting Governor and I got a rousing reception. 'This', said the President of the Federation, opening the door into a room 10' x 7', 'is the central office'.

From Zungeru, which is on the main line, we went back that night to Minna and next morning found ourselves at Badeggi on the Baro line near Bida. Here the Etsu Nupe and his council came to pay their respects and we sat in a *rumfa* and chatted to them for half-an-hour. Then after breakfast we set off by car for Agaie and Lapai which you may remember from 1950 on the Bida – Abuja road. They are the HQs of two little Emirates and at each we again got a very warm welcome. The idea I had in mind was to visit the little places and it seems to have been a success.

The coach is air-conditioned and living in it is very comfortable. The furniture and fittings are good and the sitting room and bedroom are carpeted. Moreover the windows are made of special glass so that you can see out without people outside being able to see in.

From Badeggi we went down to Baro but unfortunately the weather there was bad, a heavy overcast and later rain. Still, we went up the hill from which you get a fine view up and down the Niger. There are the ruins of a station up there with a huge Divisional Office and the DO's house perched on the very edge of the Plateau.

From there we rumbled back to Minna. The only thing I dislike about the train is that there is too much motion to make writing possible or reading comfortable. Finally on the Sunday we drove out to look at the Shiboro gorge, which proved to be more impressive than I had expected. The river breaks through a ridge that must go up nearly 1000 feet.

Not long afterwards Berrice and Robin joined him and Carolyn flew out on her own at the end of the school term.

* * * * *

Towards the end of another happy family holiday, Carolyn fell off
the horse she had been lent and broke her arm badly. The local
doctor could do little for her and told Tim he would have to take her
to the orthopaedic surgeon in Kano. That evening's flight to Kano
was unfortunately cancelled because of storms and there was no
other option but a bumpy car journey. After two further operations,
Dr Bryson was still not confident that she would regain full
movement of her arm and thought that Berrice should take her
back to the Royal National Orthopaedic Hospital in London.

Carolyn's accident was most inopportune. It meant that there
was no time for Berrice and the children to say goodbye to dear
African and ex-pat friends and Tim would be left on his own for
the independence celebrations and the final sorting and packing
up before leaving for good. Berrice was glad to be returning to the
UK because she had not been happy in her role as a senior wife,
but it was a great wrench for Carolyn and Robin who were born
in Nigeria and felt much more at home there than they did in
England. After independence all Tim and Berrice's friends, the
bastions of their childhood, would be scattered far and wide and,
with one or two exceptions, they would never see them again. It was
a difficult and unsettling time for them.

No news from you yet but I hope the journey went smoothly and
that you were met on arrival and properly looked after.

I drove back on Thursday and got home uneventfully. A
gloomy home-coming I must say, but that can't be helped. There
have been a lot of enquiries about Carolyn and I must say people
have shown great kindness and concern. I told the Premier what
had happened and said good-bye for you and he asked me to send
his sympathy to you and Carolyn. There have been a lot of other
messages too from high and low, HE at one end and Dogo the
bellboy at the other.

Well, we had a glorious holiday while it lasted and it won't
be long before I am home. I do hope poor Carolyn's arm will
mend well and not cause her any more pain or distress. At least
I think the accident has served to bring us closer to her than we
were before.

Tim's main priority now was to start thinking about employment post-independence.

> I have answered the letter from the Foreign Office thanking them for their offer but saying that I don't wish to be considered for the Beirut job. I think I told you that earlier in the year I put up a man called David Owen who is head of the UN Technical Aid Bureau. I have written to him now asking whether he thinks there are any openings for the likes of me in the UN Services and have added that after many years overseas it is a post in Europe that I should like. I still think that we could be very happy in Geneva, especially on £3000 a year tax free.
>
> It is still raining every day, usually in the evenings. There have been so many snakes round Government House that Sarkin Gardi has been summoned again from Sokoto and is now busy cleaning the place up. From the cellar where the corn is kept he produced a big cobra and then three young ones which he said were the cobra's brood. As the two which were cobras were of different sizes and as the third wasn't a cobra at all we thought that they must all have come out of his pocket. Later on, however, I did see him catch a young puff adder, which someone else spotted in one of the hedges and that I am sure was genuine.
>
> I hope all goes well – I am missing you very much but am cheered by the thought that this separation is much shorter than the last one.

A few days later he was able to report that Sarkin Gardi had got rid of all the snakes.

> S. Gardi finished his work at GH with a tally of 1 spitting cobra, 3 puff adders and 3 baby snakes. He has put down (for an extra fee of £6) *magani* at the four corners of the house which he says will keep snakes away for six years. He caught his first wild snake (as distinct from handling his father's captive snakes) when he was nine. What interested me particularly was that he had an encounter with the Tureta man-eater twenty days after it had killed the blind man. He says that he had fortunately taken his invisibility charm with him so that he was able to walk past within three yards of it and its mate without their seeing him. Having done so he had to be resolute not to turn his head because doing so breaks the spell and then he would have been done for. This sounds a very tall story but factually I am sure that he was telling the truth. Perhaps the lions just weren't hungry.

The Tiv have been staging a minor rising with arson, looting, road-blocks, and armed bands of 100-200 roaming about the country creating havoc and mayhem. The surprising thing is that only four people have been killed so far. One was shot by the police officer when about to loose an arrow off at Mike Counsell. Dent has done very well in talking to the Tiv and bringing them to their senses.

I see in the paper today more talk of a Colombo Plan[7] for Africa. Now if a new organisation were set up, a job in it (at HQ, which would probably be London) would attract me very much. I keep writing glowing testimonials for other people and I suppose it is time I stirred my own stumps.

It was now nearly the end of September and just days away from the first of October when Nigeria would become independent.

Many happy returns of our anniversary. Eighteen very happy years of which I do not regret a moment except the time we have had to spend apart.

David Muffett has been here again, this time with Kay. They both send their sympathy to Carolyn as indeed a lot of others have. It is extraordinary how word has got round: even people who have been out of the country rush up and say 'How is C's arm?' It must be about the most talked over limb in the North and if I had kept a list of the Governors, Premiers, Cabinet Ministers, Bishops, Emirs, Professors, Brigadiers and Directors who have enquired after it the roll would comprise the best part of church and state.

You remember that David took a film of the Durbar for the Gloucesters. Well, last leave they were bidden to dinner. There were no other guests and after the meal they were shown the film which apparently was very good. Afterwards Henry took David aside and made a glorious and characteristic remark. He said: 'Muffett, when you get back to Nigeria tell them that leather chairs are no good – not for a long function like that. Because of that Durbar of yours I had prickly heat on my arse for weeks afterwards'. They said he was using the worst language possible while she seemed to be watching him constantly as if expecting an appalling gaffe every moment.

Well the celebrations for independence are almost upon us. I suppose at my dinner party tomorrow I shall have to make a speech which I always dread. After dinner we adjourn to Lugard

Hall where Isa Kaita is giving a reception until midnight when I suppose the Union Jack will be hauled down and the new Nigerian flag hoisted. Tomorrow there will be a parade on the racecourse, which will be taken by Isa Kaita and at which I shall simply be a spectator. Then in the evening there will be native dancing and next day a race meeting to which, in HE's absence, I suppose I shall have to go.

While most people looked forward to starting their retirement, or a new life somewhere else, there were one or two who could not face the future.

You will be surprised to hear that this evening we have been burying the Chief Justice, even more surprised when you hear that he committed suicide last night. When I was greeted with the news this morning I found it very difficult to credit but it was true enough. Apparently his boys heard a shot very early this morning so they rang up Skinner, the Judge, and insisted on his coming over. Skinner went up to the bedroom and found that he had shot himself with his shot-gun. He was quite dead. The extraordinary thing is that he had been out to dinner last night and had seemed normal and fairly cheerful. No-one knows why he did it. It is true that he was very reluctant to retire and was rather worried about money, not because there was not enough but because his pension would not enable him to live in the style he liked; of course none of these things explain or justify what he did.

Honours have been raining down recently on my ageing head. First of all the Sultan asked me the other day if I was going to Sokoto for the Princess's visit and I said no, no-one had asked me. The Premier then cut in and said he not only invited me but insisted on my attending. Soon afterwards I heard that I was included in the lunch party for Princess Alexandra at Government House at which previously the Premier was to have been the only guest. I gather that this is because we were at Kano when the Duchess of Kent went through.

Princess Alexandra arrived in Kaduna shortly afterwards for the Northern Region celebrations.

There was the usual ceremony in Lugard Hall with a joint session of the two Houses and an address of welcome from the Premier and a reply by HRH with message from the Queen. It all went

off very well and was televised so perhaps you will see it. I
watched from one of the VIP galleries but was at the back and
couldn't see much. At lunch I found myself next to HRH. She
has such a very clipped diction that I found it difficult to
understand what she was saying and once or twice had to guess.
I hoped for an opportunity of telling her that you had driven her
to Hunstanton as a baby but none occurred. I think that she is a
nice girl but I found her questions a bit grasshopperish and
came away with the feeling that she was more concerned with
keeping the conversation going than with imbibing information.
As you know, these things leave me rather cold and I shall not be
sorry when they are safely over.

We then set off for Sokoto where the royal visit was a great
success and I do wish you could have been there to see it. We
flew up – all the guests and visitors in two chartered Dakotas
and found an immense throng at the airport waiting to greet
Princess Alexandra who was just behind in her Heron. The
route from the airport to the Residency was lined all the way, at
five yard intervals, by horsemen and when she arrived at about
5.30 she drove between them in an open car with the Premier.

Next day we had the Durbar on the *hurumi* where they
have a new (and rather ugly) grandstand. It was a fine morning,
not too hot. Yauri led off with a brave show – more dancers than
horsemen of course – and then came Argungu. Their special
turn consisted in a camel which marched past the royal box on its
knees and four horses which lay down and allowed their riders
to put them to bed by spreading sheets over them. After them
came Gwandu who had no special act but were very well turned
out, each platoon of about twenty having its own colour scheme,
different from the one in front and the one behind.

Last of all came Sokoto with the biggest and most diverse
contingent. Sarkin Gardi had found an enormous cobra which
was writhing about all over him. Occasionally he would pop its
head into his mouth as if it was an iced lolly and then he would
use it as a brush to put antimony on his eyelids.

In the final *Ja-afi* one man's girth broke and he fell very
heavily but there were no other casualties. The next event was
the Premier's lunch party in his house. He has had it all rebuilt
in permanent materials – very well too – and we sat down to a
meal of local food. This consisted of paw-paw followed by a sort
of entrée of rice and kuskus (rather like curry) followed in turn

by the main dish of guinea-fowl and rice. Finally there came an enormous variety of cakes and puddings and sweets. I must say the Princess was very sporting and had a go at almost everything though some of the confections were so large and heavy that even Muffett might have felt daunted. I sat next to the Lady-in-waiting, Lady Moira Hamilton, who was pleasant and easy to get on with but embarrassed me every now and again by asking questions, in stage whispers, like 'Who is more important, the Sultan or our host?' or 'Do you think it's safe to recommend this stuff to the Princess?'

In the evening I took Hedley Marshall to see some of the sights and at night there was a reception, given by the four Emirs, in the gardens. They had coloured lights festooned in the trees and little oil lamps along all the paths and I must say the place looked wonderful. It was nice and cool too because a storm had conveniently deposited a carpet of rain from Gusau to Sokoto Airport and then dispersed. The only difficulty was recognising the Africans in such a dim light but I was able to find a few of my old friends. Again I wished that you could have been there to see it all.

Hedley and I were put up by the PAO (Speers who was in Kano) in a double-Kaduna.[8] The spare wing is very cramped for two and the grille on the verandah keeps all the breeze out so we found it hot and stuffy but we managed. The Princess's two maids were in a nearby house in the new GRA and began creating when a few earwigs appeared. Their host and hostess did their best to pacify them but on the second night they refused to sleep in the house and had to be given a caravan in the Residency grounds which I hope they found insufferably hot. When I was consulted I said that Europeans in Sokoto had died from many different causes but none, so far as I was aware, from being savaged by earwigs. I went on to suggest that if they did not want to sleep they should sit up and improve their minds by reading Clapperton's Travels and Mungo Park's Journals.

There are now six air-conditioners in the Residency at Sokoto.

Next day the rest of the party flew on to Maiduguri and I came back to Kaduna by road.

With the celebrations safely over, it was now time for Tim to prepare for his departure.

I have made a start with the packing and I think all our household stuff will go comfortably into five big boxes, including the books,

236

and the rest into our uniform cases. I am dreading the next three weeks and wish you were here. Still, it won't be long now.

Yesterday I had a talk to the Premier and told him of my idea of writing a book about Sokoto. He said it was funny I should mention that because only the other day they (the Ministers) were talking about the need for books about the North and saying that people like Whitting and myself should be asked to do them. Anyway he has given the idea his blessing in principle though of course I shall have to be careful to write nothing to offend their susceptibilities. Sometimes this may be rather difficult but as I am not attempting a definitive history but only an impressionistic picture I think I can manage to be tactful and yet fairly honest. Anyway I am relieved to find that the Premier likes the idea.[9]

I have come to the conclusion that it is excessively mean to try to sell everything when we are retiring with a large sum of lumpers and so I have decided to give most of our surplus stuff away. I hope you won't think this too quixotic but a sale wouldn't have brought in more than £30 or £40 at the most and when it came to the point I found the whole thing rather demeaning. I therefore asked M. Ahmadu Coomassie, a senior African official, to come in this morning and I showed him our better stuff, which I had divided into about twenty lots. He said even senior Africans would be glad to have it and would not feel at all embarrassed at the offer so I told him to take his pick and he chose the camp bed with which I threw in a mattress, mosquito net and rods.

Tim's decision to give away their possessions was a good one.

I am glad I decided to give our stuff away instead of selling it because the beneficiaries have been most appreciative. I gave Ali Akilu the good saddle with stirrups, girths, martingale and two bridles and urged him to ride round Zaria as I in my day rode round Sokoto. I think he was quite touched and I must say I felt rather moved, as if I was handing on the torch to him. To my great surprise Alhaji Ladan asked for the old saddle which I had intended to sell because I thought it was not good enough to give away as a present. I felt I had to throw in something else so I told him to take the long mirror for his wife which he did. The Dikkos, by what I think was neat gamesmanship, got away with about three lots instead of one. 'What do we owe you?' they said, knowing full well that I was giving the stuff away. In reply to their next question I then had to say that two pink blankets, the

Autumn Spray china, the cot blankets, the very old curtains and one saucepan were by no means too much. Still, they seemed genuinely grateful (though they alone omitted to give the boys a dash). Curiously enough the good curtains have not gone yet, nor has the iron, nor the good mosquito net. The pots and pans and pyrex dishes I did not expect to be in much demand.

The Deputy High Commissioner – Twist of the CRO – has arrived and installed himself in the house near the water tower. It has been extensively reconstructed and no fewer than eleven air-conditioners are now embodied in it. This of course infuriates people like David Lloyd-Morgan and Hector Jelf. Twist is inclined to be pompous and he will have to be very careful if he is to avoid offending our people who are all ready to be prickly.

At the beginning of November Tim set off on his farewell tour of Sokoto.

Our first leg was Kaduna to Yelwa, about 250 miles. There is a superior Rest House there now but no DO or ADO to live in it. I had previously arranged with the Emirs of Yauri and Borgu to make an expedition to the Bussa rapids where Mungo Park is said to have perished and this I did next day. The Emir of Yauri now has a powered canoe and he put this at our disposal for the river part of the trip. You would have loved it.

Next day we drove up to Birnin Kebbi. The two big bridges have been rebuilt and some of the road has been reconstructed but the rest is worse than it used to be in our day. The car was overheating too so we had a tiresome and worrying drive.

At Birnin Kebbi the Emir laid on a dinner party in my honour. It was very well done and reminded me of the one Yahaya gave for Aunt Charlotte. I pottered round all the institutions there and saw M. Bello (whose tooth has gone), Bagudo and Umoru, the Fulani boy we had in Sokoto. There are about thirty people in the station now. The neem trees have grown up amazingly in our garden and round about. I very much enjoyed seeing it once more and the Emir and Councillors couldn't have been nicer but it made me feel sad, what with memories of the past and the thought that probably we should never see it again.

Yesterday I came on here to Argungu where I have been busy compiling historical notes. Tomorrow I go on to Sokoto.

When he got back to Kaduna, Tim was given a farewell dinner party by the Governor and another by the Premier who made a very complimentary speech about him and presented him with a riga and cap, camel hair rug, ostrich feather pouffe, and a signed colour photograph. Then there was an informal party with his friends and the next day he left Kaduna.

> The worst is now over and I am in Lagos staying with Peter Stallard.
>
> The ordeal I dreaded almost most of all was the farewell on the station because I am like Robin, waves of emotion come over me and my eyes fill with tears and my voice becomes a croak, so I was really rather afraid of breaking down. In the event I just managed to bear up. I must say I got a very good send-off and there were almost as many Africans as Europeans to see me off and of course a Hausa Farewell. Thank goodness it is all over. Lots of people, too many to remember, sent messages to you.
>
> Maiholi came down for the last few days and in addition to the oil stove I gave him my Hounsfield bed and mosquito net together with the A&N sleeping bag. He was very pleased with these. Lawan got the wireless set. To Pinci I sent a mosquito net, camel-hair blanket and the umbrella. The house is going to be turned into a lodge for the PM and VVIPs and Ali will stay on as head steward, a nice cushy job. I think Lawan wanted to stay on as cook but as he was already promised to Government House it was difficult to change. Moses has got a job at £6 a month and is quite happy so all our staff are placed. The gardeners of course will stay on. As parting presents I gave Lawan £50 and Ali £25 and of course many others a pound or two so all in all the parting has cost us about £100 which I think is about right.
>
> Peter S. has moved from his old house in Ikoyi to a flat in Lagos near GH. It is on the third floor and very airy and pleasant with a view through trees to the harbour. Lagos is hot, though, and I shall be glad to get on the now fully air-conditioned 'Aureole'.
>
> Now that I have nothing to do but get myself on board I feel relaxed and very happy at the thought of a reunion with you in two weeks time. I am longing for that.

Tim's last letter was written on board the 'Aureole' and posted from Freetown.

> We sailed at noon and the Robertsons [Governor-General] got a very good send-off with a ceremony on the quay and all the ships' sirens blaring in the harbour and finally a Hausa Farewell from the yacht club.

I found getting on board just as bloody as it was thirteen years ago. I had been told that everything was much improved but except that the porters wore red aprons it all seemed precisely the same. It was a relief to escape on to the boat, just as it was in 1947.

We are fully air-conditioned and it makes all the difference in the world. The food is good and I have a cabin to myself. I have a whole box-full of books connected with my embryonic masterpiece and therefore have plenty to occupy me. Now that Nigeria is behind me and all the tensions of parting are over and done with, my thoughts have all turned home and I am absolutely longing to see you again.

I am writing this from Freetown which we have just reached. So far we have had glorious weather and calm seas all the way and the voyage has been very pleasant. I normally work on deck in the mornings and then at noon, when most people have forsaken the pool for the bar, have a swim. After lunch I snooze and in the evenings return to the deck and do some more work. It is a pleasant life and if only you were here would be perfect. When we make our fortunes we must go and see a bit of the world in this way.

In Takoradi I kept thinking of our arrival there in 1945 and our trip to Achimota, your first night in Africa. It seems now to have been a different life, almost as remote as Coltishall.

Did I tell you that Maiholi wants to go on the pilgrimage and has asked me to give him a lump sum in lieu of four to six years pension to enable him to do so. When I pointed out that it was very arduous and that he might die he said that would be splendid because he would go straight to paradise. I think he is beginning to think of those celestial girls already. I don't know what to do, he is very keen, poor old thing.

ENVOI

Tim and Berrice remembered by friends and colleagues

Sir Bryan Sharwood Smith

'In the new structure the Secretary to the Premier would become Head of the Civil Service...

During all this time Sardauna and his ministers had been understanding and helpful. Obviously the new structure had to accord with their wishes, and its main features were the result of a joint operation. But when we came to the manning of the new ministries points of difference soon became apparent. Ministers preferred working with British civil servants of their own choice, men who had served them well in the past and to whom they felt a sense of obligation. This was understandable. But although I could compromise up to a point, I felt sure that it was my duty to leave the region with the strongest possible team of top civil servants in key posts. ...I was afraid that untrammelled power might bring temptations that would not be resisted and that favouritism or personal prejudice might one day play a part in postings and promotions...

Success would depend very much on the personality of the future Secretary to the Premier, the man to whom the British civil servants would look in times of doubt and difficulty. In Tim Johnston, at that time Resident at Kano, we had a man whom everyone would trust. Only forty-four years of age and the youngest, by far, of the senior Residents, he was already outstanding. During the war he had served with the RAF and had earned a double D.F.C. over Malta. He was both able and forceful and would always say and do what he thought was right;...' *But Always As Friends*, 1969

Sir Gawain Bell

'Throughout my time the Premier was fortunate in having as the Permanent Secretary to his office two outstandingly able and dedicated men...H.A.S. Johnston and B. Greatbatch.

'Tim' Johnston joined the Administrative Service after taking his degree at Oxford in 1936. He was released at the outbreak of war to join the Royal Air Force and served with great distinction ...He returned to Nigeria after the war and quickly rose to become a provincial resident. His mind was fertile, he had great breadth of vision and the determination to bring his ideas to fruition. He was a man of dogged tenacity, a Hausa scholar of marked ability, and he had great sympathy with the people of the North. When in 1960 he moved from being Permanent Secretary to the Premier to become Deputy Governor I came to appreciate even more his great ability and strength of character. He was as perceptive in matters of wider policy as he had been sensitive, as a district officer and a resident, to political problems in a less extensive field. Had he been born half a generation earlier he would undoubtedly have reached Governor's rank.' *An Imperial Twilight*, 1989

John Smith

'Let me give you two glimpses of Tim which made him a hero in my eyes. The death penalty still existed in Nigeria in 1960. Execution warrants had to be signed by the governor. As PS I had to draw them up, apply the black seal and put them up to the boss to sign. I hated the job and so did Tim. He would spend days before he could bring himself to sign a warrant, a task he was obliged to do constitutionally because by that time he had to take the advice of a committee when exercising the prerogative of mercy. And the committee never did, they were a hanging lot even when the case cried out for mercy. Tim would be miserable for a long time whereas others I served signed them glibly on the spot and one once even joked about executions he had himself administered. When in later life I was appointed a governor I was fortunate that the death penalty had been abolished but my experience as a PS and the agonies Tim suffered made me refuse to surrender the exercise of the prerogative of mercy before independence. Without any formal constitutional advice I was able to take my own decisions.

I had always had good Nigerian friends, something easier for my generation than earlier ones, and while PS I was invited by Hassan Katsina, son of the Emir, to stay in Katsina for salla. Tim as governor was invited by the Provincial Commissioner, still an expat. As we would both be in the same place for the same event I explained that I already had an invitation which I would like to honour and Tim was happy for me to do so. We drove up together and I performed what jobs were necessary but stayed in the city with Hassan. Oliver Hunt, the PC, was furious. He did not approve of an expat administrator having close Nigerian friends (other than on the polo field) and certainly disapproved of anyone staying in the city, but Tim was merely amused by his attitude and thought it good and normal that my generation were able to do things he might not have been able to do at my age. And, of course, it was such connections which enabled me to stay on for ten years after independence.' From a letter written in August 2006

John Chartres

'I was Acting Surgical Specialist at Kaduna when your mother Berrice arrived with an abdominal complaint. She was, I remember, a very beautiful woman.

Tim was sent to Nassarawa District in 1945 to unravel corruption in NA administration. This involved going through many files and treasury papers. The Hausa nickname he was given at the time was Kaza (= chicken) because he was always scratching little things and finding them not right!' From letters written in August 2006 and April 2008

Christopher Hanson-Smith

'I have very happy memories of Tim in Sokoto where he was my boss and invited me to take on the role of "Fulani Liaison Officer". The only snag was that I promised not to marry my fiancée for eighteen months so that I could concentrate on my rather lonely job which required much touring in the "bush".

It was Tim who encouraged my study of both Hausa and Fulfulde – the Fulani language – so that I became proficient in both.

Tim was a prolific writer and covered many sheets of foolscap with his thoughts and recommendations for his staff. His writing was fortunately bold and legible!

He was a keen and forceful tennis player who took some beating. He was not such a good rider, however, and did not take to polo.

He liked his shooting and we often went after the duck in the *fadama* – the marshes – which were fortunately plentiful – I mean both the duck, geese and the marshes.' From a letter written in September 2006

Anita Mountain

'When we were in Kaduna, our garden backed on to your parents who I seem to remember lived on Race Course Road. We occasionally "baby sat" for Robin if that is the proper word!! Berrice and Tim were constantly bemused by Robin's ability to jack up Tim's car during the lunch hour and remove the tyres!!

In Kaduna I sort of set up as a "home hairdresser" without any responsibility for what went wrong, and I occasionally did Berrice's hair – she was brave!! I never found her shy, but reserved and careful what she said. Your parents were living in the "top layer", so it was with the bosses of UAC, John Holt etc. that they would have had to entertain. There was a huge gulf between Residents and their wives and junior officers. It was all understood!!

It must have been a huge leap into being Resident's wife after her early beginnings, and the happy days in Nassarawa. The trouble was that they were so senior to us all, and yet Berrice was in fact nearer to our age, and in Kano we were quite a jolly lot of women with the same sort of war time track record.

Berrice was such a great beauty, and in those days, had she had the self-confidence she would have sailed through that life on her good looks alone. But her life was Tim, and maybe you and Robin suffered a bit for that. She relied on Tim so very much, and in Kano she had to put up a huge effort of will to entertain all the odds and sods passing through. Your Mum's nervousness was in fact uniquely masked by her reserve. I think that takes an iron will. Tim was a very loyal supporter of a junior officer if he judged he was being sensible and responsible – and that was THE thing about Tim – he may have been reserved but he was loyal to his junior officers if they put up a good case and were "straight down the middle"!

He really was a very good upright man and Derek has not worked for any other man he has admired more than Tim, but it was a trying time to get to KNOW him!' From letters and emails written in October to December 2007

Derek Mountain

'Anita and I became firm friends with Tim and Berrice, although given the restraints of such a hierarchical society, it was not easy because of the difference in rank. It seems strange now but that is how it was.

Tim was hugely respected and liked by his colleagues for his integrity and towering competence. I think all of us understood the natural shyness of both Tim and Berrice and made due allowance for it.

I read with amusement what you said in your letter about Tim not liking too many parties. We had in Kano a retired RAF officer, Air Commodore North Carter, who ran the administration of the Provincial Office. Tim had served in the RAF under North and they were very close. North was much older than the rest of us, including Tim. He was regarded as a benevolent uncle by all of us. Anita and I were living in a mud house, appropriate to the status of a junior officer! When we announced we were having a large drinks party and told others that we had invited North and Tim (Berrice was in the U.K. at the time), they said neither would come. However, both came and were the last to leave a very noisy party in the early hours.

During the Governor-General's visit, Tim told me to take Berrice and Lady Robertson and show them Kano City, that great huddle of mud pies. The two ladies got on well and sat chattering in the back of my car without doing much sight seeing. I took them up onto Goron Dutse, one of the two small hills in the centre of the city. It was dark and the city lay below us twinkling in the light of a thousand flickering oil lamps. Suddenly, the chatter in the back of the car stopped. "What are we doing here?" asked Berrice. "I thought you would find it romantic", I said. "Very well, now drive us home", she replied.

In Kaduna we saw less of them because of the nature of the place as a regional headquarters. An incident involving Robin stays in my mind. When Tim and Berrice went out for the evening their staff were told to go through the hedge and seek our assistance in an emergency. One night their steward arrived in a state of great excitement and asked me to come at once. There was a large tree in the hedge dividing our gardens and, by the light of a torch, I could see the family cat in the top branches. Robin was three-quarters of the way up trying to get it down. By the time I was half-way up the tree Tim arrived on the scene. "What's going on?" Well, it took some explaining!' From a letter written in October 2007

Pam McClintock

'When Tim was our Resident, Nicky had the greatest respect, loyalty and affection for him. Very often out there things could get difficult, but when he was working with Tim as his senior officer he knew Tim would back him up and he knew what Tim would want him to do and he knew that Tim trusted him as he trusted Tim.

I think that although Berrice was not often *seen* we all knew how happy she made Tim and their life was a pool of quiet privacy, where Tim would relax at the end of a hot, worrying day. I always felt a great respect for her and her quiet calm ways were very comforting.

I cannot imagine any people better than Tim and Berrice to have as our seniors. I still remember the wonderful feeling of safety and friendship that one always felt when we had to call at the Residency, or I had to let Nicky go off there without me. I remember Berrice as a very, very nice person who I could trust and who (I think) felt about things the way I did. I don't think I will ever forget them or stop being grateful to them for the kindness and courtesy they always showed us.' From a letter written in October 2007

Ken Vorley

'Tim certainly had a rather serious expression for much of the time, but he had a great sense of humour and his smile and laughter were very infectious. He was a man who portrayed the highest levels of integrity and of concern for those for whom he was responsible. I certainly had the utmost confidence in him for I knew he would stand by me even if I did something which was not as bright as it should have been.' From a letter written in November 2007

Manus Nunan

'I knew Tim in Kano where he was Resident and later in Kaduna where he was effectively Head of the Civil Service. He was somewhat older than me and he was almost a legend. One heard that he had been a fighter pilot during the war in Malta. In Kano he was engaged in meeting important visitors at the airport. Even then the title "Ice Queen" for his wife was known. I was told that she hated meeting people and it was said that because of that fact he would never be offered a governorship. (Such things did exist at that date.) As Permanent Secretary in the Premier's Office he was probably in the ideal job.' From a letter written in December 2007

Martin Maconachie

'When Tim had had some food and drunk his beer, on the day so graphically described in his letter, he asked after my wife. He knew that she was in England, staying with my parents, expecting our first child. In answer to further questions I explained that when the child was born a cable would be sent to the nearest Post Office, i.e. to Malammaduri, about twenty miles from Hadejia. I had arranged for a messenger to bring me the news from there.

The next morning...Tim...decided to visit all the schools...[and he said] he would do this on his own; I was to stay in Hadejia awaiting news from England. Before he left for Kano he asked me what I liked reading. For the rest of my tour he regularly sent me books from his own library.

Some months later one of America's greatest experts on water supply and engineering was visiting Nigeria – Mr William C. Lowdermilk. Tim persuaded him to visit Gumel where water supply was inadequate despite the digging of deep and expensive wells. I accompanied Lowdermilk to act as his interpreter. He asked the Emir of Gumel why the town had been built where it was. The Emir explained that his great grandfather had been riding through the bush and decided that wherever his horse had a pee that's where he would build the town. Lowdermilk was gobsmacked. "Well chief" he said "that figures – that really figures". He went on to say that what was needed was a full geological survey and if that didn't yield results "you will have to move the town". He was a big man used to spending big bucks on big solutions. In passing his advice on to the Emir I left out the bit about rebuilding the town. The Emir was proud of the town and would have been offended. When I told Tim about all this he was greatly amused and commented that it was good for these great men to be brought down to earth occasionally.

Towards the end of my time in Hadejia it was decided that an airstrip should be built just outside the town to enable visitors to get there quickly avoiding the appalling roads. I was given the money and the loan of a grader to help level the site. The surface was laterite, which you may remember was a sort of red gravelly material. It was skiddy and very unsafe after rain, but not too bad in dry weather. It would of course only take light planes. Tim flew down for the ceremonial opening in a plane piloted by a Nigerian Airways pilot. The pilot said that landing had been an unnerving experience; all he could see on approaching was a little knot of people and a large white ambulance (which I had put there in case of accidents). The landing had been bumpy and the strip not up to standard in his view. Tim seemed less concerned but agreed that further work was needed on it. He rebuked me privately later for having removed the battery from the ambulance to power the microphone for the official speeches describing this as "not very sensible".

Talking of laterite Tim was always determined to seek solutions to problems. The problem with laterite roads was that they were skiddy in the wet, but at all times the surface was liable to form into small waves under the influence of traffic. Then you had to drive fairly fast along the tops of the waves to avoid a bumpy ride. Tim persuaded Kaduna to finance a Mechanical Unit with graders, diggers, dumpers etc. to try and improve these roads. Various experiments were carried out mixing laterite with sand and clay in varying proportions to try and discover the best mix for road surfacing. This was only partially successful but was an example of his imaginative hard work in tackling problems.

The next time I had dealings with Tim was after we had left Nigeria in 1962. I was looking for a new job and he was in charge of the Resettlement Bureau helping people from all over the Empire to find jobs. Before he took control of it, the RB had been a rather airy fairy outfit. But he had worked very hard to make it more professional, developing wide contacts in Government, business and industry. He was a bit concerned that there was only one thing I wanted to do, i.e. join the Ministry of Defence, but anyway I knew that whatever he wrote about me would be fair – and in fact I did get the job!

To sum up I felt that Tim's work had a special stamp about it – competent, imaginative and the product of hard thought. He seemed to get through an extraordinary amount of work without appearing to hurry. Lunch parties and entertaining were not his scene, as far as I can recall, but he was kind and concerned about us as individuals. He was sparing with both praise and blame and whichever you got you had earned!' From a letter written in January 2008

16. Tim in 1966

NOTES

Chapter 1

1 Extracts taken from Tim's own description in *A Selection of Hausa Stories*, 1966, by permission of Oxford University Press
2 The Chief Commissioner for the Northern Provinces was W.E. Hunt CMG CBE, who was appointed on 19.12.35. However Walter Morgan CMG acted for him from 13.6.36 until the end of the year and the visit occurred in October. Blue Books, National Archives
3 In a bad Harmattan the temperature can fall below 40°F at night, but can still be in the 80s during the day – a drop of 40° in a few hours. Bello, *My Life*
4 The station was outside the town and contained the government administration offices and the residences of the Europeans
5 A tax census was carried out each year before the preparation of the budget; Village Heads assessed all the adult males according to their circumstances so the able and wealthy paid more than the old and infirm

Chapter 2

1 Tim Johnston, *Tattered Battlements, A Malta Diary by a Fighter Pilot*, was first published in 1943 by Peter Davies Ltd. A revised edition *Tattered Battlements, A Fighter Pilot's Malta Diary, D-Day and After*, by Wing Commander Tim Johnston, DFC and Bar, was published in 1985 by William Kimber & Co. Ltd. Every effort has been made to trace WK & Co. in order to obtain permission to use extracts from the book but it seems they no longer exist
2 Hausa

Chapter 3

1 Sir John Patterson was CC from 1943–47 but Commander John Carrow acted for him in 1944 and 1945/6

2   Officers and their families were not allowed to accept gifts and would always 'pay' for them by giving the donor a dash (tip) equivalent to the value of the gift

3   The WC, or rather the EC, was a small mud hut behind the main hut called a 'Bayan Gida', literally 'behind the house'. Well-kept villages had BGs within compounds. Dirty villages had nothing and people used the surrounding bush. Fortunately the dry heat and scavenger beetles sorted things out in a reasonably hygienic fashion

4   DOs always travelled with a representative of the Emir or Native Authority

5   Nigerian Constitutional Proposals, January 1946

6   Makurdi was known as the 'punishment station'

7   The Chief Commissioner no doubt considered that, because of his absence from Nigeria during the war years, Tim was 'out of touch' and that he (the Chief Commissioner) knew best!

8   Probably Sir John R. Patterson. It is not clear why Tim refers to him as Rumtus except that he often gave people nicknames

9   The Stephensons had been Tim and Berrice's nearest neighbours living about 30 miles away. With no telephone and no transport other than bicycles, Berrice and Eleanor communicated with each other by writing notes which were delivered by a runner

10 The 'Richards Constitution' had been introduced that year and for the first time Nigerians from the North were able to become members of the Central Legislature

11 Lenox-Conyngham was one of a group of four or five District Officers who were regularly passed over for promotion to Senior District Officer. They used to meet for a convivial lunch known as 'The Feast of the Passed-Overs'. (Letter from Martin Maconachi, 19.2.2008)

Chapter 4

1   H.A.S. Johnston, *The Fulani Empire of Sokoto*; Sokoto District Note Books

2   Sir A.T. Weatherhead, 'But Always as Friends', unpublished manuscript, Rhodes House Library

3   Tim's horse was called Walkiya which is Hausa for 'lightning'

4   Sir Frederick Lugard, High Commissioner, Protectorate of Northern Nigeria, 1900–7

5   Johnston, *The Fulani Empire of Sokoto*, by permission of OUP. In *Concerning Brave Captains*, 1964, David Muffett quotes another source which reported that the Waziri and chiefs were shot on the first charge of the force and, on seeing their leaders killed by the Europeans, the men fled off into the bush

6   fadi-ka-mutu means roughly 'if it drops you're dead'

7   His account of how he escaped from his Tuareg master shows how much faith the Hausas had in *layar zana*, the charm of invisibility

8   Ba'ude = A person from Ude

9　Sarkin Burmi Abdulbaki published the full account of his story in 1954 The Hausa version and the English translation are included in *A Selection of Hausa Stories*, No. 58 Abdulbaki Tanimuddarin Tureta, 1966. This abridged version is included by permission of Oxford University Press

10　A longer version is included in *Hausa Stories*, No. 44 Muhammadu Kanta, Chief of Kebbi. This abridged version included by permission of OUP

11　Hassan was Sultan from 1931–38 and Tim had known him when he was first in Sokoto in 1936–37

12　*Hausa Stories*, No. 64 The Blind Man, the Boy and the Lion and No. 65 The Packmen and the Man-Eating Lion. This abridged version included by permission of OUP

13　Private letters of Sir A.T. Weatherhead, Rhodes House Library

14　Ed. A.H.M. Kirk-Greene, *The Transfer of Power*

15　Sir A.T. Weatherhead, 'But Always as Friends', unpublished manuscript, Rhodes House Library

16　Sir Bryan Sharwood-Smith, *But Always as Friends*

17　Sir A.T. Weatherhead, 'But Always as Friends', unpublished manuscript

18　The revised constitution came into force in October 1954

19　This was a delicate matter because the wives were in purdah and consequently had little or no contact with European women who could have shown them how a flushing toilet worked

20　*Hausa Stories*, No 60, The Shamaki and the Majidadi, by permission of OUP

21　*Hausa Stories*, No 61, The Sunday Battle, by permission of OUP

22　Peggy Watt, *There is Only One Nigeria*, 1985

Chapter 5

1　Letter from the Acting Resident, Kano Province to the Civil Secretary, September 1954

2　Letters from Anita Mountain 2007

3　November–December 1954

4　Tim's hand-written translation

5　There were very few tarmacked roads in those days which meant driving on dirt roads

6　N.C. McClintock, *Kingdoms in the Sand and Sun*

7　N.C. McClintock

8　Sir Bryan Sharwood-Smith's nickname was Mai-wandon karfi, or Ironpants, which probably derived from the fact that he never sat down. Here the people were saying 'Ironpants has taken to golden pants'. The blue winter gubernatorial uniform was much grander than the white tropical one

9　*The Times*, Friday 10 June 1955

10　Probably one of the Emir's representatives

11 Letter from Martin Maconachie, January 2008
12 Letter from the Governor to the Secretary of State, 18.5.55, WAF
    97/115/01. National Archives CO554/1161
13 Note on the Conditions of Service of Expatriate Officers in the Northern
    Region, prepared at the instance of the Governor, June 1955. NA
    CO554/1027
14 Letter from the Governor to the Secretary of State, 14.2.55, WAF
    103/3/01. NA CO554/1183
15 Johnston papers
16 N. C. McClintock, *Kingdoms in the Sand and Sun*
17 Thanks to Derek Mountain for this anecdote
18 Johnston, Annual Report on Kano Province for 1956
19 Johnston papers, The Impact of Democracy on Northern Nigeria

Chapter 6

1 Letter from J.W. Robertson to Sir John Macpherson dated 12 November
   1956, CO967/318
2 If a person is not treated, cerebral malaria can be fatal in 24–72 hours.
   Children are particularly at risk
3 Sir Bryan Sharwood-Smith, *But Always as Friends*
4 K.P. Maddocks, *Of No Fixed Abode*
5 Letter from Sir Gawain Bell dated 12.5.68
6 Officers were anti the Colonial Office because it had little understanding
   of the problems of governing such a huge area and population, and no
   realistic idea about paying them properly or dealing with their conditions of
   service in an adequate way. Consequently, many of them felt very bitter
7 Minorities Commission Report, NA CO554/1541
8 *The Times*, Letter to the Editor dated Wednesday October 1, 1958
9 *The Times*, Letter to the Editor dated Saturday October 4, 1958
10 *The Times*, Saturday October 18, 1958
11 Johnston papers: The United Kingdom and Northern Nigeria: A
   Balance Sheet
12 In Tim's opinion it was inconceivable that Captain Mundy should have
   left them on the battlefield. In all probability he presented one to the
   Battalion and kept the other for himself
13 Johnston papers – Correspondence between HASJ and Maj. Gen. Exham
14 A.T. Clark, *Was It Only Yesterday* – 'The Call of the Drum' contribution
   of Dom Alberic
15 Letter from John Smith, 17.8.2006
16 A note on matters affecting the attainment and reflective exercise of
   Self-Government by the Northern Region. Sharwood-Smith, May 1957
17 Gilbert Stephenson spent two and a half years at the Colonial Office
   around this time and he wrote: 'Having described in detail our own

system of government, it would be pointed out to these visiting officials how this, our Westminster pattern of government, had been evolved over centuries of trial and error, and was thus suited to our own particular conditions. It would be suggested, politely, that as the traditions and generally-held assumptions in their countries were very different, that perhaps a different form of government would be more suitable. The reaction to this well-intended suggestion was always the same – a declaration that whatever system suited us best in Great Britain was the system they wished to instal in their own country. They would not be fobbed off, they would declare, with any inferior pattern of government. …And so it was, in spite of all our efforts at the CO, that unfortunately it was our own Westminster system of government that so often came to be inaugurated as the first type of government in many developing countries, especially in Africa; whereas some other system would probably have been far more suitable.' (G.L. Stephenson, Rhodes House Library, MSS.Afr.s.1833)

18 Muhammadu Shefe 1953–59. In 1951 the senior councillor of Argungu had been removed for leading the NA into a web of intrigue and nepotism. After a purge of the administration Muhammadu Shefe was appointed Emir in 1953 but five years later a rift opened between him and his Council which led to his resignation

Chapter 7

1 Maiholi would have been thrilled that Tim had become Deputy Governor, not least because he could bask in his reflected glory!

2 Johnston papers. Letter 530/II/425 dated 8 February 1960 from HASJ to The Rt Hon Iain Macleod, Secretary of State for the Colonies. CO554/2428

3 When she died, their son became Chief of Daura and he in turn had six sons who founded six of the seven original Hausa States, the Hausa Bakwai. These were Daura, Kano, Zazzau, Gobir, Katsina and Rano. The seventh, Garun Gabas, was founded by the son of Abuyazidu's first wife. Abridged version included by permission of OUP

4 Northern Nigeria Review of Affairs. Dep-Gov of the Northern Region of Nigeria to Secretary of State for the Colonies, 11 July 1960. National Archives CO554/2391

5 Letter of 14 July 1960 from HASJ to C.G. Eastwood. NA CO554/2391

6 Sylvia Leith-Ross wrote a memoir entitled: Stepping Stones, Memoirs of Colonial Nigeria 1907–60

7 A Colombo Plan would mean that nations outside the Commonwealth would be able to participate and Nigeria could continue to receive American aid. Tim's feeling was that if the wealthy nations of the Commonwealth were not prepared to make sacrifices in order to help the

poorer members, they had no right to stand between the poorer members and the bounty of the United States

8   A double-Kaduna was a type of bungalow with a central living room and bedrooms on either side

9   *The Fulani Empire of Sokoto*, HASJ, OUP. Only recently, a letter was discovered which Tim wrote to Philip Mason shortly before he died and which Berrice never posted. In it he said: 'After so long an interval, the appearance of this presentation copy [of *The Fulani Empire*] will probably come as a surprise to you, especially when you find that the book is not the one you saw in draft. That earlier effort fell between the historical and popular stools. When it had proved to be a near-miss with three or four publishers, I decided to re-write it as a straight history and this is the result.'

GLOSSARY

Alhaji	Courtesy title accorded to any man who has been on the Pilgrimage to Mecca
Alkali (pl. Alkalai)	Native court judge administering Muslim law
Birni	A walled town. The town wall
Canteen	Shop selling European goods
C(h)iroma	Princely title
Dan	The 'son of'; also used as diminutive
Dash	A tip
Dodo	A pagan ghost, mythical spirit
Dogari (pl. Dogarai)	Old-time uniformed retainers of emirs whose functions were escort duties, guard duties and police duties in general, the personal bodyguards, household police of the Emirs
Fadama	Floodplain of a river; well-watered perennially fertile ground; marshland
Fulani (sing. Ba-Fillache)	Semi-pastoral people whose ancestors overcame the native rulers of Hausaland
Galadima	Principal minister, DH or NA official
Gaskiya Ta Fi Kwabo	The Hausa newspaper, literally 'Truth is worth more than a penny'
Gida – Maigida – Uwargida	House – master of the house – mistress of the house or head wife
Habe	The Hausa as distinct from the Fulani (used to mean non-Muslim too)
Haj, haji	Pilgrimage to Mecca
Haraji	General/individual tax, tax revision
Harmattan	Dry, dust-laden wind that blows from the Sahara from November to February or even later

Hausa (pl. Hausawa) – Ba-Haushe	The land or language of the people of Hausa-speaking tribes – a Hausa
Hurumi	The communal grazing ground that lies immediately outside the walls of a town. The farmland is beyond the Hurumi
Ibo	An ethnic group of SE Nigeria
Ja'afi or Jafi	The 'charge' on ceremonial occasions
Jihad	Holy war
Kofa	Doorway, hole; intermediary, representative
Kuku	Hausa version of English 'cook'
Lamido	Fulani word meaning Chief; Chief of Adamawa
Ma'aji	Treasurer
Madaki (pl. madawaki)	Village head; deputy, master of the horse
Magani	Medicine or magic
Mai- (pl. masu)	Owner of; also Chief in Bornu
Maigida	Owner of the house
Makama	An important title high in the hierarchy in several emirates, e.g. Bida, Kano, Sokoto
Maliki	Founder of a school of Muslim law
Ramadan	Muslim month of fast
Riga	Man's gown
Rumfa	A shelter made of zana mats
Sabon Gari	New town
Salla babba	Great festival that celebrates the commencement of the new Muslim year
Sardauna	A princely title implying leadership in war
Sarki (pl. sarakuna)	Chief, Emir in Hausa
Sarkin Barriki	Rest House keeper
Sarkin Kano	Chief of Kano
Sarkin Yaki	Chief in War
Shari'a	Justice, Muslim law
Shehu	A religious leader often possessing temporal authority; sheikh

Shettima	A Bornu title
Turawa (sing. Ba-Ture)	All white-skinned people
Uwargida	Mother of the house; head wife
Wakili (pl. wakilai)	Representative, deputy, trad. title
Waziri	Vizier. Title given to the most important man in the emirate after the Emir
Zana	Straw (mat)
Zaure	Entrance hut to a man's compound
Zazzau	Old Hausa name for Zaria

ABBREVIATIONS

ADO	Assistant District Officer
A&N	Army & Navy Stores
AG	Action Group
AOC	Air Officer Commanding
ATS	Auxiliary Territorial Service
CAS	Colonial Administrative Service
CD&WF	Colonial Development & Welfare Fund
CO	Colonial Office; Commanding Officer
CRH	Catering Rest House
CRO	Commonwealth Relations Office
CS	Colonial Service
DDT	Dichloro-diphenyl-trichloroethane, a highly toxic insecticide whose use is now banned in most countries!
DO	District Officer
FCO	Foreign and Commonwealth Office
GH	Government House
GRA	Government Reservation Area
HE	His Excellency, used for a Governor or a Governor-General
HH	His Honour, used for a Chief Commissioner or Lieutenant Governor
HMG	Her/His Majesty's Government
HMOCS	Her Majesty's Overseas Civil Service
HRH	His or Her Royal Highness
MOO	Medical Officers
NA	Native Administration/Native Authority
NCNC	National Council of Nigeria and the Cameroons
NEPU	Northern Elements' Progressive Union, the Northern opposition party

NPC	Northern People's Congress, the main Northern political party
OAG	Officer Administering Government
OSRB	Overseas Service Resettlement Bureau
PEO	Principal Education Officer
PS	Private Secretary
PSC	Public Service Commission
PWD	Public Works Department
RAFVR	Royal Air Force Volunteer Reserve
R/T	Radio-telephony
RWAFF	Royal West African Frontier Force
SDO	Senior District Officer
UAC	United Africa Company

Note on Spellings

Although the words 'Moslem' and 'Mohammedan' were generally used at the time, the former sounds old-fashioned and the latter may even be considered offensive now, so I have changed them to 'Muslim'.

'Usuman dan Fodiyo' is the spelling Tim used in his *The Fulani Empire of Sokoto*, but there are other variations e.g. Usman dan Fodio.

CONSTITUTIONAL PROGRESS

(Source: John P. Mackintosh, Nigerian Government and Politics, 1966)

Richards Constitution, January 1947

Based on the views of the previous Governor, Sir Bernard Bourdillon, it aimed to combine the Native Authorities by bringing their representatives together into a Regional Council and then to summon regional representatives to a single legislature in Lagos. The three Regional Councils could advise on their own problems, consider Bills and financial legislation for their own Region but they had no power to legislate or vote taxes. This was done by the Central Legislature.

Macpherson Constitution, June 1951

After an extensive consultation process from village meetings right up to Regional Conference level, a final General Conference, held in Ibadan in January 1950, recommended increased regional autonomy and the creation of larger Regional Legislatures. The new Constitution set up bi-cameral legislatures in the North and West and a single chamber in the East, which were empowered to legislate on local government, health, education and agriculture. They also sent representatives to the Central Legislature in Lagos.

Lyttelton Constitution, 1953–54

By 1953 it was clear that the Constitution would have to be changed to provide for greater regional autonomy. The East and West proposed, and the North agreed to, a federal system which would allocate specified powers to the central government and leave all other powers to the regions. Agreement was

263

also reached on a system of revenue allocation and on the regionalisation of the Civil Service and the Judiciary.

London Constitutional Conference, May–June 1957

The Conference decided on full regional self-government for the East and the West by October. The North would aim for self-government in 1959. It was also agreed that at the centre there should be a bi-cameral Parliament with a Senate and a House of Representatives. The central Executive Council would consist solely of politicians appointed by a Prime Minister. Commissions were set up to look into fiscal matters and the question of minorities.

Resumed London Conference, September–October 1958

The Conference accepted the proposals of the Fiscal Commission: Regional Governments would have exclusive control of income tax. The Federal Government would be allocated company profits and death duties. It would also be responsible for collecting all import and excise duties, mining rents and mineral royalties, 30% of which had to be paid into a Distributable Pool to be divided between the Regions.

The recommendations of the Minorities Commission were also accepted: No more states would be created within the Federation before independence, the Nigeria Police Force would become a single Federal Force, and a list of Fundamental Rights would be included in the Constitution to protect minorities.

Northern Regional Self-Government, March 1959

Federal Independence, October 1960

BIOGRAPHICAL NOTES

Abdulbaki, Sarkin Burmi. District Head

Abubakar, Alhaji Sir, GCON, GBE, CMG. Sultan of Sokoto from 1938.

Abubakar Imam, Alhaji, Editor Gaskiya Ta Fi Kwabo 1945. Writer and respected academic.

Abubakar Tafawa Balewa, Alhaji Sir, PC, KBE, MP. Prime Minister of Nigeria 1959–66.

Achimugu, Peter S. NPC Northern Regional Minister.

Adams, Richard. Administrative Officer.

Adams, Sir Theodore Samuel CMG. Chief Commissioner, Northern Provinces.

Ahmadu Bello, Alhaji Sir, Sardauna of Sokoto and cousin of the Sultan. Premier Northern Region 1954–66.

Ali Akilu, Northern Regional Administrative Officer. Head of the Civil Service [on independence] and later OAG of Northern Nigeria.

Aliyu Makaman Bida, Alhaji, CBE. Leading NPC Politician. Minister of Finance Northern Region 1957–66.

Aminu Kano, Alhaji, Leader of NEPU, the opposition party in Northern Region from 1950. Became Whip in Sir Abubakar's coalition government 1959.

Barlow-Poole, Richard, CBE. Administrative Service Northern Nigeria 1947–59, dep perm sec Min of Health 1959–62, perm sec min of Lands & Survey 1962–6, commr of Native Courts 1966–68.

Bell, Sir Gawain Westray. Governor Northern Region 1957–62.

Bello Dan Amar Kano, Muhammadu, CBE. Teacher. Northern Regional Minister. Kano District Head.

Beresford-Stooke, Sir George, KCMG. Chief Secretary.

Bourdillon, Sir Bernard Henry, GCMG, KBE. Governor Nigeria 1936–43.

Browne, Sir Algernon Thomas, Kt. Chief Justice Northern Nigeria 1955–60.

Bukar Shaib. Vet from Bornu. Later became a Permanent Secretary and went on to a distinguished career with FAO.

Carrow, Commander John, CMG DSC. Administrative Officer.

Carter, North, Air Commodore. Ran the administration of the Provincial Office, Kano.

Chartres, Dr John. Medical Officer involved in the Sleeping Sickness survey.

Clark, A. Trevor. Administrative Officer.

Cole, C.W. ('Foxy'). Administrative Officer.

Counsell, Mike. Administrative Officer.

Dikko, Dr Russel Aliyu Barau. Northern Regional Medical Officer and joint Founder of NPC.

Eastwood, Christopher G., CMG. Assistant Under-Secretary of State Colonial Office 1945–52 and 1954–66.

Egremont-Lee, Major Antony James Barker. King's Shropshire Light Infantry. ADC to Governor Bell 1960.

Ellison, Randall. Chairman of the Public Service Commission.

Foot, Hugh Mackintosh (later Lord Caradon) GCMG KCVO OBE PC. (1907–90) Chief Secretary Nigeria 1947–51.

Ford, 'Bill'. Administrative Officer.

Gardner-Brown, A.G.H. Administrative Officer and Deputy Governor-General.

Gorsuch, Leslie. Salaries Commissioner.

Greatbatch, Bruce G. (later Sir, KCVO, CMG, MBE). Senior Resident Kano 1955–59, Secretary to Premier and Head of N. Nigeria Civil Service 1959–63.

Greswell, Richard G., CMG. Administrative Officer.

Grey, Sir Ralph Francis Alnwick (later Lord Grey of Naunton). Chief Secretary Federation of Nigeria 1955–57 and Deputy Governor-General 1957–59.

Grier, Pat. Administrative Officer.

Hanson-Smith, Christopher. Administrative Officer 1951–59. Liaison Officer with Fulani 1951–55.

Harragin, Sir Walter, CMG. President of West African Court of Appeal and Salaries Commissioner.

Hassan, Sultan of Sokoto 1931–38.

Humphreys, Frank. Administrative Officer.

Hunt, E. Oliver W, DSO. Administrative Officer.

Isa Kaita, Alhaji. NPC Politician and Northern Regional Minister.

Jelf, Hector G. CBE. Administrative Officer.

Kashim Ibrahim, Alhaji Sir (Shettima Kashim) KCMG, CBE. NPC Politician, Regional and Federal Minister, Waziri and Governor of Northern Region.

Lennox-Boyd, Alan Tindal (later Viscount Boyd of Merton PC CH) Secretary of State for the Colonies 1954–59.

Lenox-Conyngham. Administrative Officer.

Letchworth, Tom, CMG. Administrative Officer.

Lloyd-Morgan, David. Administrative Officer.

Longmore, T. Robert ('Bob'). Administrative Officer.

Lugard, Frederick Dealtry (later Lord Lugard). High Commissioner and C-in-C of Northern Nigeria 1900–06. High Commissioner Northern Nigeria 1912–14. Governor of Nigeria 1914–19.

Lyttelton, Oliver (later Lord Chandos). Secretary of State for Colonies.

McClintock, Nicholas Cole, CBE. Administrative Officer.

Macdonald, [?]. Resident Makurdi.

Macleod, Iain. Secretary of State for Colonies.

Maconachie, Martin O. CBE. Administrative Officer.

Macpherson, Sir John Stuart. Governor of Nigeria 1948–54. Governor-General 1954–55.

Maddocks, Kenneth P. (later Sir, KCMG, KCVO). Civil Secretary Northern Region 1955–57. Deputy Governor 1957–58. Acting Governor 1956 and 1957.

Marshall, Hedley H., CMG, QC. Legal Secretary then Attorney General Northern Region 1954–62.

Michie, Charles W. CMG. Administrative Officer.

Mountain, Derek. OBE. District Officer, Kano City. Acting Resident, Sardauna Province, Northern Cameroons.

Muffett, Dr David JM, OBE. Administrative Officer.

Muhammad Mukhtari Dambatta, Sarkin Bai, NPC Politician.

Muhammadu Ribadu, MBE. NPC Politician. Appointed Federal Minister 1952.

Muhammadu Sanusi. Chiroma and Emir of Kano.

Muhammadu Shefe. Emir of Argungu 1953–59.

Nelson, St Elmo. Administrative Officer.

Nunan, Manus, QC. Solicitor-General Northern Nigeria.

Owen, David. Chairman UN Technical Assistance Board.

Patterson, Sir John R. KBE, CMG. Chief Commissioner Northern Provinces 1943–48.

Perham, Dame Margery, DCMG, CBE. Reader in Colonial Administration and Fellow of Nuffield College, Oxford 1939–63, and leading authority on the system of colonial administration by Indirect Rule.

Pleass, Sir Clement John, KCMG, JCVO, KBE. Governor Eastern Region 1952–54.

Pott, D.A. ('Duggie') OBE. Administrative Officer.

Poynton, Hilton. Deputy Under-Secretary, Colonial Office.

Rankine, Sir John Dalzel, KCMG KCVO. Governor Western Region 1954–60.

Richards, Sir Arthur Frederick (later Lord Milverton) GCMG. Governor of Nigeria 1943–47.

Robertson, Sir James Wilson, KT, GCMG, GCVO, KBE. Governor-General Federation of Nigeria 1955–60.

Scott, Peter Heathcote Guillum. Administrative Officer and Northern Regional Financial Secretary 1952–57.

Seaford, Harry. Administrative Officer.

Sharwood-Smith, Sir Bryan Evers, KCMG KCVO KBE. Resident, Lieutenant Governor Northern Nigeria 1952–54, Governor 1954–57.

Smith, John H. CBE. Administrative Officer.

Stallard, Peter J.G. (later Sir, KCMG). Administrative Officer, Secretary to the Prime Minister.

Stapledon, Sir Robert, KCMG CBE. Governor Eastern Region 1955–60.

Stephenson, Gilbert L. Administrative Officer.

Temple, C.L. CMG. Resident and Lt Governor Northern Province.

Thompstone, Sir Eric Westbury. Chief Commissioner Northern Region 1947–51, Lt Governor 1951–52.

Usman Nagogo, Alhaji Sir, Kt., CMG, CBE. Emir of Katsina.

Vorley, Rev'd K.A. Administrative Officer.

Wallace, Julian. Administrative Officer.

Weatherhead, Sir A. T. ('Waddle'). Resident Sokoto and Kano. Deputy-Governor.

Willink, Sir Henry, PC. Chairman Minorities Commission.

Wilson, Gordon D. Administrative Officer.

Wrench, Hector. Administrative Officer.

Yahaya, Emir of Gwandu.

BIBLIOGRAPHY AND
FURTHER READING

Sources

The letters and diaries of Tim and Berrice Johnston dated from 1936 to 1960. Official papers of H.A.S. (Tim) Johnston held privately and in the National Archives.

Johnston books

Johnston, H.A.S., *A Selection of Hausa Stories*, 1966
— *The Fulani Empire of Sokoto*, 1967
— and Muffett, D.J.M., *Denham in Bornu*, 1973
Sturton, Hugh (HASJ), *Zomo, the Rabbit*, 1966

Unpublished Memoirs in Rhodes House Library

Stephenson, G.L., 'Nigerian and Other Days', MSS.Afr.s.1833
Watt, L.S. 'Diaries', MSS.Afr.s.1412
Weatherhead, A.T., 'But Always as Friends' (also titled 'Possessors of Power'), MSS.Afr.s.232
— 'Letters', MSS.Afr.s.2028

Published Memoirs

Arrowsmith, K.V., *Bush Paths*, 1991
Ball, David R., *Into Africa and Out – Northern Nigeria 1956–62*, 2002
Bell, Sir Gawain, *An Imperial Twilight*, 1989
Bello, Sir Ahmadu, *My Life*, 1962
Brook, I., *The One-Eyed Man is King*, 1966
Evans, Jean, *Not Bad for a Foreigner*, 1996
Hollis, Rosemary, *A Scorpion for Tea*, 1973
Kerslake, R.T., *Time and the Hour*, 1997
Leith-Ross, Sylvia, *Stepping Stones: Memoirs of Colonial Nigeria, 1907–60*, 1983
McClintock, N.C., *Kingdoms in the Sand and Sun*, 1992

Maddocks, K.P., *Of No Fixed Abode*, 1988
Maddocks, Patricia, *So Many Worlds*, 2004
Maslen, J., *Beating about the Nigerian Bush*, 1994
Meehan, Myra, *My Nigerian Journey*, 1993
Meehan, Tony, *Goodbye Maigida*, 1991
Morley, John, *Colonial Postscript: Diary of a D.O. 1935–56*, 1992
Niven, Sir Rex, *Nigerian Kaleidoscope*, 1982
Perham, Margery, *West African Passage*, 1983
Robertson, Sir James, *Transition in Africa*, 1974
Rowling, Noël, *Nigerian Memories*, 1982
Russell, Elnor, *Bush Life*, 1978
Sharwood-Smith, Sir Bryan, *But Always as Friends: Northern Nigeria and the Cameroons 1921–1957*, 1969
Sharwood-Smith, Joan, *Diary of a Colonial Wife*, 1992
Smith, J.H., *Colonial Cadet in Nigeria*, 1968
Terrell, R., *West African Interlude*, 1988
Watt, Peggy, *There is Only One Nigeria*, 1985
White, S., *Dan Bana: The Memoirs of a Nigerian Official*, 1966
Wright, R.H., *Then the Wind Changed in Africa*, ed. R. Pearce, 1992

Collective Memoirs

Clark, A.T. (ed), *Was It Only Yesterday? The Last Generation of Nigeria's Turawa*, 2002
Kirk-Greene, A.H.M., (ed), *The Transfer of Power in Africa: The Colonial Administrator in the Age of Decolonization*, 1979
— *Glimpses of Empire*, 2001

General Works

Achebe, Chinua, *The Trouble with Nigeria*, 1983
Callaway, Helen, *Gender Culture and Empire: European Women in Colonial Nigeria*, 1987
Clark, Trevor, *A Right Honourable Gentleman – Abubakar from the Black Rock*, 1991
Crowder, Michael, *The Story of Nigeria*, 1962
Hatch, John, *Nigeria – A History*, 1971
Heussler, Robert, *The British in Northern Nigeria*, 1968
Hogben, S.J. and Kirk-Greene, A.H.M., *The Emirates of Northern Nigeria: A Preliminary Survey of their Historical Traditions*, 1993
Kirk-Greene, Anthony, *Symbol of Authority: The British District Officer in Africa*, 2006
Lupton, Kenneth, *Mungo Park – The African Traveler*, 1979

Meek, C.K., *The Northern Tribes of Nigeria*, 1925

— *Tribal Studies in Northern Nigeria*, 1931

Morel, E.D., *Nigeria Its Peoples and Its Problems*, 1911 and 1968

Muffett, D.J.M., *Concerning Brave Captains*, 1964

— *Let Truth Be Told: The Coups d'Etat of 1966*, 1982

Peel, Richard, *Old Sinister – A Memoir of Sir Arthur Richards*, 1986

Perham, Margery, *Native Administration in Nigeria*, 1937

Smith, John (ed), *Administering Empire: The Colonial Service in Retrospect*, 1999

Temple, O. (ed by C.L. Temple), *Tribes, Provinces, Emirates and States of the Provinces of Northern Nigeria*, 1919

INDEX

The text of illustration 14 on page 164 should read:
"Tim, the Emir of Kano and the Govenor-General"